The Perennial Philosophy
Series

World Wisdom
The Library of Perennial Philosophy

The Library of Perennial Philosophy is dedicated to the exposition of the timeless Truth underlying the diverse religions. This Truth, often referred to as the *Sophia Perennis*—or Perennial Wisdom—finds its expression in the revealed Scriptures as well as the writings of the great sages and the artistic creations of the traditional worlds.

The Sacred Foundations of Justice in Islam: The Teachings of 'Ali ibn Abi Talib appears as one of our selections in the Perennial Philosophy series.

The Perennial Philosophy Series

In the beginning of the twentieth century, a school of thought arose which has focused on the enunciation and explanation of the Perennial Philosophy. Deeply rooted in the sense of the sacred, the writings of its leading exponents establish an indispensable foundation for understanding the timeless Truth and spiritual practices which live in the heart of all religions. Some of these titles are companion volumes to the Treasures of the World's Religions series, which allows a comparison of the writings of the great sages of the past with the perennialist authors of our time.

The Sacred
Foundations of
Justice in Islam:

The Teachings of 'Ali ibn Abi Talib

By M. Ali Lakhani, Reza Shah-Kazemi
and Leonard Lewisohn

Edited by

M. Ali Lakhani

Introduction by

Seyyed Hossein Nasr

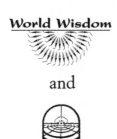

World Wisdom

and

Sacred Web

The Sacred Foundations of Justice in Islam:
The Teachings of 'Ali ibn Abi Talib
© 2006 World Wisdom, Inc. and Sacred Web Publishing

Most recent printing indicated by last digit below:
10 9 8 7 6 5 4 3 2

For complete bibliographical information on the articles
in this anthology, please see the List of Sources
at the end of the book, pp. 165-176.

Library of Congress Cataloging-in-Publication Data

Lakhani, M. Ali., 1955-
 The sacred foundations of justice in Islam : the teachings of 'Alī ibn Abī Ṭālib /
by M. Ali Lakhani, Reza Shah-Kazemi and Leonard Lewisohn ; edited by M. Ali
Lakhani ; introduction by Seyyed Hossein Nasr.
 p. cm. -- (Perennial philosophy series)
Includes bibliographical references and index.
 ISBN-13: 978-1-933316-26-0 (pbk. : alk. paper)
 ISBN-10: 1-933316-26-8 (pbk. : alk. paper)
 1. 'Alī ibn Abī Ṭālib, Caliph, 600 (ca.)-661--Views on justice. 2. 'Alī ibn Abī Ṭālib,
Caliph, 600 (ca.)-661--Teachings. 3. Islam and justice. I. Shah-Kazemi, Reza. II.
Lewisohn, Leonard.
III. Title.
BP193.1.A2L35 2006
297.6'48--dc22

                                                                    2006020340

Printed on acid-free paper in The United States of America.

For information address World Wisdom, Inc.
P.O. Box 2682, Bloomington, Indiana 47402-2682

www.worldwisdom.com

Sacred Web Publishing
147, 3300 Capilano Road, North Vancouver, B.C., Canada, V7R 4H8

www.sacredweb.com

Imam 'Ali with his sword (*Dh'ulfaqar* or *Zulfikar*); fragment from the *Du'a-ye Sabah*, or morning prayer, by Imam 'Ali; contemporary calligraphy from Iran. The veiled face symbolizes the self-effacement and absorption of the realized Self into the mysteries of Transcendence. The two-pronged sword, Zulfikar, given by the Prophet Muhammad to 'Ali at the Battle of Badr, is an emblem of spiritual chivalry, of piety and virtue, and of the realized Self's vanquishment of inner passions and outer desires. It can be understood as the symbol of the Imam's commitment to the principles of Truth and Justice.

TABLE OF CONTENTS

PREFATORY NOTE

The first two studies in this anthology are revised versions of essays commissioned for the International Congress on Imam 'Ali and Justice, Unity and Security, convened from March 13 through 16, 2001, organized by the Institute for Humanities and Cultural Studies in Iran. The essays were adjudged the two best English language essays at the International Congress, and were awarded the first and second prizes, respectively, at a special ceremony held in Tehran, Iran, in 2002. An expanded version of the essay by Dr. Shah-Kazemi appears in his book, *Justice and Remembrance—Introducing the Spirituality of Imam 'Ali* (IB Tauris, in association with the Institute of Ismaili Studies, London, 2006).

The third study was specially commissioned for this anthology.

Kufic calligraphy of the name 'Ali.

Tile from the Friday Mosque of Isfahan displaying the *hadīth*: "I am the City of Knowledge and 'Ali is the Gate".

INTRODUCTION

To be fully human is to have an innate sense of justice and a yearning for justice. And yet when it comes to the question of what justice is, it becomes difficult to define it except in its relation to accepted and defined legal and social norms. What is difficult is to comprehend the meaning of justice metaphysically, in relation to the Divine Principle, in itself, and also in its rapport with various levels of manifestation down to the terrestrial and the human. When we speak of justice, we have the intuitive sense of putting things aright and in their appropriate place, of re-establishing a lost harmony and equilibrium, of remaining true to the nature of things, of giving each being its due. But what about God, who is considered by 'Ali ibn Abi Talib (d. 661 C.E./ 40 A.H.), to whose ideas this book is devoted, to be not only "just" but also "Justice" itself, the assertion that he is both al-'Adil (Just or Equitable) and al-'Adl (Justice) to use Islamic terms? Only through metaphysics can such an assertion be understood and not through the legal or formal understanding of justice.

From the metaphysical point of view it can be said that the Divine Nature is one and completely Itself. It has in fact no parts that need to be put in their appropriate place through justice. If justice means to place everything in its place according to its nature and in following Divine cosmic and human laws, then the Divine Nature is pure justice in the highest sense, being the One without any parts which could be out of place and needing justice according to their nature to return to their appropriate state. What is Justice? One could respond that on the highest level it is the Divine Reality Itself. The Divine is also the Source of all laws according to which we judge what is just or unjust.

Harmony results from the manifestation of the One in the many and since all things come ultimately from the One, harmony pervades all things to some degree. God is the ultimate source of all harmony and equilibrium. But He is also in Himself perfect equilibrium and peace and absolute Beauty, which means also perfect harmony, although He has no parts which could be out of equilibrium or lack harmony. If justice be conceived as the establishment and, when necessary, re-establishment of equilibrium and harmony, then the Divine Reality may be said to be not only just but also perfect justice itself, for It is not only the source of equilibrium and harmony but also has the qualities of Peace and Beauty which are Divine Attributes. Being perfect equilibrium and perfect harmony the Divine is also Justice, for there is no peace without equilibrium and no beauty without harmony. Furthermore, justice is inseparable from the truth and the Divine is Truth as such.

This metaphysical doctrine can be brought home through the analysis of the word *al-haqq* in Arabic. To pay each thing its due (*al-haqq*) is identified with justice, and the rights of various beings whether human or otherwise, which have to be respected if there is to be justice is also called *al-haqq* (pl. *huquq*). Now, God according to the Qur'an is *al-Haqq*, the Truth, and this necessitates Him having the quality of justice and being the source of all justice. As *al-Haqq*, God is Justice itself, and as source of the *huquq* of His creatures and the laws by which His creation is governed, He is just, as well as being ultimately the source of all justice on the human plane.

Justice is inseparable from truth in human life. This is the consequence of the fact that human beings are united in the Divine Nature. Therefore in this world there can be no justice without truth. In all traditional religious and sapiental traditions justice is associated with truth, while truth itself *is* reality in the metaphysical sense. Again, this fact is made the clear in the double meaning of the Arabic term *al-haqq* which means both truth and reality. To be just is to conform to the nature of the Real and not to the transient and the illusory. In a sense it might be said that injustice is related to ignorance of the truth and real nature of things, while the practice of justice is impossible without truth which would enable us to know beings in their reality. And since that is not possible for the human collectivity in this period of history to achieve by itself, revelations have been sent to guide man in the understanding of the truth, of what is real and of justice.

It is the nexus between justice and truth that has caused certain traditional philosophers of the ancient world to call justice the highest virtue which in Islam is preserved for truth itself. One cannot be just without truthfulness and on the metaphysical level one cannot understand justice without knowledge of the truth. Conversely, those who are truthful must of necessity be also just if truth is to embrace their will and their actions as well as their intelligence.

In all traditions, while the notion of the essential reality of justice is related to metaphysics and the inward nature of man where the innate sense of justice resides, on the plane of action laws have been sent to guide human beings in such a way that their actions conform to the nature of things, to cosmic laws and to the Divine Will. Lest one think that revealed law, which determines justice in a particular traditional ambience, is emphasized only in the Abrahamic world, it is necessary to recall the Laws of Manu in Hinduism, the cosmic character of Confucian ethics, the cosmic nature of the law of *karma* in Buddhism, the origins of Zoroastrian laws and the relation between law, revelation and justice in early Greek philosophy, especially in Pythagoras (d. circa 475 B.C.) and Parmenides (d. circa 450 B.C.). Furthermore, the extensive and profound discussions of Plato (d. 347 B.C.) about justice are related to his understanding of laws, which for him are not simply man-made agreements. One sees this clearly in his exposition of law in its cosmic dimension in his *Dialogues*, especially the later ones such as *Laws*, which interestingly enough was translated into Arabic as "*Kitab al-nawamis*" ("Book of Laws"), *namus* (the Greek *nomos*) (Law or Revelation) being considered by Muslims to be the same as the laws revealed by God to His prophets. Also the word "canon" in Greek, which gave rise to the Arabic word *qanun*, meaning law, is a Pythagorean term related to harmonics. Justice is related to both metaphysics and laws, and in all traditional worlds laws themselves descend from the Source and are related to cosmic laws and the harmony that pervades creation. The justice that dominates this world, despite all appearances to the contrary, is a necessary dimension of manifestation at all levels, precisely because manifestation *is* the manifestation of the Principle which is Justice Itself. There must be justice in the world in the same way that there must be existential reality in all beings by virtue of their existentiation by the absolute Being.

It must be added that justice dominates over the whole cosmos except in the human world where we are given the free will to be unjust, to rebel against Heaven, to flout the true nature of various beings because of selfish ends and most of all because of the possibility given to us as beings reflecting the Divine to possess free will, to forget who we are and to live in a state of negligence and ignorance. All human injustice begins in the deeper sense with our being unjust to our own deeper self, to the Divine "image" we bear deep down in the very substance of our soul, to the inner man whom we have forgotten through our spiritual blindness, the inner man whose rights we trample so easily under foot.

*

*   *

The present book deals not with justice in general, but with justice according to the words and deeds of 'Ali ibn Abi Talib. The Qur'an and *Hadith* are replete with references to justice and such terms as *al-'adl* (Justice), *al-qist* (Just Portion) and *al-mizan* (Balance or Scale) appear often in various contexts in these sacred sources of Islam. The latter term, meaning "balance," has many meanings, but is especially related to the aspect of justice that concerns balance, that is, putting things in their rightful place and of the measure of good and evil acts which are also related to justice and injustice. Needless to say, numerous commentators of the Qur'an and *Hadith* have dealt over the centuries with the meaning of these and other terms associated with justice. But in early Islam it was left most of all to 'Ali ibn Abi Talib to expound, on the basis of the Word of God and the teachings of the Prophet, the meaning of justice in its deepest metaphysical sense as well as in its social applications. His words and letters collected by Sayyid Sharif al-Radi in the 4th/10th century in a single volume entitled *Nahj al-Balaghah* ("The Path of Eloquence") are, after the Qur'an and *Hadith,* the most inspired and influential writings on justice in the annals of Islamic history.

'Ali was at once a metaphysician of the highest order and a man involved fully in the practical matters of this world, including being the caliph for five years until his assassination. His discussion of justice ranges therefore from the most sublime metaphysical and spiritual teachings to matters of practical, political, and social concern. His letter to Malik al-Ashtar, who was appointed by 'Ali as governor of Egypt, has been held up as model for a just ruler in both Sunni and Shi'ite circles since the first Islamic century. It is, therefore, especially amazing that no thorough and in-depth study had been devoted in any European languages to his understanding of justice until the appearance of this book. One can take a step further and claim more generally that, despite a few books that have appeared in Europe and America, little serious attention has been paid in the West to the understanding of the Islamic meaning of justice on various levels and its relation to both the spiritual and the practical life, to both the greater *jihad* (Striving in an inward sense) and the lesser *jihad* (Striving in a more external sense).

The present book is therefore, a very welcome addition to the field of Islamic studies, having been written with authenticity and in a scholarly manner from within the Islamic tradition by three authors with somewhat different perspectives. In the first essay, M. Ali Lakhani deals with perspicacity with the more metaphysical aspects of the subject, delving into the nature of the human being, the structure of reality and the universal significance of justice according to 'Ali. In the second essay, which complements the first, Reza Shah-Kazemi deals with the significance of justice in both the contemplative and active lives, which complement each other in principle, and especially as seen in the life of 'Ali. He also deals with 'Ali's emphasis on the relation between justice and faith and analyzes many passages from the letter to Malik al-Ashtar to illustrate the profound observations that he makes about 'Ali's views.

It is astonishing that the *Nahj al-balaghah,* which is one of the most important works in Islamic civilization, has never been translated into elegant English directly from the Arabic, an English which would be worthy to some extent of the remarkable eloquence of the original Arabic. It is also strange that so little exists in European languages on 'Ali in general while there are hundreds of books on him in Arabic, Persian, Urdu, Turkish and other Islamic languages[1]. The first two essays of this book are among the best writings on this extraordinary figure in Western languages and are obligatory reading for anyone interested in 'Ali but not familiar with Islamic languages.

The third essay deals with a somewhat different aspect of the subject. In many contexts, justice is identified with retribution, not only legally and practically in human society but also in the theological and eschatological sense. Sufism and spiritual chivalry have, however, always emphasized the aspect of God as the Merciful and how Divine Mercy complements Divine Justice. The sacred *hadith* "verily My Mercy precedeth My wrath" is a constant refrain in numerous Sufi texts. Leonard Lewisohn deals with this subject on the basis of the words and deeds of 'Ali as well as classical Sufi sources. He emphasizes the importance of forbearance, tolerance and forgiveness and makes notable comparisons of Islamic teachings on Divine Mercy and Forgiveness with material drawn from English literature. His treatment of the subject is especially important these days when some people in the Islamic world commit heinous acts in the name of justice, being impervious to Islam's emphasis upon Divine Mercy and Forgiveness. Such people strengthen the hands of those in the West who harbor enmity against Islam and who identify God as simply a tribal god of revenge and retribution without the love and mercy that they identify

---

[1] Reza Shah Kazemi's *Justice and Remembrance—Introducing the Spirituality of Imam 'Ali* (London: I.B. Tauris in association with the Institute of Ismaili Studies, 2006) will be the first such work on 'Ali in any European language.

with Christianity. In fact nothing could be farther from the truth as the final essay in this book demonstrates amply.

The traditionalist writers such as René Guénon (d. 1951), Ananda K. Coomaraswamy (d. 1947), Frithjof Schuon (d. 1998), Titus Burckhardt (d. 1984), Martin Lings (d. 2005) and others, have expounded traditional metaphysics and the perennial philosophy in its metaphysical, cosmological, anthropological and artistic dimensions in a magisterial manner for some eight decades. But strangely enough, none of them has devoted a major work to the subject of justice, although they have made many valuable allusions to it. This book, especially its first two chapters written from a strictly traditional point of view, is an important addition to the corpus of traditional literature in that it deals almost exclusively with the subject of justice, although only in the context of Islam and not on a global scale.

I congratulate the authors of this book for their important contributions and hope that this book will reach a wide audience. Let us hope that it will be read by those interested in the meaning of justice from the traditional perspective as well as students and devotees of Islam in general and 'Ali in particular. Let us also hope that Muslims themselves, especially those brought up in the West and not well acquainted with Islamic languages, will gain through this book a deeper understanding of the life and thought of 'Ali and the deepest meaning of justice in the Islamic tradition.

Seyyed Hossein Nasr
Bethesda, Maryland, U. S. A.
December 2005
Dhu'l-qi'dah, 1426 A.H.

"Muhammad marries his daughter Fatima to his nephew ʿAli." From the Turkish manuscript *Siyer-i Nebī, volume IV, original Ms. p. 24b*, 16th century. Istanbul, Top-kapi Saray Museum.

THE METAPHYSICS
OF HUMAN GOVERNANCE:
IMAM 'ALI, TRUTH AND JUSTICE[1]

M. Ali Lakhani

No individual is lost and no nation is refused prosperity and success
if the foundations of their thoughts and actions rest upon piety
and godliness, and upon truth and justice.[2]

'Ali ibn Abi Talib

I. Introduction

The aim of this essay is to demonstrate, through the writings[3] of 'Ali
ibn Abi Talib[4] (referred to herein as "Imam 'Ali" or "the Imam") and
the sources he venerated, how his conception of "justice" is informed
by certain principles of traditional metaphysics, and to touch upon its
relevance to our modern times.

---

[1] This is a revised version of a study that was submitted and delivered to the International Congress on Imam 'Ali and Justice, Unity and Security, held in Tehran, March 13 through 16, 2001, organized by the Institute for Humanities and Cultural Studies.

[2] Sermon 21, *Nahjul-Balagha*, Sermons, Letters and Sayings of Imam 'Ali, translated by Syed Mohammed Askari Jafery, Tahrike Tarsile Qur'an, New York, Second American Edition, 1981 (henceforth referred to as *Nahjul-Balagha*, Jafery). There are variant translations in English of Imam 'Ali's writings as rendered by Sharif ar-Radi. We will also refer to the translation by Sayed Ali Reza, Tahrike Tarsile Qur'an, New York, Fifth American Edition, 1986 (henceforth referred to as *Nahjul-Balagha*, Reza).

[3] We have used the term "writings" to designate the compendium of sermons, letters and sayings attributed to Imam 'Ali, collected and preserved by Sharif ar-Radi under the title *Nahjul-Balagha* in 420 A.H. There is evidence that the words of Imam 'Ali were gathered during his own lifetime and preserved in writing within 30 years following his death. Many of the sermons and orations of Imam 'Ali have unfortunately been lost, but it is now generally accepted by scholars that the compendium of Sharif ar-Radi, based on earlier reliable sources, contains the words of Imam 'Ali, and it is in this sense that we refer to these as Imam 'Ali's "writings", though these are not his "writings" *stricto sensu*.

[4] 'Ali ibn Abi Talib (c.600 - 661) was the son-in-law of Prophet Muhammad, and the Fourth Caliph of Sunni Islam. Shi'ite Muslims venerate 'Ali as their first Imam, the political and spiritual successor of the Prophet. Imam 'Ali is generally venerated by all Muslims as one of the foremost sources of Islamic spirituality.

A preliminary observation will serve to place this discussion in its proper context: at the heart of every traditional religious or metaphysical quest lie two categories of question central to human existence. The first has to do with the discernment of reality. It can be formulated variously as "What is the nature of reality?", "Who am I?", "What is the world?", "How can one know what is real?", "What is truth and what is the criterion for its discernment?" and so on. The second has to do with our relationship to the reality we have discerned. It can be formulated variously as "What is the purpose of life?", "How should we relate to others?", "How should we govern ourselves?" and so on. Answers to both these categories of question must be provided by any traditional religious or metaphysical system that claims to be comprehensive. In other words, the system must address both sets of questions by providing, respectively, two elements of response: a *doctrine of truth* by which reality may be truthfully discerned, and a *method of transformation* by which one may integrate with and conform to the reality that one has truthfully discerned.[5]

It is undoubtedly a claim of Islam, as one of the world's major universal religions, to offer not merely a theological but also a comprehensive metaphysical answer to the central questions of human existence: thus the Qur'an claims to be both a "clear proof"[6] (of reality) and a "manifest light"[7] (guiding all true believers upon the Straight Path[8]). Consistent with all other revealed religious traditions and with

---

[5] Seyyed Hossein Nasr states: "...every religion possesses two elements which are its basis and its foundation: a doctrine which distinguishes between the Absolute and the relative, between the absolutely Real and the relatively real...and a method of concentrating upon the Real, and attaching oneself to the Absolute and living according to the Will of Heaven, in accordance with the purpose and meaning of human existence" - *Ideals and Realities of Islam*, Beacon Press, Boston, 1972, at page 15.

[6] *Al-An'am*, VI:157; *An-Nisa'* IV:174.

[7] *Ash-Shura* XLII:52; *An-Nisa'* IV:174.

[8] The concept of the "Straight Path" or *al-Sirat al-Mustaqeem* (which will be referred to elsewhere in this paper from time to time) derives from the *Surat al-Fatihah*, the opening chapter of the Qur'an, recited by all devout Muslims in their daily prayers. The Qur'anic supplication: *ihdina's-sirat al-mustaqeem (Al-Fatihah* I:6) is translated as "Guide us on the Straight Path", which is explained in the next Qur'anic verse as "The Path of those upon whom You have bestowed your grace, not of those who have earned Your wrath nor of those who have gone astray". Allowing for the exception that God's grace is like the wind that "bloweth where it listeth", it can be said that the precondition of being on the Straight Path is that the supplicant must merit God's grace by having a pure heart. Those "who have gone astray" can be understood as those who have not awakened to the perception of their intellects and who thereby fail to discern the real from the illusory; while those "who have earned Your wrath" can be understood as those who, in the face of external guidance from the divine

---

the universal principles of traditional metaphysics, the central doctrine of Islam is of the unity of reality, and its sacramental method is
aimed at the union with that reality. Doctrine and method, unity and
union: these relate back to the two sets of questions of human existence as we have defined them. In answering the first of these—the
questions about the *discernment of reality*—we are taught that reality
is essentially integrated and accordingly that we must refine our perceptions to discern reality as One. This discernment has implications
for the second set of questions—which relate to our *relationship with
reality*—for, unless we conform to the reality we have discerned, we
cannot lead integrated lives. The two sets of questions are therefore
metaphysically linked, and we shall have more to say about the nature
of this linkage later in this paper.

For the moment, the key point we wish to emphasize is that
Imam 'Ali time and again in his writings articulates his twin mission
as being that of "truth and justice"—a phrase used repeatedly in his
khutbas and other writings compiled by Sharif ar-Radi under the title
Nahjul-Balagha[9]—and, in so doing, he addresses both themes that are
required to be addressed by a comprehensive metaphysical or religious tradition, namely, Truth (or the discernment of the nature and
structure of reality) and Justice (or the conforming of humanity and
all creation to the order of reality). Let us now examine each of these
themes in turn.

II. Truth: The Discernment of Reality

Before one poses any questions about the nature of reality, it becomes
necessary to consider an epistemological question: "How can reality be
known?" Common experience teaches us about the unreliability of
the five senses, and a moment's reflection makes it clear that discursive reason cannot yield any answers to questions about the ultimate
nature of reality, which is transcendent[10]. How is it possible, then, to
discern reality truthfully? The answer provided by traditional meta-

---

messengers and the inner discernment of their intellects, yet refuse to perfect their
submission to God, in other words those who enslave their intellects to the dictates
and temptations of their egoic wills.

[9] Refer to note 3 (*supra*) for a brief explanation of the collection titled *Nahjul-
Balagha.*

[10] Frithjof Schuon writes: "Reason obtains knowledge like a man walking about and
exploring the countryside by successive discoveries, whereas the Intellect contemplates
the same countryside from a mountain height" (*Stations of Wisdom*, Frithjof Schuon,
World Wisdom Books, Bloomington, Indiana, 1995, at page 65). In a well-known

physics is simple: truth, being of a universal order, is inscribed within our deepest self—that within us which is transcendent and universal, our primordial nature, the core of our very being. Knowledge of reality is therefore equated with self-knowledge or gnosis, and can at one level be understood as the centripetal and radial reconnection of the circumference with the Center through the grace of the primordial intelligence that constitutes our very being. That faculty which is capable of discerning reality in its most subtle nature—bearing in mind that the merely human is not privileged to know the Divine—is not the human faculty of the common senses or of the discursive reason, but the transcendent faculty of the supra-rational Intellect[11], the core of our discerning self, which is sometimes labeled the "Heart".[12]

The Islamic response to the epistemological question is completely in accord with the response of traditional metaphysics: true knowledge resides in the "Heart" or spiritual core of our being. Muslim theosophy starts with the Qur'anic teaching that the divine breath is the

---

phrase, Meister Eckhart has defined the Intellect as "something in the soul which is uncreated and uncreatable". It is the Intellect alone that is adequate to Truth. Reason alone cannot discover Truth: this is as futile as "a fool who seeks the luminous Sun/ In the desert with a lamp in his hand" (an image from Shabistari's *Gulshan-i raz*).

[11] "Metaphysic is supra-rational, intuitive and immediate knowledge. Moreover, this pure intellectual intuition, without which there is no true metaphysic, must never be likened to the intuition spoken of by certain contemporary philosophers, which, on the contrary, is infra-rational. There is an intellectual intuition and a sensory intuition; one is above reason, but the other is below it; this latter can only grasp the world of change and becoming, namely, nature, or rather an inappreciable part of nature. The domain of intellectual intuition, by contrast, is the domain of eternal and immutable principles, it is the domain of metaphysic. To have a direct grasp of universal principles, the transcendent intellect must itself belong to the universal order; it is thus not an individual faculty, and to consider it as such would be contradictory, since it cannot pertain to the possibilities of the individual to transcend his own limits": René Guénon, *Le Métaphysique Orientale*, p. 11, quoted by Whitall N. Perry in his magisterial anthology, *A Treasury of Traditional Wisdom*, Perennial Books, Middlesex, Second Edition, 1981, at page 733.

[12] The center of oneself, symbolically the "Heart", is in traditional cosmology also understood to be the metaphysical center of the world, symbolically the "Sun". This radiant Center is, like an eye, the visionary core of one's being, which, in Meister Eckhart's terminology, is simultaneously "the eye by which I see God" and "the eye by which God sees me". The symbolism of the "Heart" is universal: some examples are: "I am seated in the hearts of all", *Bhagavad Gita*, XV:15; "His throne is in heaven who teaches from within the heart", St. Augustine, *In Epist. Joannis ad Parthos*, cited by A.K. Coomaraswamy in 'Recollection, Indian and Platonic', Supplement to the *Journal of American Oriental Society*, No. 3, April-June, 1944, p.1; and the *hadith qudsi* of the Prophet: "My earth and My heaven contain me not, but the heart of My faithful servant containeth Me", cited in Whitall N. Perry, *A Treasury of Traditional Wisdom, supra*, at p. 822.

very spirit that is infused into our Adamic clay: "Then He fashioned him in due proportion and breathed into him of His Spirit."[13] This divine spirit is our *fitra*—our primordial and innate spiritual nature[14] —which pre-existentially affirms and testifies to its Origin in the Qur'anic episode of the Covenant of Alast[15], and is endowed with an innate knowledge of its fiduciary obligations—the *Amanah*[16] or Divine Trust, the duties entrusted to humanity and to each of us individually and which constitute our *raison d'être*. This is the primordial self of whom the Prophet has said: "Every child is born according to *fitra*. Then its parents make it into a Christian, a Jew, or a Magian (Zoroastrian)."[17] It is a self already endowed with the knowledge of its Maker (in other words, of the ultimate integrity of reality—in Islamic terms, *tawhid*) even before its entry into this world. It is the spirit or *ruh*, whose discerning faculty is *'aql* or Intellect, not merely the discursive reason or the senses. This is the center and "Heart" of our consciousness, referred to in the famous *hadith qudsi*: "My earth

---

[13] *As-Sajdah* XXXII:9.

[14] Note the *hadith*: "God created mankind in His own image": Bukhari, *Isti'dhan* 1; Muslim, *Birr* 115.

[15] The Covenant of Alast refers to a primordial covenant between each human being and God, referred to in the Qur'anic Verse, *Al-A'raf* VII:172—"And (remember) when your Lord took their offspring from the loins of the children of Adam and made them testify as to themselves (saying): 'Am I not your Lord?'—They said: 'Yea, verily, we so testify', lest you should say on the Day of Resurrection: 'Verily, we have been unaware of this'." The term "Alast" derives from the key Arabic phrase that appears in the quoted verse: *alastu bi-rabbikum* ('Am I not your Lord?'). By attesting to the essential nature of reality, humanity affirms its pre-existential bond with God, as both supra-temporal Origin and supra-spatial Center. This attestation requires of humanity an existential re-affirmation of its Source and Nature through discernment, remembrance and virtue, the central features of religious life, which constitute, allowing for the grace of God, the means of all salvation.

[16] The Islamic concept of *Amanah* or the Divine Trust derives scripturally from the following Qur'anic Verse, *Al-Ahzab*, XXXIII:72—"We offered the Trust to the heavens and the earth and the mountains, but they refused to carry it and were afraid of it. And the human being carried it. Surely he is very ignorant, a great wrongdoer." Humanity, being privileged by the grace of revelation and intellection to know the transcendent and to recognize creation as a manifestation of transcendence, also bears the responsibility of stewardship towards creation. This is an aspect of the principle of *noblesse oblige*. To know God is also to know all things in God, and God in all things, and to treat all God's creatures as sacred. The origin of morality is predicated on the discernment that "all that lives is holy" (*William Blake*), which in turn is premised on the discernment of the sacred as the radiance of the divine. That humanity in general is content to accept the privilege of its creaturely superiority without accepting the responsibility that such superiority confers, explains the Qur'anic comment at the end of the quoted verse.

[17] Bukhari, *Jana'iz* 80; Muslim, *Qadar* 22.

and My heaven contain me not, but the Heart of My faithful servant containeth Me"; and again in those Qur'anic *surahs* that refer to the inscription of faith upon the "hearts" of men[18]. This is the Heart which, while capable of "containing" that in us which is divine, is also capable, in Qur'anic terms, of being "diseased"[19] or "rusted"[20] or "locked"[21]. It is this knowing Heart—the seat of our conscience—that "fallen" man, now in a state of "heedlessness"[22] (*ghafla*), must strive, by divine grace, to awaken. This "awakening" operates as both an illumination and a liquefaction of the heart, simultaneously dispelling the darkness of its ignorance and melting the carapace of its existential hardness[23] with the tender love of the spirit[24]. Truth is an awakening into a state of Presence and the awareness of Presence, into a state of Self-remembering wholeness (or holiness) that is imbued with a sense of the sacred[25], a sacramentally charged all-absorbing and immersed awareness of the Omni-Presence of the Divine Countenance[26], so that

[18] *Al-Mujadilah* LVIII:22 – "...For such, He has written Faith in their hearts..."

[19] *Al-Baqarah* II:10 – "In their hearts is a disease..."

[20] *Al-Mutaffifin* LXXXIII:14 – "...what they were earning has rusted upon their hearts."

[21] *Surat Muhammad* or *Surat Al-Qital* XLVII:24 – "Do they not deeply ponder the Qur'an? Or is it that there are locks upon their hearts?"

[22] *Al-Hajj* XXII:46 – "...Verily, it is not the eyes that grow blind, but it is the hearts which are in the breasts that grow blind."

[23] Frithjof Schuon writes: "The world is made up of forms, and they are as it were the debris of a celestial music that has become frozen; knowledge or sanctity dissolves our frozen state and liberates the inner melody. Here we must recall the verse in the Qur'an which speaks of the 'stones from which streams spring forth', though there are hearts which are 'harder than stones', a passage reminiscent of the 'living water' of Christ and of the 'well of water springing up into everlasting life' in the hearts of saints" (*Understanding Islam*, Frithjof Schuon, Unwin, London, 1976, at page 41).

[24] Grace operates as a Divine Ray of Love that is operative within the serenity of the contemplative mind and in the vigilance of spiritual ardor. Frithjof Schuon writes in *Spiritual Perspectives and Human Facts*, translated by P. N. Townsend, Perennial Books, Pates Manor, Bedfont, Middlesex, 1987, at page 158: "Peace is absence of dissipation. Love is absence of hardness. Fallen man is hardness and dissipation...In the peace of the Lord, the waves of this dissipation are calmed and the soul is at rest in its primordial nature, in its center. Through love, the outer shell of the heart is melted like snow and the heart awakens from its death; hard, opaque and cold in the fallen state, it becomes liquid, transparent and aflame in the Divine life."

[25] The term "sacred" denotes the theophanic radiation and resonance of the Absolute in the contingent: "The sacred is the presence of the Center in the periphery, of the Motionless in the moving" (*Understanding Islam*, Frithjof Schuon, *supra*, at page 48).

[26] The notion of the theophanic Countenance of the Divine derives scripturally from the following Qur'anic Verse, *Al-Baqarah*, II:115 – "Wherever you turn, there is the face of God."

its consciousness is illuminated with and moistened by the knowledge of its Maker. This realizational knowledge (gnosis), which the believer had pre-existentially affirmed in the Covenant of Alast, now (that is to say, in this privative existence) becomes incumbent on the devout Muslim as an existential affirmation in the first part of the *shahadah*. The formula for this affirmation is the testament, *la ilaha illa 'llah*— literally, "There is no god if not *the* God", which could, for this purpose, be rendered esoterically as: "Nothing is real if it is not discerned as a manifestation of Absolute integrated reality." In other words—to anticipate our argument—Truth is to be discerned as a theophany. This is a point that we will elaborate upon later.

Having dealt with the epistemological question about the basis of knowledge, one can begin to deal with the substantive question of the nature of reality itself. From the viewpoint of traditional metaphysics, creation progressively exteriorizes that which is principially interior. Reality, while being essentially One, is at the same time a hierarchical descent or objectivization from the subtle and transcendent Essence to gross and immanent Form—an unfolding concretization of the Absolute to the Infinite, from the Center to the periphery. At its most subtle level, Supreme Reality is beyond knowledge, indefinable and ineffably mysterious, and all human approaches to this ultimate knowledge are therefore characterized by paradox and bewilderment: the Absolute cannot in any ultimate sense be apprehended by man, as such, being transcendent and beyond-being. However, because Supreme Reality is Absolute, it is necessarily Infinite, and all possibilities are prefigured within it at an archetypal level that can be said to be relatively-absolute—to admit of which is not in any way to derogate from the essential Self-Sufficiency, Ipseity and Oneness of Supreme Reality. The forms and possibilities of all beings are thus gathered within this qualified level of reality and are projected or manifested out of principial Reality, in a given or defined measure, as creatures within existence. This projection has a reality that is entirely contingent on the Absolute, which is its fount and, more accurately, the Sole Existent. Creaturely or contingent existence is thus a theophany, a radiation of transcendence through which all creation sacrally partakes of and reflects the metaphysical transparency of the Divine.

This metaphysical view of reality is affirmed within Islam. The Qur'anic view accords perfectly with the metaphysical view by distinguishing between transcendent reality (*tanzih*)[27] and immanent

---

[27] See, for instance, *Ash-Shura* XLII:11 – "Nothing is like Him."

reality (*tashbih*)[28]. God is the Supreme Reality, whose essentially unconditioned quiddity (*dhat*) is distinguished from His qualified attributes (*sifat*) but without in any way derogating from His essential metaphysical Oneness (*tawhid*). As Absolute and unconditioned reality, God is without likeness or peer or privation or cause: this is the Absolute reality of the *Surat Al-Ikhlas*[29]. But as Absolute reality, God is also Infinite, both transcendent and immanent. The Qur'an therefore speaks of the attributes of God, ascribing to Him various names and qualities[30]. It is these names and qualities, prefigured within the archetypal or imaginal realm of the Infinite (the "storehouses" of God's creation[31]), that are projected into existence by divine fiat or Command[32] —but "only in a known measure"[33]. And it is through these names and qualities—which human beings are privileged among all creatures to know[34] —that man can attain the humanly possible knowledge of God: in other words, the created world (the macro-

---

[28] See, for instance, *Al-Hadid* LVII:4 – "He is with you, wherever you are"; or *Al-Baqarah*, II:115 (*supra*) – "Wherever you turn, there is the face of God."

[29] The *Surat Al-Ikhlas* is Verse CXII of the Qur'an, the Verse of Divine Purity or Metaphysical Oneness. It forms part of the daily prayer of devout Muslims, a reminder of the principle of the integrity of reality (*tawhid*) and of the Absolute uniqueness, self-sufficiency and transcendence of the Deity. The Verse states: "In the Name of God, the Most Gracious, the Most Merciful. Say: He is God, (the reality that is metaphysically) One; God, the Self-Sufficient; He does not begat, nor was He begotten; and there is none that can be compared to Him." As to the notion of Metaphysical Oneness, Imam 'Ali states in Sermon 190 (*Nahjul-Balagha*, Jafery): "He is one but His unity is not a mathematical quality..." Metaphysical Oneness is thus "a true whole (which) is logically anterior to, and independent of, its parts", as explained by René Guénon in *The Multiple States of Being*, Larson Publications Inc., New York, 1984 (translation by Joscelyn Godwin from the French book "*Les etats multiple de l'etre*").

[30] These are the *asma wa sifat*, sometimes referred to as the Ninety-Nine Names of God (though there are many more), such as the Compassionate, the Merciful, and so on.

[31] The reference to "storehouses" relates to *Al-Hijr*, XV:21 of the Qur'an -- "There is no thing whose storehouses are not with Us, but We send it down only in a known measure." This is the archetypal realm in which existence is prefigured in the "Mind of God" (if we can be permitted to use this expression, without intending to anthropomorphize the Divine).

[32] *An-Nahl*, XVI:40 – "Verily, Our Word to a thing when We intend it, is only that We say unto it: "Be!", and it is."

[33] See *Al-Hijr*, XV:21, *supra*.

[34] According to Islamic tradition and scripture, humanity is privileged among all creatures by the scope of its knowledge and by an intellect that is adequate to the Absolute. The Qur'anic Verse *Al-Baqarah*, II:31—"And He taught Adam the names of all things..." attests to the symbolic knowledge endowed upon humanity. This presumes the requirement of a "symbolist spirit" of interpretation. One should bear in

cosm) is constituted of "signs" which resonate within the pre-existential memory of man (the microcosm) as the names and attributes of God, which are reflections of the spiritual realities of the Divine (the metacosm). It is by the grace of spiritual literacy that man, not through merely human intelligence but through the blessing of the innate spiritual intellect, can know God. This gnosis (*irfan*) is the drop's knowledge of the Ocean that it contains within itself. Man, as such, cannot know the Divine Essence or Godhead[35], but the transcendent spiritual faculty—the Intellect operating within man—is privileged to know Itself. This is the "knowledge of unveiling" (*kashf*), which operates *externally* as the perception of the revealed reality as a theophany, as a sacred text comprising of "signs"[36] pointing to God—and *internally*,

---

mind that the "names" of things signify an anagogical understanding of reality because, as the Qur'an states, in *Al-A'raf*, VII:180, for example, "the Most Beautiful Names belong to Allah". Seyyed Hossein Nasr, commenting on *Al-Baqarah*, II:31, notes that man "was given power and dominion over all things by virtue of being God's vicegerant (*khalifah*) on earth. But with this function of *khalifah* was combined the quality of *'abd*, that is, the quality of being in perfect submission to God. Man has the right to dominate over the earth as *khalifah* only on condition that he remains in perfect submission to Him who is the real master of nature" (from the essay, *Who is Man?: The perennial Answer of Islam*, by Seyyed Hossein Nasr. The essay was delivered by Nasr as a Noranda Lecture at Expo 67 in Montreal on September 4, 1967, later published in the traditionalist journal, *Studies in Comparative Religion*, Winter 1968, Volume 2, No. 1, and reprinted in *The Sword of Gnosis*, edited by Jacob Needleman, Penguin Metaphysical Library, Penguin Books, Baltimore, 1974, at page 203. The quoted passage appears at page 207).

[35] Thus we see in the Qur'an that even the Holy Prophet, during his exalted *mi'raj* in which he journeyed to the seventh heaven, was proscribed from transgressing the bounds of a lote tree (*Sidrat-ul-Muntuha*), and was thereby veiled from Supreme Reality—see *An-Najm*, LIII:17. This is in keeping with the *hadith*: "God has seventy veils of light and darkness. Were they to be removed, the glories of His Face would burn away everything perceived by the sight of His creatures": al-Ghazali, *Ihya* 1:144. Man, as such, is veiled from the Godhead—though man can know the attributes of God, as these are disclosed by revelation and experience—though even here it is important to emphasize that the Divine Attributes are qualitatively different from their human equivalents, which are their existential approximations. Only God—or that which is transcendent within man—can know God. Thus Schuon has noted that "the individuality as such will always be a veil before the Divine Reality, for the individual as such cannot 'know God'. The Intellect, whether it is envisaged in its 'created' aspect or in its 'uncreated' reality, is not the individual. The individual experiences it in the form of a fulgurating darkness and he grasps only the flashes which illumine and transfigure him." (*Spiritual Perspectives and Human Facts*, by Frithjof Schuon, *supra*, at page 155).

[36] There are numerous passages in the Qur'an that speak of created things as the "signs" of God. See, for instance, *Surat Yunus*, X:6 and 67 (night and day); *Ash-Shura*, XLII:32 and 33 (ships in the sea); *Al-Jathiyah*, XLV:3 – "Verily, in the heavens and the earth are signs for the believers."

through sacred recollection[37], as self-identification with the spiritual nature of these "signs". This is one of the meanings of the Verse: "We shall show them Our signs upon the horizons and in their selves."[38]

Thus far we have set out a traditionally metaphysical response to the first category of questions central to human existence, namely, the questions dealing with how to discern reality, and we have argued that this metaphysical response is in accord with the Islamic response based on Qur'anic scripture and the *hadith*. As both of these sources were venerated by Imam 'Ali and are referred to deferentially in his writings, it might suffice to argue that Imam 'Ali's response corresponds to the metaphysical and Islamic schema we have outlined earlier. However, a few illustrations of Imam 'Ali's views will serve to better demonstrate this correspondence.

On the issue of the epistemological question of the basis of knowledge, it is well known that the 'Alid tradition is an intellectual tradition, and there are numerous references throughout Imam 'Ali's writings to demonstrate that he advocated an intellectual approach to the discernment of reality. For instance:

> Use your intellect to understand something when you hear about it—the intellect that examines, that is, and not just the intellect that repeats what it hears, for surely there are many who repeat the knowledge that they hear, and there are few who examine it.[39]

Intellectual appreciation occurs through examination and understanding, not through unexamined acceptance, even if the latter involves mental processes. It is significant in the following excerpt that the Imam distinguishes between the mind and intellect. Censuring his recalcitrant followers, he states:

---

[37] The practice of divine invocation or *dhikr* is a method of "realizing reality", of awakening to the Presence of the Divine Countenance and of being experientially one with the Divine Substance. The connection between the practice of invocation and the notion of "names" is derived from various traditions and Qur'anic passages, for example, *Al-Isra'*, XVII:110—"Say: Invoke God or invoke the Most Gracious, by whatever name you invoke Him (it is the same), for to Him belong the Best Names..."

[38] *Surat Fussilat*, XLI:53. There are three sources of Truth in Islam, all rooted in God: these are the Revelation as Scripture (the Qur'an, in Islam, which is the "criterion" of Truth), as the Objective Creation (the "horizons" or macrocosm), and as the Subjective Self (the microcosm).

[39] From *The Sayings and Wisdom of Imam 'Ali*, The Muhammadi Trust, Zahra Publications, ISBN 0946079919.

O people! You behave as if you have bodies and minds but no intellects: as if you have extremely divergent views and do not want to gather round and obey an authority.[40]

Implicit here is the notion that intellection is to be distinguished from the ordinary functioning of the mind. The "authority" to be obeyed can thus be understood, not only externally, as the spiritual authority of the Caliph or Imam, but also internally, as the transcendent and critical intellect—the discerning eye of the spirit, which is distinguished from the discursive reasoning capacity of the merely human mind. It is the universality of this intellect that endows it with the criterion of objectivity, hence the capability to resolve "divergent views". Note also that this view of the superiority of the transcendent intellect over the merely rational mind accords with the metaphysical hierarchy of the spirit, mind and body, the ascendancy of the spiritual over the psychic and corporeal, or *spiritus vel intellectus* over the "psycho-physical *res*."[41]

Similarly, Imam 'Ali expressly acknowledges the Heart as the locus of the intellect, the source of innate metaphysical knowledge of reality. For instance, a celebrated prayer that is ascribed to Imam 'Ali, known as the *Dua Kumayl*,[42] contains the assertion that the "heart has been filled with (pure) knowledge" of the Maker. This accords with the Qur'anic descriptions of the Adamic clay being infused with the divine Spirit[43], and of archetypal man being taught the "names" of all things[44]. In the celebrated First Sermon, Imam 'Ali describes the process of creation and of the infusion of the divine Spirit into Adam: "...He infused into it the Divine soul (intellect) and the figure stood up as a man."[45] It is this spiritual Center within humanity,

---

[40] Sermon 100, *Nahjul-Balagha*, Jafery.

[41] This universal cosmological principle is found in all religious traditions. For example, a clear statement of this principle is to be found in the *Bhagavad Gita*: "It is said that the senses are powerful. But beyond the senses is the mind, beyond mind is intellect, and beyond and greater than intellect is He (the Spirit)" (translated by Shri Purohit Swami, 1994, Shambhala, Boston, Massachusetts, Chapter 3, pages 35 and 36).

[42] According to tradition, the prayer known as *Dua Kumayl* was a supplication attributed by Imam 'Ali to the Prophet Khidr and was taught by the Imam to his disciple, Kumayl ibn Ziyad Nakha'i, by whose name the prayer is now generally known.

[43] *As-Sajdah*, XXXII:9 – "Then He fashioned him in due proportion and breathed into him of His Spirit."

[44] See note 30, *supra*.

[45] Sermon 2, *Nahjul-Balagha*, Jafery. See *Nahjul-Balagha*, Reza, Sermon 1: "Allah collected from hard, soft, sweet and sour earth, clay which He dripped in water till it got pure, and kneaded it with moisture till it became gluey. From it He carved an

with its privileged pre-existential faculty of intellectual, intuitive, and profound knowledge (called gnosis or *irfan*), that enables human beings to discern reality to its core and to testify as to its spiritual basis—thereby reaffirming the knowledge attested to in the Covenant of Alast[46]. To know one's essence is to know the substance of all reality, the metaphysical Center and Origin, which are One. Echoing the hermetic maxim of self-knowledge as the path to realization[47], the Imam states:

> Whosoever knows himself well knows his Maker.[48]

And the intrinsic nature of this intelligence is salvific. Because true knowledge is transformative, as we shall later see. Thus Imam 'Ali states:

> God does not entrust
> anyone with intelligence
> without saving him thereby someday.[49]

The *khutbas* contain numerous passages in which Imam 'Ali describes the spiritual basis of reality, that is to say, the nature of God, the supreme and manifest reality discernable by the human Intellect. For instance, in one sermon, we read:

> Praised be God who knows the secrets of things, and the proofs of whose existence shine in various phases of nature. No physical

image with curves, joints, limbs and segments. He solidified it till it dried up for a fixed time and a known duration. Then He blew into it out of His Spirit whereupon it took the pattern of a human being with mind that governs him, intelligence which he makes use of, limbs that serve him, organs that change his position, sagacity that differentiates between truth and untruth, tastes and smells, colours and species. He is a mixture of clays of different colours, cohesive materials, divergent contradictories and differing properties like heat, cold, softness and hardness."

[46] See note 15, *supra*.

[47] Thus, for example, the metaphysician, Frithjof Schuon writes: "to know the intellect is to know its consubstantial content and so the nature of things, and this is why Greek gnosis says, 'Know thyself', the Gospels say 'The Kingdom of Heaven is within you', and Islam 'Who knows himself knows his Lord." (*Understanding Islam*, Frithjof Schuon, *supra*, at page 109).

[48] Quoted by Whitall N. Perry in *A Treasury of Traditional Wisdom, supra*, at page 863.

[49] *Living and Dying with Grace: Counsels of Hadrat Ali*, translated by Thomas Cleary, Shambhala, 1995, page 103.

eye has or will ever see Him. But those who have not seen Him physically cannot deny His existence, yet the minds of those who have accepted His existence cannot grasp the real essence of Divine Nature. His place is so high that nothing can be imagined higher. He is so near to us that nothing can be imagined nearer. The Eminence of His position has not placed him further away from His creatures, and His Nearness has not brought them up to His Level. He has not permitted the human mind to grasp the Essence of His Being, yet He has not prevented them from realizing His Presence.[50]

In this eloquent passage, we see that Imam 'Ali describes the reality of God as both transcendent—and therefore places His Essence beyond our mere human faculties[51] —and immanent—and therefore places us intimately within His Presence, for the discerning spiritual Intellect. In this description, we also glean that there are levels in the structure of reality, the highest being "His Level", in other words the transcendent Essence; and also that there are degrees of intimacy or "Nearness". The significance of the polarities (High/Low and Near/Far) and the continuum of gradations implied by these polarities will be discussed later. For the moment, it suffices to note that reality is metaphysically hierarchical, that it has verticality.

In a famous passage from the First Sermon, Imam 'Ali emphasizes the doctrine of *tawhid*—that is, the essential integrity and Unity of reality, notwithstanding its apparent differentiation through multiplicity—when he states:

The first step of religion is to accept, understand and realize Him as the Lord. The perfection of understanding lies in conviction and confirmation, and the true way of conviction is to sincerely believe that there is no god but He. The correct form of belief in His Unity is to realize that He is so absolutely pure and above nature that nothing can be added to or subtracted from His Being. That is, one should realize that there is no difference between His Person and His attributes, and His attributes should not be differentiated or distinguished from His Person.

---

[50] Sermon 54, *Nahjul-Balagha*, Jafery. This appears as Sermon 49 in *Nahjul-Balagha*, Reza (*supra*).

[51] Affirming the primacy of the transcendent Intellect, Imam 'Ali has said: "God is not that which can enter under one of the categories of knowledge. God is That which guides reasoning toward Himself" - cited in *Bihar al-anwar* of Majlisi, Tehran, 1305 - 15, vol. II, p. 186.

> Whoever accepts His attributes to be other than His Person actually forsakes the idea of the Unity of God...[52]

Elsewhere, he states:

> Remember that He is Absolute and Infinite, a Being without limitations, attributes or qualities of His creatures.[53]

Through these, and many other, passages in the *Nahjul-Balagha*, Imam 'Ali affirms a view of reality that corresponds to the traditionally metaphysical view found in the Qur'an and *hadith*—of a reality whose substance, notwithstanding any outward differentiation, is spiritual. This spiritual foundation is, as it were, a radiance or effulgence that is discernable by the spiritually critical intellect. It is the ontological conviction that undergirds cognition: the knowledge of the very foundation of being. It is the discernment that all of creation is wondrous, imbued with an intelligence that resonates sacramentally within the spiritually receptive intellect. The Imam invites us to open our eyes to wonder at the design of creation, to be alive to the Sacred Ocean in which we all swim. Thus, for example, there are many passages in the *khutbas* that deal with the intricate architecture of creation and how these creations (whether a bat, an ant, a date palm, a locust or a peacock) are all "signs" pointing to a supreme Architect. For instance, after describing the marvelous design of an ant, Imam 'Ali states, in a passage that is interesting to read in today's post-Nietzschean and neo-Darwinist world:

> It is a pity that man refuses to accept the existence of the Grand Architect of this universe and this Mighty Creator of nature. It is a pity that he either believes his own existence to be an accident, or that he has come into being of his own accord and none has created him...Can there be a building without a builder? Can there be an effect without a cause?[54]

In another wonderfully evocative passage, illustrative of the wondrous qualities of spiritually sensitive observation and vision, he

---

[52] Sermon 1, *Nahjul-Balagha*, Jafery.

[53] Sermon 191, *Nahjul-Balagha*, Jafery. See Sermon 185 in *Nahjul-Balagha*, Reza (*supra*) - This Sermon describes the nature of God in sublimely apophatic language.

[54] Sermon 190, *Nahjul-Balagha*, Jafery. See Sermon 184 in *Nahjul-Balagha*, Reza (*supra*): "...woe be to him who disbelieves in the Ordainer and denies the Ruler."

arouses in his audience an appreciation of what is meant by the omniscience and omnipresence of God, in these terms:

> He knows where and how the smallest living organisms pass their lives. He knows where ants pass their summers and worms sleep out the winter seasons. He hears the sorrowful cries of speechless animals and footsteps of persons walking quietly and soundlessly. He knows how every bud develops under the covering of green folds and how it blooms into a flower. He is aware of the habitat and the den of every beast in the caves of mountains and in the density of jungles. He knows under which leaf and inside the bark of which tree, mosquitoes live and multiply. He knows from which part of a branch a bud will shoot, and which sperm will pass through its normal and natural course and form (a foetus). He knows which drops of water (from an ocean) will rise (in the form of steam) to form clouds, and which of these clouds gather together and which part of the land they will fertilize. He is aware of the life history of every drop of rain, every particle of sand, how it has started its individual existence, how the wind has blown it from place to place and how one day it will come to an end. He knows all those marks and places that have been destroyed or leveled by floods. He recognizes footprints of insects on sand hills, nests of birds on lofty mountain peaks, and songs of birds singing in the shades of green trees. He knows which shell holds pearls and which does not, what is hidden in the depth of the ocean, what the dark nights try to conceal, what the sun's rays reveal...He fully knows every detail of all this gigantic organization and sees that each part of it works according to the plan set out by Him, His power, His might, and His desire, to organize, govern and influence every part, every phase and every aspect of this mighty creation, and His favors and His benevolences reach them all. And they are not able to thank Him as much as His Kindness and Mercy deserves, and to show as much gratitude as they should.[55]

In these gloriously eloquent passages that draw our attention to the intricate detail of the wondrous design of nature—whether it be the artistic arrangement of a peacock's feathers, or the construction of a bat's wings or a locust's limbs—we are drawn inevitably to one conclusion:

> The Grand Architect of the universe has displayed clear, obvious and tangible signs of Elegance and Grace in every design of creation

---

[55] Sermon 94 (*Khutba-e-Ashbah*), *Nahjul-Balagha*, Jafery. See Sermon 90 in *Nahjul-Balagha*, Reza (*supra*).

and the Greatness and Glory of His Power in every form and system that He gave existence to...

and we are invited by the Imam to:

> ...wonder at its grandeur, admire its greatness, bow before its sublimeness and accept one Sole and Supreme Intellect, One God behind all this.[56]

It is significant that, despite this theophanic view of creation, which emphasizes its essential homogeneity, Imam 'Ali clearly maintains, in keeping with traditional metaphysics, that creation is arranged hierarchically. We have noted earlier that the Imam speaks of the possibility of being "Near" or "Far" from God. Similarly, describing the process of creation, the Imam observes:

> As soon as things came into existence, every one of them was allotted properties and their place in nature...Thus every creature and every object had a place permanently fixed, was assigned a position in nature which none can change.[57]

In this scheme, man is pre-eminent, not because of his material superiority, but because of his spiritual intelligence. Describing the creation of Adam, archetypal man, the Imam states:

> ...then He infused into it the Divine soul (intellect) and the figure stood up as a man. This creation was an intelligent and rational being, using intellect instead of instinct and having complete control of his mental faculties and full command over his limbs. He further had natural sagacity and wisdom, to differentiate between right and wrong, between truth and falsehood and between justice and inequity...
>
> Having created such a being, He ordained the angels to hand over to him the trust committed to their care and to fulfill the promise they had made, which was to accept the superiority of man and to recognize his greatness. He therefore ordered them all to pay

---

[56] Sermon 168, *Nahjul-Balagha*, Jafery. See Sermon 164 in *Nahjul-Balagha*, Reza (*supra*): "Allah Has provided wonderful creations including the living, the lifeless, the stationary, and the moving. He has established such clear proofs for His delicate creative power and great might that minds bend down to Him in acknowledgment thereof and in submission to Him, and arguments about His oneness strike our ears".

[57] Sermon 1, *Nahjul-Balagha*, Jafery.

their homage to him and bow down before him. They all obeyed His command except Satan...[58]

The "greatness" of humanity derives from its transcendent intellect, its pre-existential "natural sagacity and wisdom". Implicit in the notion of "greatness" is the concept of hierarchy, inherent in the notion of the ordering of reality, and this concept, premised as it is on the metaphysical principle of verticality[59] is, as we shall see, crucial to the Imam's understanding of justice.

Nature then is depicted as a theophany, arranged hierarchically and radiating the sacred Presence of the Divine, though the Essence of the "Grand Architect" remains transcendent. However, that which is transcendent within humanity, namely, the spirit, can, by the grace of its intellectual vision, the "Eye of the Heart", intuit that which is ontologically evident, that is to say, it can know its own pervasive nature and substance. And by knowing itself, as the Imam has noted, it can know its Maker. In the face of this sacred Presence, man, as such, is reduced to insignificance, and must therefore have an appropriate attitude of humility and wondrous gratitude, while at the same time, by virtue of the intellect's discernment of the pervasive nature of its substance—the sacred Presence in all—, must also have compassion towards all beings. Humility and compassion, detachment and love:

[58] Sermon 2, *Nahjul-Balagha*, Jafery. See *Al-A'raf*, VII: 11 and 12: "And surely, We created you and then gave you human form; then We told the angels 'Prostrate yourselves to Adam', and they prostrated themselves, except Iblis, he refused to be of those who prostrated themselves. God said: 'What prevented you (O Satan) that you did not prostrate yourself when I commanded you?' Iblis said, 'I am better than him (Adam). You created me from fire, and him You created from clay'". Satan's sin is one of metaphysical blindness, the inability to recognize the spiritual foundation of humanity. This opacity of vision is the genesis of pride.

[59] "The principle of verticality, which is a fundamental principle of traditional wisdom, is based on the affirmation of transcendence as an aspect of a comprehensive and integrated reality that is Absolute. According to this understanding, reality has both a transcendent Origin and an immanent Center, which are one, rather than being reduced to the merely horizontal dimension of its existential or quantitative elements. Verticality implies both Heaven and Earth, a worldview in which meaning and purpose are defined principally by both height and depth, and secondarily by breadth—that is, principally by man's relationship to God, who is simultaneously 'above' and 'within' creation, and who therefore governs all creaturely relationships – rather than by breadth alone – that is, solely in terms of the relationship between the subject and the world. It also implies that the horizontal is subordinate to the vertical, that is to say, the relationship between man and the world is premised on the primary relationship between God and man: to restate this in Christian terms, the love of one's neighbor is premised on one's love for God."—from the Editorial, "The Principle of Verticality", by M. Ali Lakhani, in *Sacred Web 14*, Vancouver, Canada, 2004

these qualities are the foundational elements of the piety that, as we shall see later, constitute the basis of Imam 'Ali's view of Justice.

To summarize: Imam 'Ali's view of reality, which is fully consonant with the principles of traditional metaphysics articulated within the Qur'an and *hadith*, point to an essentially unified and integrated view of reality, in which the structure of reality can be differentiated in terms of polarities rooted within its very structure, as the Divine Subject objectivizes Itself, by deploying from the Absolute to the Infinite and from Essence to Form. The whole of the continuum of this deployment is a hierarchically constituted theophany, reflecting the sacred core of our innermost spiritual nature.

III. Linking Truth and Justice

We now come to a crucial point in our discussion. We have thus far been examining the first of the two categories of questions central to human existence—dealing with the discernment of reality, or, to use Imam 'Ali's terminology, the question of Truth. We have earlier identified two categories of questions—dealing with the conforming of human beings to discerned reality, or, to use Imam 'Ali's terminology as it relates to governance, the question of Justice. We have mentioned that these two categories of questions are metaphysically linked, and we will now examine the vital nature of this linkage.

Simply put, the link between Truth and Justice is based on the universal doctrine that "man is made in the image of God" and *thereby* is "God's representative on earth". In this word "thereby" lies the connection between one's "nature" and one's "responsibility" (in the sense of one's "ability to respond" to the dictates of one's nature). To discern one's true or primordial nature (symbolized in the Qur'anic episode of the Divine Covenant of Alast, discussed earlier) is to understand the underlying spiritual foundation and hierarchical order of things and thereby to accept one's natural responsibility in terms of that order (symbolized by the Qur'anic Divine Trust or *Amanah*, discussed earlier). To restate this differently, *Iman* (faith or spiritual vision) is the foundation of *Amanah* (the commitment to conform to one's true nature). Or one might say, *Amanah* is the corollary of *Iman*. The connection between knowing and conforming to that knowledge is an ontological connection—that is to say, it exists at the level of being; so that all true knowledge (gnosis) is transformative: knowing and being are one. In this ontological oneness, all contraries are reconciled and all things are placed in their "proper order", that is to say, in conformity with Truth or hierarchically ordered reality. As we shall see, it is this "proper order" or equilibrium that constitutes Justice, both outwardly and inwardly. Hence, there is a correspondence between Truth and Justice, which is reflected in the two senses of "right" (a word that is etymologically rooted in the Sanskrit, *rt*, which is also the basis of the terms "rite" and "ritual", both denoting conformity with metaphysical order), namely, "right" as "true" or "correct", and "right" as "fair" or "just" (similarly, in Arabic, the term *al-haqq* is used in both senses).

Let us briefly examine this notion of an equilibrium based on "ontological oneness"—how the contraries within reality can be said to be reconciled ontologically. In the metaphysical view of reality, equilibrium is defined as "Heart-centeredness"—the idea of a Center that is predicated in Oneness: all that exists is merely an articulation of the Divine Breath—a spiritual expansion from the Center to the Periphery, from the Hidden to the Manifest, from Essence to Form. In the words of the Christian mystic, Meister Eckhart (1260-1329 A.D.), "Form is the revelation of Essence". The Holy Qur'an speaks of the link between ultimate reality and its objectivization in similar terms, where reality is a spiritual expansion or deployment from a Hidden divine Origin into a Manifest theophanic Presence:

He is the First and the Last, the Hidden and the Manifest.
And He is the Knower of all things.[60]

The terms *batin* ("Hidden") and *zahir* ("Manifest") are sometimes translated as "Most High" (implying transcendence) and "Most Near" (implying immanence), respectively. They refer to a spatial dimension of reality, whereby one can conceive of it as Center or as Periphery. These correspond to the polarities (High/Low and Near/Far) referred to in the passage quoted earlier from Imam 'Ali. These polarities stem from the very structure of reality itself. They are universal polarities, expressed in all traditions, perhaps the best-known being the yin-yang polarity in Taoism. To speak of reality as transcendent (*tanzih*) is to emphasize its "masculine" qualities—severity, distance, Absoluteness—while to speak of reality as immanent (*tashbih*) is to emphasize its "feminine" qualities—compassion, intimacy, Infinitude. The crucial point is that a comprehensive view of reality requires the reconciliation of the metaphysical polarities that constitute the archetypes of masculine and the feminine, activity and passivity, and

---

[60] *Al-Hadid*, LVII:3.

so forth. This reconciliation takes the form of envisioning reality as an integrated whole within which the differentiated polarities co-exist in a complementary fashion within a synthesis of opposites[61], or *coincidentia oppositorum*. In Islam, it has therefore been said that: "God cannot be known except as a synthesis of opposites."[62] The locus of this synthesis is the Heart, and its knowledge is that of its primordial nature or *fitra*. The significance of this for a proper understanding of the linkage between Truth and Justice will be made clear shortly. However, before turning to this in greater detail, let us first continue with our examination of the Qur'anic passage just quoted.

In the Qur'anic passage quoted above, the terms *awwal* ("First") and *akhir* ("Last") correspond to the temporal notion of the Origin and Return. As in the symbol of a Circle, these two points are the same—the Alpha and Omega are One[63]. In the passage from the point of Origin to the point of Return, there are two trajectories to be considered. The first corresponds to the "sending down" (*tanzil*) or the concretization of the Absolute into this world of "congealed essences": this is the trajectory of divine descent, of the manifestation of Essence into Form. The second corresponds to the "return" (*ma'ad*) or the transformative alignment of ourselves with our spiritual nature (*fitra*): this is the trajectory of human ascent, of the return to our spiritual Origin. These two trajectories correspond to the cosmic substance itself—what Ibn al-'Arabi terms the "Breath of the Merciful" or *Nafas Rahmani*[64], the expiration and inspiration

---

[61] *Al-insan al-kamil* or the Universal Man, symbolic of the original androgynic state, is the complete human state in which the metaphysical polarities are perfectly reconciled. The Universal Man corresponds to the primordial nature or *fitra* of humanity, whose locus is the Heart.

[62] Abu Sa'id al-Kharraz (quoted by Ibn 'Arabi in *Fusus al-Hikam*, Cairo edition, 1321 A.H, with the commentary of al-Qashani, at page 64; also cited by Toshihiko Izutsu in *Sufism and Taoism*, University of California Press, Berkeley, 1984, at page 75).

[63] "In my beginning is my end" from T.S. Eliot's *East Coker*, one of the celebrated *Four Quartets* by Eliot, emphasizes this universal truth of the correspondence of the point of Origin and the point of Return. Eliot's grave inscription begins with the quoted words from *East Coker*, and ends: "In the end is my beginning". This also recalls Heraclitus' saying: "The beginning and the end are one", and the motto of Mary Stuart, "En ma fin est mon commencement."

[64] Ibn al-'Arabi uses the image of the Divine Breath to explain how Being bursts forth from God's merciful nature in the same way that air explodes from our chests when we hold our breath for long. Thus Izutsu explains: "Just as air bursts forth from the chest of man, the compressed existence within the depths of the Absolute, taking the form of Mercy, gushes forth from the Absolute. This, (Ibn al-'Arabi) calls the 'breath of the Merciful' (*al-nafas al-rahmaniy*)" —see Toshihiko Izutsu's *Sufism and Toaism*, University of California Press, 1984, in Part I, Chapter IX, 'Ontological Mercy', at

of God, through whose spiritual breath[65] the Cosmos expands and contracts in a compassionate cycle of creation and reabsorption, of prefigurement, projection and reintegration. Though God cannot be limited by any attributes, His quintessence might be said to possess a Quality transcending all qualities—that is to say, a Quality beyond the ken of mere human knowledge, but which is synonymous with the cosmic substance and constitutes our innermost core, the "Heart" or *fitra*, discernable by our spiritual Intellect. This Supreme Quality, within which all polarities are extinguished, and which is none other than the Essence of God or the Divine Quintessence, is a quality that closest resembles Compassion or Mercy because, lacking nothing in His Self-Sufficient and Infinite Plenitude, the nature of God is Beneficence. He is like a Light that shines. This is why God is said to be both intrinsically and extrinsically Compassionate—both *Rahman* and *Rahim*[66]. And it is this Quality that constitutes the motive force of creation, as in the celebrated *hadith qudsi* or sacred saying of the Prophet: "I was a Hidden Treasure and I loved to be known, and so I created the world so that I could be known."

In the Hadith of the Hidden Treasure, God created the world, not out of privation (for God suffices unto Himself) but out of His gra-

---

page 131. See also William Chittick's *The Sufi Path of Knowledge*, State University of New York Press, 1989, at page 19, where he states: "The evanescent and changing nature of existence, or the cosmos as ever-renewed creation and never-repeated divine self-disclosure, is evoked by Ibn al-'Arabi's best-known names for the substance of the universe, the "Breath of the All-merciful" (*nafas al-rahman*). God breathes out, and while breathing, He speaks. But only His Speech is eternal, not His spoken words as words. Every word appears for an instant only to disappear from the cosmos forever (though it remains immutably present in His knowledge)."

[65] Schuon elaborates on the connection between the 'remembering' and 'breathing': "The 'remembrance of God' is like breathing deeply in the solitude of high mountains: here the morning air, filled with the purity of the eternal snows, dilates the breast; it becomes space and heaven enters our heart. This picture includes yet another symbolism, that of the 'universal breath': here expiration relates to cosmic manifestation or the creative phase and inspiration to reintegration. To the phase of salvation or the return to God." (*Understanding Islam*, Frithjof Schuon, *supra*, at page 59).

[66] Ibn al-'Arabi distinguishes between two aspects of God's Mercy: (1) the "Mercy of gratuitous gift" (*rahmah al-imtinan*), which is God's essential Mercy extended to all things, not as a reward for some act. Thus existence is synonymous with Mercy, as in the Qur'anic passage "My Mercy covers everything" (*Al-A'raf*, VII:156). This aspect of Mercy is referred to by the name *Rahman*; and (2) the "Mercy of obligation" (*rahmah al-wujub*) which is conferred according the creature's state of readiness to receive it. This aspect of Mercy is referred to in the Qur'anic passage "He has pre-scribed Mercy for Himself" (*Al-An'am*, VI:12) and is referred to by the name *Rahim*. See Izutsu's *Sufism and Taoism*, *ibid.*, at pages 121 to 123.

cious bounteousness (the Hadith refers to love as His motive), in order "to be known" (the object of knowledge, the known)—but again this must not be understood in any privative sense, since God is the Absolute possessor of all knowledge. Thus, as is stated in the Qur'anic passage we have been discussing, He is also the "Knower of all things" (the subject of knowledge, the knower). We (his creatures) live in the knowledge of God, not merely as the objects of His knowledge (for "He is the Knower of all things") but also potentially as the transcendent Subject, the only "Knower". Imam 'Ali thus states:

> I know God by God, and I know that which is not God by the light of God.[67]

Gnosis can thus be understood as pure vision[68], which is the sight of our illumining Heart—itself illumined by the "light of God" ("Light upon Light", from the famous Qur'anic parable in the Verse of Light[69]). Symbolically, the Eye and the Light are one. Knowledge is Being. It is only sacred or primordial knowledge that is ontological and integrated. This is the unitive kardial knowledge of the Tree of Life[70]. By contrast, the knowledge of the Tree of Good and Evil[71] is the knowledge of a fragmentary consciousness, "that of a fragmented

---

[67] Quoted by Hujwiri in *Kashf al-Mahjub*, translated from the Persian by Reynold A. Nicholson, London, Luzac, 1911, 1936, 1959, at p. 296, and by Whitall N. Perry in *A Treasury of Traditional Wisdom, supra*, at page 751.

[68] Knowledge is *theoria* or pure vision. It is not merely an abstraction (as is implied by the devalued modern sense of the word "theory"), but the Inner Eye of reality. It is in this sense that the ancient sages were said to be "seers". For a Qur'anic reference to the visionary basis of gnosis, see *Surat At-Takathur*, CII: 5-7.

[69] *Al-Nur* XXIV:35 – "God is the Light of the heavens and the earth. The parable of His Light is, as it were, that of a niche containing a lamp; the lamp is enclosed in a glass, the glass like a radiant star; lit from a blessed tree—an olive-tree that is neither of the east nor of the west—the oil of which would almost give light even though fire had not touched it: Light upon Light! God guides to His Light the one who whom He wills; and God offers parables to human beings, and God knows all things".

[70] See the *Book of Genesis*, Chapter 2, Verses 8 and 9: "And the Lord God planted a garden eastward in Eden; and there he put the man whom he had formed, And out of the ground made the Lord God to grow every tree that is pleasant to the sight, and good for food; the tree of life also in the midst of the garden, and the tree of knowledge of good and evil."

[71] See the *Book of Genesis*, Chapter 2, Verses 16 and 17: "And the Lord God commanded the man, saying, Of every tree of the garden thou mayest freely eat: But of the tree of the knowledge of good and evil, thou shalt not eat of it: for in the day thou eatest thereof thou shalt surely die." And refer to the story of the Fall in the *Book of Genesis*, Chapter 3, in particular Verses 4 through 7: "And the serpent said unto the woman, Ye shall not surely die: For God doth know that in the day ye eat thereof,

unity, of things unreferred to the center and valued for their own sake as if they were self-sufficing entities" (*Marco Pallis*)[72]. The unitive knowledge symbolized by the Tree of Life refers all things back to their metaphysical Origin and Heart-Center, the Divine Principle or the transcendent Self. Each level of reality derives its value from the higher dimensions from which it issues to the extent that these refer back to their supra-ontological Source. Value thus corresponds to and issues from structure, Justice from Truth. Similarly, one can say that all qualities of worth or significance derive from metaphysical archetypes, rooted in the Absolute, which is the source and font of all value, quality, meaning and purpose. These transcendental attributes of worth, excellence, significance and telos, increase in value in correspondence to their metaphysical reality, that is, in terms of their proximity to the Center. The locus of this correspondence within man is the Heart. This is why the criterion of Justice or order is kardial responsibility (responding to one's primordial or Heart-centered nature): one must first be Just in order to do Justice.

It is the ontological knowledge of our theomorphic nature that is testified to in the Covenant of Alast and inscribed within our Hearts. It is this knowledge, discernable by our Intellects, that enables us to envision reality as an integrated whole, as a synthesis of opposites and a theophany of sacred radiance[73]. And it is this very same knowledge that constitutes the foundation of our creaturely privileges and our viceregal responsibilities of stewardship in relation to the divine order. To know the spiritual foundation of things is to participate ontologically in a spiritual Oneness, whose radiance permeates the whole of creation, and whose discernment corresponds to what is termed "the sense of the sacred." The recognition by us of our theomorphic nature

---

then your eyes shall be opened, and ye shall be as gods, knowing good and evil. And when the woman saw that the tree was good for food, and that it was pleasant to the eyes, and a tree to be desired to make one wise, she took of the fruit thereof, and did eat, and gave also unto her husband with her; and he did eat. And the eyes of them both were opened, and they knew that they were naked..."

[72] For an excellent discussion of the symbolical significance of the story of the Fall in the Book of Genesis, see Marco Pallis' essay, "*Is there a Problem of Evil?*", published in the traditionalist journal, *Tomorrow*, Autumn 1963, Volume 11, No. 4, reprinted in *The Sword of Gnosis*, edited by Jacob Needleman, Penguin Metaphysical Library, Penguin Books, Baltimore, 1974, at page 230. The quoted passage appears at page 237.

[73] Schuon states: "Intelligence as such is above all the sense of priorities and proportions... it implies *a priori* a sense of the Absolute and of the hierarchy of corresponding values" (Frithjof Schuon, *To Have a Center*, World Wisdom Books, 1990, Bloomington, Indiana, USA, p. 29). Note that the hierarchy of values corresponds to a metaphysical ordering of reality derived from the sense of the Absolute.

gives rise within us to the compulsion to reorder ourselves, both internally and externally, so that Outer Man may conform to the Inner Man—as it were, to the Source of Light, and thereby shine for others. To borrow a universal symbol, the Moon (the Heart of man, which corresponds to his spiritual nature) reflects the Light of the Sun (the Divine Principle) and casts this Light (the Divine Light of Mercy and Justice) upon Earth (all creation). Universal Man, the embodiment of Truth as Presence, and of Light, is thus the vehicle of Justice. The human is a reflection of the divine and of the archetypal possibilities of cosmic existence. Conformity to our primordial nature is thus our true purpose, and the very basis of our relation to the divine order[74].

To summarize, the metaphysical linkage between Truth and Justice—the twin mission of Imam 'Ali[75]—must therefore be understood as ontological in nature: in other words, it is a harmonization that occurs at the level of being. To speak of Justice is to assume that there is a certain order to things. To speak of Truth, in the metaphysical manner of the Qur'an and the writings of Imam 'Ali, is to understand that knowledge is sacred, that there is an ontological order and integrity within reality, which is the foundation of Justice. Truth is the journey to the Center, the removing of veils, and it is only from the Center of the unveiled and primordial Self that Justice can be done. There, within our innermost Heart, the harmonization of apparently contradictory elements within reality is possible, and this complementarity of polarities within reality is based on an ontological outlook that will be vital to a proper understanding of Justice, as we shall see.

---

[74] "Primordial man is the archetype of creation as he is its purpose and entelechy. That is why according to a *hadith*, God addresses the Prophet of Islam, whose inner reality is the primordial man par excellence in the Islamic tradition, in these terms: 'If thou wert not, I would not have created the world'" (Seyyed Hossein Nasr in *Knowledge and the Sacred*, SUNY, Albany, NY, 1989, at page 166).

[75] See Sermon 38, *Nahjul-Balagha*, Jafery: "My mission, today, is the same as it was at the time of the Prophet (a.s.). I shall strive till I eradicate impiety and injustice, and till I establish a rule of justice and truth, - a humane and heavenly regime." Though this phrase does not appear in the corresponding passage in the Reza translation, there are other passages in the Reza translation that support this mission - for instance, in Sermon 130, Imam 'Ali laments to his followers: "How hard it is for me to uncover for you the secrets of justice, or to straighten the curve of truthfulness". In another significant passage, the Imam states: "...do not abstain from saying a truth or pointing out a matter of justice because I do not regard myself above erring" (*Nahjul-Balagha*, Reza, Sermon 215), emphasizing thereby the pre-eminence of Truth and Justice.

IV. Justice: Re-establishing a Proper Order

We have earlier argued that Justice is metaphysically linked to Truth and that the nature of this connection is ontological. Being Just is the foundation of doing Justice. We will now attempt to demonstrate how these principles were central to Imam 'Ali's view of government.

Imam 'Ali's writings explicitly make the connection between Justice and Truth in the sense of the proper ordering of things. Defining Justice, he states:

Justice puts things in their places.[76]

Elsewhere, he defines "intelligence" in terms of the ability to "put things in their proper places."[77] Justice is thereby an attribute of intelligence.

This begs the question: "What are the proper places of things?" Or to restate the question: "What are the criteria of Justice for the proper ordering of things?" The answer to these questions depends on one's vantage, which in turn is a matter of one's orientation. The world-view or orientation of traditional man is based on a metaphysical view of reality, that is to say, a perspective that takes into account the essential interconnectedness of all things at a spiritual level which transcends the formal and merely material world of ordinary perceptions—the latter being therefore considered deceptive and illusory. Put differently, one might say that the proper order of things can only be metaphysically discerned from the vantage of one who is at its spiritual Center. The locus of this spiritual Center is understood to be ontological, that is to say, residing at the deepest level of one's being: according to tradition, it is the centered vision of the Heart that alone can interpret the spiritual significance of the textual world or, if we prefer, the existential "con-text"—that is to say the "signs" of God.

What, then, is the existential context? Imam 'Ali likens it to that of a voyager embarked precariously upon a storm-tossed sea. We are told in one of the sermons:

---

[76] Cleary, *supra*, page 64. This quotation recalls Confucius' definition of "the art of government" as consisting in "making things right, or putting things in their right places", in *Liki*, XXVII, cited by Whitall N. Perry in *A Treasury of Traditional Wisdom, supra*, at page 970.

[77] Cleary, *ibid.*, page 44.

O people! I counsel you to fear God. I want to warn you of this world. Sooner or later you shall have to part with it. It is not a place of permanent residence and not a place for perpetual happiness and comfort. Those who are residing here are actually travelers, halting temporarily during their journey—which they are bound to continue. Actually it is not a safe place even for a temporary sojourn. Like a boat in a furious storm, this world is throwing its passengers from side to side; many of them have fallen overboard, some of whom are drowned while others are being tossed by the waves and winds which are playing havoc with their lives. Those who are drowned will never come back and those who are still floating are not out of danger.[78]

The view that the world is not a "permanent residence" and that humanity is "journeying" to some distant shore of "perpetual happiness and comfort" is in accord with the traditional view we have discussed earlier. Human beings are in exile from their Origin, and their passage through this world may be viewed as a journey of Return. They are, however, buffeted by the "furious storms" of the world and, we are told, are "not out of danger". What is this "danger" that renders one's position so precarious?

The "danger", according to Islamic tradition, is twofold: firstly, the forgetfulness of our spiritual patrimony, that "man is made in the image of God"; and secondly, of our spiritual responsibilities (in the kardial sense we have discussed earlier) that result from knowing our nature, which include loving and serving God and His creation for "man is God's representative on earth". The first of these dangers corresponds to our forgetfulness of the Divine Covenant (in Qur'anic terms this translates into our breach of the Covenant of Alast referred to earlier[79], whereby man undertook to remember his spiritual Origin, which is also the Center of his being). The second of these dangers corresponds to our neglect of the Divine Trust (in Qur'anic terms this translates into our repudiation of our vow of *Amanah* referred to

---

[78] Sermon 201, *Nahjul-Balagha*, Jafery. This appears as Sermon 195 in *Nahjul-Balagha*, Reza (*supra*): "I advise you, O creatures of Allah, to have fear of Allah, and I warn you of this world which is a house from which departure is inevitable and a place of discomfort. He who lives in it has to depart, and he who stays here has to leave it. It is drifting with its people like a boat whom severe winds dash (here and there) in the deep sea. Some of them get drowned and die, while some of them escape on the surface of the waves, where winds push them with their currents and carry them towards their dangers. So, whatever is drowned cannot be restored, and whatever escapes is on the way to destruction."

[79] See footnote 15, *supra*.

earlier[80], whereby man assumed the responsibility to regard creation as a theophany and to treat it with the respect owed to it on account of its sacred Origin). The commitment of the Covenant entails for humanity the burden of the Trust. To ignore the Covenant implies an abrogation of one's divine responsibilities towards the creatures of God[81]. The forgetfulness of our Divine Covenant can be understood as an intellectual failure: the failure of the intellect (whether through blindness or hubris) to affirm the transcendent Source that gives ontological value to all reality and manifests in the spiritual being of both man and creation; while our neglect of the Divine Trust can be understood as a failure of the will (through the temptations of placing the "flesh" over the "spirit" in an inversion of values) to conform to its spiritual nature and its concomitant spiritual responsibilities. Both these "dangers" correspond to what the Qu'ran refers to, respectively, as the "blindness" and "hardening" of the Heart.[82] It is the translucent and tender Heart that is faithful, and it is faith (*iman*) that constitutes the foundation of the Divine Trust (*Amanah*).

In terms of our previous analysis, we might note that the two forms of error, namely, the error of the blind or hubristic intellect and the error of the unprincipled and unyielding will falling into temptation, correspond respectively to errors in regard to the two categories of questions central to human existence that we have discussed earlier. Thus, the weak intellect errs by virtue of its failure to discern reality—that is, it is cut off from the transcendent vision of the spiritual integrity of reality that binds humanity to all creation; and the weak will errs by virtue of its failure to conform to reality—that is, it abrogates its responsibility to sacralize life through action.

From a metaphysical standpoint, creation is a cosmic veil which—depending on our perception—can either conceal or reveal the spiritual light of compassion by which the whole of creation is sustained. It is faith that "opens our eyes", thereby enabling us to become spiri-

---

[80] See footnote 16, *supra*.

[81] Commenting on the answer given by mankind to God in the Qur'anic episode of the Covenant of Alast ("Am I not your Lord? They said Yea, verily"—*Al-A'raf*, VII:172, see footnote 15, *supra*), Seyyed Hossein Nasr states: "In this 'yea' is to be found the secret of human destiny, because by iterating it man accepted the burden of trust (*amanah*) which none in creation but he dared accept"—(from the essay, *Who is Man?: The perennial Answer of Islam*, by Seyyed Hossein Nasr, reprinted in *The Sword of Gnosis, supra*, at page 209).

[82] *Az-Zumar*, XXXIX:22 – "...woe to those whose hearts are hardened against remembrance of Allah! They are in plain error!" See also footnote 22, *supra*.

tually literate, so that we perceive creation with the eyes of faith, with spiritual "imagination"[83] or metaphysical transparency, by looking beyond the apparent opacity of the veil to the transcendence beyond, in an act of divine grace—for as the scripture states: "God guides to His Light whom He wills."[84] It is thus given to each of us to conform our individual wills to the Divine Will, so that we are open to His grace while remaining critically engaged by our intellects. It is through this combination of receptivity and alertness that true faith operates.

It is reported that Imam 'Ali was once asked by one of his companions, Dhi'lib al-Yamani, "Have you seen your Lord?" The Imam replied, "I would not worship a lord whom I have not seen." He was then asked, "How did you see Him?" The Imam replied, "The eyes cannot see Him according to outer vision; rather, it is the hearts that perceive Him, through the verities of faith."[85] This affirmation of the ontological evidence[86] (or faith[87]) of metaphysical realities is also an illustration of the Imam's view of the correspondence between metaphysical knowledge and imaginal vision[88].

---

[83] The term "imagination" is not intended to evoke the illusory world of fantasy, but to suggest the spiritual capability of the insightful perception and intuition of "invisible realities" by the "eye of the heart". This mode of perception is sometimes referred to as spiritual "unveiling" (*kashf*). This is the gnostic vision that fuses knowing and seeing: see footnote 68, *supra*.

[84] *An-Nur*, XXIV:35.

[85] This passage is cited in *Doctrines of Shi'i Islam*, by Ayatollah Ja'far Sobhani, I. B. Tauris & Co. Ltd., 2001, translated and edited by Reza Shah-Kazemi, at page 43.

[86] "Metaphysical truths are not accepted merely because they are logically evident, but because they are ontologically evident; their logical evidentness is only a trace of these truths imprinted on the mind. The ontological evidentness is something contained in our very existence, something contained in the universe, something of God." (Frithjof Schuon in *Spiritual Perspectives and Human Facts, supra*, at page 133).

[87] The term "faith" denotes not merely conviction, but Presence and the engagement that is its corollary. "A man may have metaphysical certainty without possessing 'faith', that is, without this certainty residing in his soul as an ever-active presence. But if metaphysical certainty suffices on the doctrinal ground, it is far from being sufficient on the spiritual plane, where it must be completed and brought to life by faith. Faith is nothing other than the adhesion of our whole being to Truth...One who has faith acts as if he were in the presence of what he believes—or knows—to be true... For every man, whether he 'knows' or 'believes', perfection is 'to adore God as if you saw Him and, if you do not see Him, He none the less sees you.'" (Frithjof Schuon in *Spiritual Perspectives and Human Facts, supra*, at page 134).

[88] Commenting on the foundations of *islam* and *iman* as the practical and theoretical foundations of Sufi practice, William C. Chittick remarks: "Once seekers have gained sufficient grounding in these two dimensions, they can focus their efforts on 'worshiping God as if they see Him.' Eventually, sincerity and love may take them to the place where the 'as if' ceases to apply. In other words, they will worship Him

In a key passage among his Sayings, Imam 'Ali includes "justice" as one of the four pillars of "faith"[89]. In that passage, he discusses the basis of "justice" in the following terms:

> Justice is also based on four disciplines:
> immersion in understanding,
> penetration of knowledge,
> brightness in judgment,
> and firm establishment of thoughtfulness.
> For one who understands
> knows with penetrating knowledge,
> and one who knows with penetrating knowledge
> proceeds judiciously from the start.
> And one who is thoughtful
> has not been negligent of his trust
> and lives a benign life among the people.[90]

Corresponding to the Imam's understanding that Truth is perceived through "the verities of faith", is his understanding that Justice is linked to Truth through gnosis or "penetrating knowledge", that is to say, through the discernment of reality in accordance with "the verities of faith". Note the necessity of "immersion", "penetration" and "firm establishment", all pointing to the nature of faith as "the adhesion of one's whole being to Truth". The Imam notes that "immersion in understanding" (which implies a sense of visionary clarity or sapiential awareness[91], and not merely an abstract or conceptual understanding) leads to "penetrating knowledge", that is to say, an awareness of the very heart of things (which implies seeing both the foundation and the

---

while seeing Him. An often cited model here is the Prophet's cousin and son-in-law Ali, who said, 'I would not worship a Lord whom I do not see.'"(*Sufism: A Short Introduction*, by William C. Chittick, Oneworld, Oxford, 2000, at page 15).

[89] The four pillars of faith are patience, certitude, justice and struggle.

[90] Cleary, *supra*, at pages 66 and 67. This text is a portion of Saying No. 31 from the Collected Sayings of the Imam included in the *Nahjul-Balagha* , Reza.

[91] Other translators render this as "clearness of mind" (see, for example, Jafery, *Nahjul-Balagha, op. cit.*). The sense that is conveyed is of the clarity of the serene contemplative, whose distilled vision apprehends spiritual Presence and the hierarchic relationships that a spiritually-constituted cosmos entails. This discernment is sapiential in its etymological sense, which signifies an experiential dimension (from the Latin '*sapere*', meaning 'to taste'). Remarking on the relationship between calm and contemplation, Schuon states: "When the mind is perfectly calm—or perfectly simple—Truth is mirrored in it, just as objects are reflected in calm water" (in *Spiritual Perspectives and Human Facts*, by Frithjof Schuon, supra, at page 158).

proper order of things, referring them to their metaphysical Center[92]), which in turn leads to judicious behavior (which can be understood as faithfulness or conformity to the spiritual order). "Thoughtfulness" (better rendered as spiritual "alertness"—what the Buddhists call "wakefulness", the awareness of Presence) precludes "negligence" (in the sense of "forgetfulness", spiritual slumber or inertness) of one's spiritual nature and responsibilities. (The "trust" of which the Imam says that the just man must not be negligent is none other than the Qur'anic Trust, the *Amanah* referred to earlier.) Only by living "thoughtfully" (or in "remembrance" of Truth as Presence, in the Qur'anic sense of *dhikr*[93], that is to say, by invoking, summoning, witnessing and embodying the spiritual Presence of the Divine Self) can one live judiciously and in peace.

In contrast to the "thoughtfulness" that the Imam advocates, existence itself is the condition of heedlessness (*ghafla*): hence the famous *hadith*—"All men are asleep (in this world); only when they die do they wake up." Though humanity is veiled from God, this veil, though it may appear opaque, is virtually translucent in view of the innate capacity of the Intellect to penetrate through the veil into the realm of metaphysical transparency: this is indicated by the *hadith*—"My eyes slept, but my heart did not sleep." However, forgetful man—ensnared by the cosmic veil and the opacity of his vision—is heedless and slow to accept counsel. Imam 'Ali states:

> Between you and spiritual counsel
> is a veil of heedlessness.[94]

Time and again in his sermons, Imam 'Ali reminds the faithful that the world is fickle[95] and that humanity will be called upon to account for their actions in the hereafter. For instance:

> Remember that this world is a place where there is no safety from
> its sorrows and afflictions while one is engulfed in it. Whatever

---

[92] Schuon defines intelligence (which corresponds to the sapiential awareness of "penetrating knowledge") as "above all the sense of priorities and proportions", the former implying "a priori a sense of the Absolute" and the latter, a sense "of the hierarchy of corresponding values" (*To Have a Center*, by Frithjof Schuon, World Wisdom Books, Bloomington, Indiana, 1990, at page 29).

[93] See footnote 37, *supra*.

[94] Cleary, *supra*, page 93.

[95] In a letter to Salman Farsi, Imam 'Ali states: "This world is like a serpent, so soft to touch, yet so lethal in its bite"—Letter 68, *Nahjul-Balagha*, Jafery.

worldly gains anybody acquires here cannot secure salvation for him. Human beings are tested here with calamities and sorrows and are being tempted with impiety and sin. Those who have collected worldly pleasures around themselves will have to leave them and on the day of reckoning they will have to give an account (of how they came in possession of such wealth and power and what they did with it). And those who have spent their lives in good deeds shall find their rewards waiting for them in Heaven, which they shall enjoy forever.[96]

In another passage, we read:

Hear me once again that this world is perishable and destructible, its phases change quickly, often leaving behind nothing but sad lessons behind them...Glory be to God! How alluring and delusive are the pleasures of this world; how every enhancement and increase of wealth and position here increases greed and avarice; and how the protection offered here very often ends in punishment and pain; what a place is it where neither death can be averted nor the past can be brought back...[97]

In these passages, we see that Imam 'Ali's view accords with the metaphysical world-view: when the formal, material world is viewed in isolation—apart from its transcendent Origin—, it is a transient world, of limited duration: human beings are confronted by their mortality and the ephemerality and decay of all things. Beset by sorrows, humanity can take small comfort in the pleasures of this world, which are merely fleeting, detaching humanity from God[98]. Salvation, then, lies in the recognition that there is a Return and a "day of reckoning"—for this recognition is a spur to piety.

Here we come to a key aspect of Imam 'Ali's view of Justice: piety[99] is a prerequisite of Justice. Only the good-hearted can be just.

---

[96] Sermon 66, *Nahjul-Balagha*, Jafery. This appears as Sermon 62 in *Nahjul-Balagha*, Reza (*supra*): "People are tested in (the world) through calamities...For the intelligent, this world is like the shade - one moment it is spread out and extended, but soon it shrinks and contracts".

[97] Sermon 117, *Nahjul-Balagha*, Jafery. This appears as Sermon 113 in *Nahjul-Balagha*, Reza (*supra*). See also, Sermons 110 and 112, *ibid*.

[98] Frithjof Schuon writes in *From the Divine to the Human*, translated by Gustavo Polit and Deborah Lambert, World Wisdom Books, Bloomington, Indiana, 1982, at page 8: "Man is by definition situated between an intellection which connects him to God and a world which has the power to detach him from God."

[99] William Wordsworth's celebrated Ode, *Intimations of Immortality from Recollections of Early Childhood*, commences with a quotation from his poem, *My Heart Leaps Up*,

As one traditionalist writer puts it, "The heart is the point where justice resides. It is in the heart that we must preserve the equilibrium which corresponds to the harmonic unity of the entire creation."[100] Just as God is Compassionate (as *Rahman*) in terms of His intrinsic nature in a way that is metaphysically prior to His extending this Mercy (as *Rahim*) to His creatures[101], so man must be true to his spiritual nature before he can be true to others[102]. Only he who knows that he is nothing in the face of God (that is, the one who embodies the spiritual poverty or humility that is evoked by the transcendent Majesty of God) is worthy, by the devotion and God-fearing awe inspired in view of that knowledge, to be the receptacle for God's Presence. (This is why the blessing of spiritual expansion and illumination, even among the great prophets and saints who have experienced this, is preceded by the blessing of spiritual constriction and darkness.) Paradoxically, it is only the pious servant (*'abd*) who can wear the mantle of the ruler (*khalifah*). It is only the empty vessel[103] of the dark[104]

which states:

> The child is father of the man;
> And I could wish my days to be
> Bound each to each by natural piety.

In William Blake's marginalia to this poem, Blake sees Wordsworth as opposing the Natural Man against the Spiritual Man, and he comments: "There is no such thing as Natural Piety because the Natural Man is at enmity with God." He continues: "... Imagination is the Divine Vision not of The World nor of Man nor from Man as he is a Natural Man but only as he is a Spiritual Man. Imagination has nothing to do with Memory" (*The Complete Poetry & Prose of William Blake*, David Erdman, ed., New York: Anchor Books, 1988, 665). Imam 'Ali's view of piety is that it is an attribute of one's primordial nature (*fitra*); one might say that this is Wordsworth's "natural piety" understood as corresponding to the nature of Blake's "Spiritual Man".

100 Tage Lindbom in *The Tares and the Good Grain*, translated by Alvin Moore, Jr., Mercer University Press, 1983, at pages 122-123.

101 See footnote 65, *supra*, for a comment on the two aspects of God's compassionate nature. The concept of metaphysical priority should not be construed as derogating temporally or spatially from God's Unity, which transcends all temporal and spatial restrictions.

102 This universal truth is memorably iterated in Polonius' advice to his son, Laertes, in Shakespeare's *Hamlet* (Act 1, Scene 3, lines 78 to 80):

> "This above all: to thine own self be true,
> And it must follow, as the night the day,
> Thou canst not then be false to any man."

103 This is one of the symbolisms of the Holy Grail. It is also symbolized by the Virgin Womb.

and pure Heart, detached in terms of the things of the world, which has the infinite capacity to be spiritually illumined and filled by the Presence of God. This Presence, though unperceived by those who are heedless, pervades all of created reality and informs and inspires piety and justice. It is only he who is at the Center that can perceive the Order deployed by the emanation of this Presence.

When we think of Justice, it is natural to think of it only in relation to the external: for instance, doing justice between contesting parties, or being fair in the treatment of others. However, the Imam's view, consistent with traditional metaphysics, was that the ability to judge others in an external context, must be preceded by the judicious internal re-ordering of oneself—and this can only be accomplished by recourse to the Intellect, our primordial faculty of discernment. In one passage, Imam 'Ali states:

> Beware of disobeying God when alone,
> for the witness is the Judge.[105]

Who is the "witness" that is with us when we are alone? To whom must we account when we transgress in private? The Qur'an reminds us that our very limbs will testify as to our deeds[106]. We can never be beyond the sight of God—though we may be beyond the sight of man—for God has breathed His Spirit into man, which, as the transcendent Intellect, constitutes our "conscience", our "witness"[107] and our Judge. As Schuon observes:

---

[104] This is not the darkness of obscurity—the obscurity of the ego, akin to "the false light" of vacuity—but the darkness of the Void—what in Buddhism is referred to as *Sunyata*, in Islam as *fana*, the naught that God fills and illumines with His Plenitude (*baqa*).

[105] Cleary, *supra*, page 98.

[106] "Today, We shall set a seal upon their mouths; and their hands will speak to Us, and their legs will bear witness to what they have earned" (*Ya-Sin*, XXXVI:65). "They shall have immense torment on the Day when their tongues and their hands and their legs bear witness against them for what they had been doing" (*An-Nur*, XXIV:23-24).

[107] The term "witness" recalls for us the pre-existential testament of each unborn soul, referred to in the Qur'anic episode of the Covenant of Alast (see footnote 15, *supra*). The pre-existential "witnesser" is the transcendent Intellect, that faculty of discernment by which mankind is able to perceive its spiritual origin and to recognize the pervasive radiance of the spiritual Presence within itself and in all things, just as an eye can discern the radiance of the supernal Sun that enlivens its sight and lights its world.

That which really judges us is our own norm that we carry within ourselves and which is at once an image of the whole Cosmos and of the divine Spirit shining at its center.[108]

In order to be true to ourselves, we must align our perceptions to our *fitra*, to "our own norm that we carry within ourselves", which is our spiritual Center, and thereby also to the spiritual order of things. Knowledge must correspond to being, and the "thoughtfulness" implicit in such knowledge must direct all actions. Unless one has the integrity and veracity to conform to Truth, the result will be hypocrisy. Time and again in his sermons, Imam 'Ali castigates hypocrisy and advocates piety. In one instance, he states:

...even the smallest hypocrisy towards God is a kind of polytheism...[109]

In other words, the lack of integration of thought and action—intellect and will—is a devaluation of the sacred, a veil between man and God[110]. To regard any aspect of created life in isolation from, and existing independent of, its spiritual existence is in effect to deify it—hence the reference to polytheism. The integration of thought and action is possible only through referring all contingent faculties to their spiritual locus, the Heart; and by regarding existence itself as the reverberation of a higher order, to which one is connected and which connects all things: one cannot isolate oneself from the spiritual order of things. This integral connection of man to the divine order is ontological and therefore in the nature of a participatory reality. It entails a knowledge that is transformative. Imam 'Ali says this of knowledge:

Knowledge is linked to action,
so one who knows acts,
as knowledge calls for action
and will depart
if it is not answered.[111]

---

[108] Frithjof Schuon, *In the Tracks of Buddhism*, George, Allen & Unwin Ltd., 1968, translation from the French by Marco Pallis, at page 56.

[109] Sermon 89, *Nahjul-Balagha*, Jafery - rendered by Reza as "You should know that even the smallest hypocrisy is like believing in more than one God..." in Sermon 85 in *Nahjul-Balagha*, Reza (*supra*).

[110] In this metaphysical sense, "a veil is anything other than God" (William C. Chittick in *Sufism: A Short Introduction*, supra, at page 145.)

[111] Cleary, *supra*, page 58.

Of such knowledge, Frithjof Schuon remarks, in an oft-cited passage:

> Knowledge only saves us on condition that it engages all that we are: when it constitutes a way which works and transforms, and which wounds our nature as the plough wounds the soil.[112]

Or again, commenting on the immersive quality of this knowledge in a passage that recalls the famous *hadith* that "faith (*iman*) is to acknowledge with the heart, to voice with the tongue, and to act with the limbs", Imam 'Ali states:

> Lower knowledge
> is what stops at the tongue;
> more elevated knowledge
> is what is evident in the limbs and organs.[113]

Knowledge must be actualized as action, Truth must be actualized as Presence. The implication is that it is nothing less than the reconstitution of the self that is called for by the linking of knowledge to action—of the discerning intellect to the conforming will. To see the world as sacred entails the sacralization of oneself. This is the basis of the refrain within the writings of Imam 'Ali for the need to develop piety. There are numerous exhortations in those writings for the faithful to cultivate the virtues of temperance, generosity, patience, compassion, and other similar qualities that manifest piety. Justice, according to Imam 'Ali, requires the cultivation of virtue and veracity. In a *khutba* in which he describes the qualities of a true Muslim, one who is favored by God, he states:

> Such a person makes it incumbent upon himself to be always just, and the first act of justice he will do is to remove immoderate desires and craving from his mind and to speak the truth and act accordingly.[114]

---

[112] *Spiritual Perspectives and Human Facts, supra,* at pages 144-5.

[113] Cleary, *supra,* pages 13 and 14.

[114] Sermon 90, *Nahjul-Balagha,* Jafery. This appears as Sermon 86 in *Nahjul-Balagha,* Reza (*supra*): "The first step of his justice is the rejection of desires from his heart. He describes right and acts according to it."

We have seen that, according to Imam 'Ali, "Justice puts things in their places", and therefore the proper placement of oneself in relation to God is an essential requirement for the accomplishment of Justice[115]. In one passage, Imam 'Ali notes:

> For those who put in order
> what is between them and God,
> God will put in order
> what is between them and other people.
> And for those who put in order
> their task for the Hereafter,
> God puts in order
> their business in this world.
> And those who have caution from themselves
> have protection from God.[116]

The admonition of "caution from oneself" is a caution against anthropocentrism and the hypertrophism of the self. It is also a warning against the abuse of freedom, of the failure of the egoic self to be subordinated to or effaced within the spiritual Self. Man as such is nothing in the face of God, but possesses worth only as vehicle for the Spirit. The usurping or overreaching self, by becoming detached in its perceptions from its spiritual foundation, risks losing "protection from God". This "protection" is nothing less than the grace of spiritual certitude, which manifests in our submission to the spiritual ordering of the universe, enabling us to thereby withstand the perils of this fickle and illusory world. To misunderstand reality is to risk being disappointed by its illusory nature. By contrast, to conform to reality by aligning ourselves with our spiritual Center—by being Heart-centered—is to make us impervious to the effects of the world. In spiritual submission lies strength and salvation. By transcending the world through piety, we achieve "protection from God".

Note the relationship in the quoted passage between spiritual alignment and judiciousness, and the dependence and derivation of the "horizontal" ordering of creaturely relations on the "vertical" ordering of man's relationship to God:

---

[115] Nasr writes: "Man's responsibility to society, the cosmos, and God issues ultimately from himself, not his self as ego but the inner man who is the mirror and reflection of the Supreme Self, the Ultimate Reality which can be envisaged as either pure Subject or pure Object since It transcends in Itself all dualities, being neither subject nor object." (Seyyed Hossein Nasr in *Knowledge and the Sacred, supra*, at page 168).

[116] Cleary, *supra*, page 71.

> For those who put in order
> what is between them and God,
> God will put in order
> what is between them and other people.

To know and love God (i.e. to properly order oneself in relation to Truth) means to know and love "other people" (i.e. to engage in Just dealings with His creatures)[117]. As the traditionalist Marco Pallis states, "the love of God contains the love of neighbors 'eminently', as cause contains effect"[118].

To this point, we have been discussing Justice primarily in terms of its inner dimension, that is, as the *government of oneself*. Let us now turn more directly to Imam 'Ali's view of the external dimension of Justice, that is, as *social governance*.

It will be apparent from our earlier discussion that, in the metaphysical perspective of the Imam, Justice is predicated on Truth. To restate this point, if we consider the issue of Justice from the perspective of the second category of questions central to human existence, namely, the questions of our relationship to reality, the criterion of Justice must be located, not in the contingent realm of human subjectivity or consensus, but in an objective reality that admits of transcendence. The Imam puts it this way:

> The world was created
> for other than it;
> it was not created for itself.[119]

---

[117] This relationship between spiritual alignment and judiciousness is implicit in the central teaching of Christ: "Thou shalt love the Lord thy God with all thy heart, and with all thy soul, and with all thy mind. This is the first and great commandment. And the second is like unto it, Thou shalt love thy neighbor as thyself. On these two commandments hang all the law and the prophets" (*The Gospel of St. Matthew*, Verse 22:37-40).

[118] From Marco Pallis' essay titled *The Catholic Church in Crisis*, first published (as a commentary on the book *The Vatican Oracle* by Rev. Brocard Sewell) under the title, *Thinking around a Recent Book*, in the traditionalist journal, *Studies in Comparative Religion*, Autumn 1970, Volume 4, No. 4, and reprinted in *The Sword of Gnosis*, edited by Jacob Needleman, Penguin Metaphysical Library, Penguin Books, Baltimore, 1974, at page 57. The quoted passage appears at page 71. Note also the following comments by the Swedish traditionalist, Tage Lindbom: "'To love one's neighbor' does not cease to be an empty formula until we effectively accept the same Father and when in consequence our neighbors are our brothers." (*The Tares and the Good Grain*, by Tage Lindbom, *supra*, at page 90).

[119] Cleary, *supra*, page 107.

The meaning of things, the criterion by which relationships should be governed, must, in other words, be sought outside of the things themselves[120]. The locus of meaning and the objective criterion of Truth and Justice are, in this metaphysical view, to be found in transcendence. It is only when the world is understood to be rooted in transcendence that the underlying pattern of all things can be revealed. It is only the eyes of faith that perceive the Center, and therefore the order that unfolds from the Center[121]. Only these eyes are attuned to discern the hidden pattern beneath the cosmic veil. This hidden pattern is the sense of the sacred that illumines Truth (understood as the theophanic view of creation) and Justice (understood as the compassionate response to that theophany). To regard transcendence as a criterion of knowledge thus reinforces the Imam's view that knowledge is ontological and is embodied as virtue or piety[122].

We have remarked earlier that the structure of reality according to Imam 'Ali comprises levels and polarities associated with these levels. Thus one might be said to be "near" to the Divine Origin or "far" from It, at a "higher" level on the trajectory of Return, or "lower". In this sense, all polarities within the structure of reality correspond to the dialectic of discontinuity and continuity[123]—or transcendence and immanence—and create a correspondence between structure

---

[120] This recalls Gödel's Theorem, which suggests that there is a limit to knowledge through merely discursive, physical or mechanical means. There must be a transcendent dimension that constitutes the criterion by which a system can be validated. The essence of Gödel's Theorem, in the words of the physicist, Paul Davies, is that "there will always exist true statements that cannot be proved to be true" (see Davies' *The Mind of God*, 1993 edition by Touchstone, NY, at page 103). See also, Ananda K. Coomaraswamy's dictum: "a first cause, being itself uncaused, is not *prob*-able but axiomatic (from Coomaraswamy's *Time and Eternity*, Ascona, Switzerland, Artibus Asiae, 1947, at page 42).

[121] Gai Eaton has noted: "Faith is central, unbelief is eccentric in the sense of being ex-centric, far from the Center, out in the wilderness" (*Remembering God: Reflections on Islam*, Charles Le Gai Eaton, ABC International Group Inc., Chicago, 2000, at page 142).

[122] Gnosis is equivalent to the eye's knowledge of itself through the very act of its seeing. Antonio Machado: "The eye you see is not an eye because you see it; it is an eye because it sees you" (from *Times Alone: Selected Poems of Antonio Machado*, translated by Robert Bly, Wesleyan University Press, 1983). In this regard, it is interesting to recall what W.B. Yeats wrote to Lady Elizabeth Pelham on January 4, 1939, less than three weeks before his death: "Man can embody truth but he cannot know it".

[123] Frithjof Schuon refers to metaphysical reality as a "discontinuous continuity": "things are in God and God is in things with a kind of discontinuous continuity" - *Logic and Transcendence*, translated by Peter N. Townsend, London, Perennial Books, 1984, at page 61.

and value, which we discuss below. These polarities in turn give rise to a certain tension[124], the harmonization of which is the métier of Justice.

The classic manifestation of such tension from the perspective of social governance is to be found in the apparently competing interests between the individual and the collective—in more general terms, one might restate these as the conflict between the respective needs of freedom and restraint[125]. The fundamental issue for social governance, namely, the constitution of a just society, can therefore be viewed in terms of the basis for the reconciliation of this conflict.

Applying a metaphysical analysis to this conflict, to emphasize the transcendence of reality is to emphasize the importance of the "other" and correspondingly to diminish the importance of the "within". This is the motive force of restraint. By contrast, to emphasize the immanence of reality is to emphasize the importance of the "within" and correspondingly to diminish the importance of the "other". This is the motive force of freedom. We have argued earlier that reality is in fact a *coincidentia oppositorum*, a "synthesis of opposites"—a complementarity that, in Islamic terms, is the essence of *tawhid*. The reconciliation of freedom and restraint, based on this view, is accomplished by arriving at a balance predicated on a divine archetype (described by Imam 'Ali as a "way-mark", as we shall see later) that is none other than our spiritual nature or *fitra*. The criterion for the reconciliation of tensions stemming from the polarities within reality is therefore ontological: it is resolved not by an outward criterion or

---

[124] Commenting on this tension, Gai Eaton writes: "As between the Divine and the human, distance and proximity are never divided and do not contradict each other. He is the Far and He is the Near. We, for our part, are – as it were – suspended between the two in a state of dynamic tension. We worship Him who is far from us, the utterly transcendent, and we communicate with Him who is near, "closer than the jugular vein", never at rest till we reach God, yet already at home in His Presence. And though we see Him not, nothing – if we are set on the Straight Path – can prevent us from living as if we saw Him." (*Remembering God: Reflections on Islam*, Charles Le Gai Eaton, *supra*, at page 175).

[125] The Yemeni Ismaili, Jafar b. Mansur al-Yaman (d. 914), writes in his *Kitab al-'Alim wa'l-ghulam* (*The Book of the Master and the Disciple*, translated by James W. Morris, I.B. Tauris, London, 2001, in Section 266, at pages 116 and 117) that Justice is the harmonious balancing between "two points", divine determination and human freedom. Morris remarks (*ibid.*, at page 189) that this "echoes a famous phrase of the Imam Ja'far al-Sadiq referring to the proper understanding of the subtle balance between divine determination and human freedom and responsibility" '*It is a point between these two points, neither (total divine) determination nor (total) delegation (of freedom to human beings).*'" This "subtle balance" is, as the Imam teaches, the primordial norm of the *fitra*.

by a set of moral rules or societal laws, but by the inward dimension of conformity to our transcendent spiritual nature, which is the all-pervasive Being.

This leads us to a key point in the Imam's metaphysics, namely, the notion of an ontological *tawhid*[126] in which the only Being is God in His Ipseity, the Sole Existent, the Eternal Witness, the ground of all that is contained within Its unfolding from essence to form. According to this understanding, the metaphysical degrees of manifestation within reality possess an ontological value, commencing with the Highest Level (the Supreme transcendence of essential reality in which the Godhead can be understood as the supra-ontological Subject) and proceeding through various hypostatic degrees of unfolding to formal or material reality, through a process of solidification from the subtle (*latif*) to the gross (*kathif*). In metaphysical cosmology, this unfolding is the derivation of the classification into the spiritual, psychic and corporeal realms, which correspond microcosmically, within man, to the dimensions of the Spirit ("animus" or *ruh*), the psyche ("anima" or *nafs*), and the body ("corpus" or *jism*). Based on this schema, the spiritual quest of man corresponds to the path of Return, referred to earlier. This path is a process of ontological growth to the highest ontological status attainable by self-effaced man, described by the Imam in a *hadith qudsi* attributed to him:

> Who seeketh Me findeth Me.
> Who findeth Me knoweth Me.
> Who knoweth Me loveth Me.
> Who loveth Me, him I love.
> Whom I love, him I slay.
> Whom I slay, him must I requite.
> Whom I must requite, Myself am his Requital.[127]

---

[126] According to the exposition of Ibn al-'Arabi, the concept of ontological or esoteric tawhid (*tawhid wujudi*) is to be distinguished from that of theological or exoteric tawhid (*tawhid uhuli*). The latter emphasizes the being of God in contradistinction to that of other beings (His creatures), while the former refers to the uncreated Being of God in His Ipseity (*wujud mutlaq*), who, while uncreated, is (paradoxically) the Only Existent. Thus, there is no being but God (*laysa fi al-wujud siwa allah*). In an esoteric sense, the Absolute is "absolved from the determinations that it actualizes, for there can be no being *other* than being" (commentary by Henry Corbin, from the anthology, *Shi'ism: Doctrines, Thought and Spirituality*, edited, annotated and introduced by Seyyed Hossein Nasr, Hamid Dabashi, and Seyyed Vali Reza Nasr, SUNY Press, NY, 1988, chapter 13, at page 198).

[127] Quoted by Abu Bakr Siraj Ed-Din in *The Book of Certainty*, Samuel Weiser, NY, 1974, at page 93.

The path of ontological growth envisioned by the Imam entails an egoic death (being nothing before the Face of God) before it culminates in the Divine Self-Disclosure of Requital, the "unio mystica" that dissolves the seeker into the spiritual Substance. What is outwardly a journey to annihilation (*fana*) is inwardly a passage to spiritual rebirth (*baqa*). This rebirth, the spiritual journey of Return to the Center, occurs in the Heart of the seeker ("the heart which contains Me").

The above passage confirms the intellective nature of the 'Alid tradition: love is an aspect of knowledge, an expansion of knowledge—as it were, a kind of "moral intelligence". It is through this moral intelligence that one can appreciate both the metaphysical imperatives of necessity and the metaphysical boundaries of freedom. Freedom and necessity are correlatives, whose synthesis lies in a moral intelligence premised on height and depth—in other words, on verticality. Now, it is this intelligence that legitimizes authority[128]. Simply put, the appeal to authority is the appeal to an intrinsic moral intelligence—an intelligence that recognizes the ontological equilibrium that underlies and harmonizes freedom and necessity, continuity and discontinuity—, whose extrinsic criterion is virtue. Moral intelligence and the virtue it manifests constitute the very basis of Justice, and express the ontological criterion for the equilibrium underlying the just governance of all creaturely relationships. Virtue entails conformity to one's primordial nature (or *fitra*). Authority, and thus value, increases in its proximaty to Heart-Centeredness, and declines in proportion to one's distance from the Heart-Center. Decentered man is therefore detached from the criterion of value and, while no doubt capable of possessing power, is nevertheless lacking in genuine authority.

In an interesting passage, Imam 'Ali observes:

---

[128] In the Shi'ite tradition, authority is vested in the Imam, the interpreter of the scripture. We have remarked above that the 'Alid tradition is an intellectual tradition, and it is through deep knowledge (*ma'rifah* or *irfan*) that the wisdom of interpretation is attained. In the Shi'ite tradition, it is the Imam who possesses the interpretive authority (*ta'wil*) that connects the formal text or sign to its spiritual Center or Origin, its archetype (*awwal*). Imam 'Ali refers to the Holy Qur'an as a "bright beacon, a lasting cure for warped minds and a draught which will fully quench the thirst for knowledge" (Sermon 159, *Nahjul-Balagha*, Jafery), but in the Shi'ite tradition, it is the Imam who interprets the scripture for the Community. The Shi'ite Imam is not merely the interpretive authority and articulator of the *usul* or metaphysical principles for his *murid* (disciple), but also the focus of the *murid's* love, the expander of his kardial consciousness.

It is right that the king should govern himself before governing his subjects.[129]

Self-governance, or piety, is a precondition to the right to govern others. Justice and authority rest upon the foundation of virtue, or conformity to Truth. In another passage, the Imam remarks:

> O people! From amongst you only he deserves to be caliph who possesses moral strength to maintain peace and to carry on good government based on equity and justice; and who has best understood the orders of God for this purpose.[130]

We see here that the possession of proper understanding (the correct orientation of the intellect) and moral strength (the correct orientation of the will) are the pre-requisites of the governor. Right thinking and right doing are both attributes of right being, again pointing to an ontological, inner re-orientation of the self.

In his famous epistle to Malik al-Ashtar on the occasion of the latter's appointment as the Governor of Egypt, the Imam articulated in detail the nature of his views on government and Justice. Exhorting his Governor to rule in accordance with "the principles of equity and justice", he states:

> Malik, you must never forget that if you are a ruler over them (the people), then the Caliph is the ruler over you, and God is the supreme Lord over the Caliph.[131]

Here we observe a clear statement of the hierarchical nature of authority, which incorporates the traditional distinction between spiritual and temporal authority: the Commons defer to the authority of the Regnum, which in turn defers to the authority of the Sacerdotium[132]. Order implies hierarchy. Equality, therefore, is intrinsic[133] and not to be sought on the horizontal plane.

---

[129] This quotation attributed to Imam 'Ali, and is quoted in Perry's *A Treasury of Traditional Wisdom, supra,* at page 921.

[130] Sermon 178, *Nahjul-Balagha,* Jafery.

[131] Letter 53, *Nahjul-Balagha,* Jafery.

[132] For an illuminating discussion of the traditional view of the relationship between temporal and spiritual authority, refer to the article, *Spiritual Authority and Temporal Power in the Indian Theory of Government,* by Ananda K. Coomaraswamy, American Oriental Series, Volume 22, published by the American Oriental Society, New Haven, Connecticut, 1942.

In a *khutba* dealing with the basic principles of rights and obligations, Imam 'Ali elaborates on the difference between the two metaphysical dimensions of authority: the *vertical dimension* of man's absolute subservience to God, and the *horizontal dimension* of man's reciprocal obligations to man. He writes:

> The Almighty God, by entrusting your affairs to me has given me a right over you. And as I have a right over you, so you have a right over me. This incumbency of duties between us is mutual... One-sided obligation is possible only with God. He has rights over His creatures, but they in turn have no rights over Him. This is His privilege. His Power and Authority over His creatures and His equitable assignment of attributes and qualities to each one of them, and His Justice in allotting just rights to every creature, has placed every one of them under obligation to Him. And this obligation upon human beings takes the form of their implicit obedience to Him performed faithfully and sincerely.[134]

Rights and obligations therefore pertain to hierarchies rooted in metaphysical structures. Later in the same *khutba*, speaking of the reciprocal rights and obligations of the ruler and the ruled, he states:

> This obligation, when discharged, forges a link of affinity and love between the ruler and the governed, it raises the prestige and honour of their religion and enhances the happiness and contentment of the subject. But remember that no subject will be happy and contented unless the system of government is sympathetic, humane and congenial. And no ruler can introduce a good form of government unless the subjects are ready to meet their obligations readily, sincerely and faithfully.

What these passages demonstrate is a view of social governance premised on a hierarchy in which the "Divine Principle", the supreme authority, is projected upon the human plane as "affinity and love", the true basis of obligation, creating thereby the basis of a system of government that is "sympathetic, humane and congenial". The bond between the ruler and the ruled is principially rooted. It is the vertical dimension of conformity to our spiritual norms (intrinsically, our pri-

---

[133] In the words of the Tyrolian Catholic philosopher, Nicholas of Cusa (1401-1464): "Equality is by nature prior to inequality; ... it is also naturally prior to diversity. Equality, it must be concluded, is eternal".

[134] Sermon 221, *Nahjul-Balagha*, Jafery. This appears as Sermon 215 in *Nahjul-Balagha*, Reza (*supra*).

mordial nature or *fitra*) that legitimizes the horizontal dimension of our reciprocal relationships (extrinsically different, because based on an "equitable assignment" of archetypal "attributes and qualities", yet intrinsically circumscribed by the "link of affinity and love"). Those who have greater authority do so by virtue of their concomitant obligation to reflect this authority in a "system of government that is sympathetic, humane and congenial." Authority is therefore an expression of the principle of *noblesse oblige*, an aspect of *Amanah*, the Divine Trust, itself rooted metaphysically in the "Divine Principle."

The Imam's viewpoint restates the traditional perspective that hierarchy, which is the basis of both authority and governance, is rooted in transcendence. Thus we find the following summary of this perspective, in the words of Frithjof Schuon:

> The "High" accepts the homage of the "low" only on condition that, on the plane of the "low", the "left" pays homage to the "right". That is to say that God accepts the homage of men only on condition that the inferior man pays homage to the superior man; the rectitude of the vertical relationship requires that of the horizontal relationship. That is the principle of every human order; whoever says human order, says hierarchy.[135]

Schuon's description emphasizes the view that hierarchy is a matter of spiritual devolution, and that this devolution entails spiritual obligations. Again, we return to the correspondence of structure and value. If the quintessence of God is Compassion, it is one's "homage" to that quintessence[136] that permits one to respect differences of "attributes and qualities" on the horizontal plane. Pluralism is thus premised upon the bonds of "affinity and love" of which the Imam teaches. God's authority, in terms of His vertical relationship with man, requires a hierarchical differentiation in terms of man's horizontal relationships with his neighbors and fellow creatures. To restate this view in the Imam's terminology, Justice is based on Truth—which is to say that the Divine Trust is derived from the metaphysical "witnessing" that is the essence of the Divine Covenant. Order implies hierarchy, which is the compassionate devolution of the Divine Substance[137]. Outer

[135] From *Echoes of Perennial Wisdom*, a collection of excerpts from the writings of Frithjof Schuon, 1992, World Wisdom Books, Bloomington, Indiana, at page 82.

[136] God demanded this "homage" of the angels, when He commanded them to bow before Adam. This is the essence of all prayer and worship.

[137] As Nasr has noted, "The world is ultimately good, as asserted by various orthodox

differences veil an inner Substance that is One, that radiates, by its compassionate devolution, as the sacred nature of all creation. The bonds of "affinity and love" that qualify Justice and government as truly "sympathetic, humane and congenial" are thus a reflection of this intrinsic Substance, which constitutes the primordial nature of man. In this sense, one might say that it is in the nature of humanity to be humane.

But is Justice attainable in a world that is apparently so inequitable in its treatment of human beings? For example, how can one ever hope to redress the inequities of some people having greater material comforts and others greater sorrows? From a metaphysical stand-point, ostensible inequities are inherent within the very fact of divine manifestation—in the deployment of the Absolute to the relative and in the expression of Its infinite possibilities—and, in this sense, what we might term the injustice of evil is to be understood as the priva-tive aspect of creation, or what we have earlier termed the trajectory of divine descent. All apparent inequities are, however, reconciled in the intrinsic freedom of human beings to be reintegrated with their spiritual Origin—at which point all outer or quantitative differences vanish, rendered inwardly or qualitatively insignificant in the face of the spiritual Quality or quintessence that unifies all. From this per-spective, Justice then is a matter of judging by the inner dimension, not superficially from the outward appearance of things. And one must bear in mind that God's justice is unfathomable to the human mind, as such.[138] As Ibn 'Ata'illah states: "Sometimes He gives while depriving you, and sometimes He deprives you in giving"[139].

Imam 'Ali deals with the question of these apparent inequities, and he states:

traditions, because it descends from Divine Goodness." (Seyyed Hossein Nasr in *Knowledge and the Sacred, supra,* at page 135).

[138] Recall here the Qur'anic episode of Moses and Khidr, in *Surah Al-Kahf,* XVIII:60-82, in which Moses discerned the outer meaning of certain acts, interpreting them as unfair, until their inner significance was explained to him by Khidr. The spiritual significance of this episode is that Khidr symbolizes the transpersonal Intellect, the sole criterion of justice.

[139] Ibn 'Ata'illah's Sufi Aphorisms (*Kitab al-Hikam*), translated and with an introduction and notes by Victor Danner, and Foreward by Martin Lings, Leiden, E.J. Brill, Netherlands, 1984 edition (first published 1973), chapter IX, no. 83, page 36. There are several similar aphorisms from Ibn 'Ata'illah that counsel against judging with the "eyes of the flesh" but rather with the "eyes of the spirit"; for example: "Deprivation hurts you only because of the lack of your understanding of God in it" (*ibid.,* chapter X, no. 94, page 37).

The Almighty God apportioned livelihood and sustenance to each and every creature. Some are assigned more and some less. Therefore there are some who are well-to-do while others are poor. But this kind of distribution is based upon equity. The fact is that He has tested people in these ways. Some were tried through opulence, while others through poverty[140]. He wants to find out whether wealth makes people grateful to God and persuades them to show their gratitude through their words and deeds; and poverty brings out patience and endurance in man, and whether he remembers to be thankful to Him even in straitened circumstances. Always mixed along with great riches and wealth are dangers of poverty and starvation. Lurking in the folds of peace and prosperity are monsters of calamities unknown and misfortunes unseen; and usually sorrows and sufferings are found mingled with joys and comforts; in short, no happiness and blessing in this world is unmixed. One must remember this and must not give way either to vanity and arrogance or to despair and despondency.

As is the condition with wealth, comfort and happiness, so it is with age. He has fixed different periods of lives for different people. Some are given longer spans while others are assigned shorter durations; some will always go ahead and others will follow. But life will always end in death.[141]

Thus we see that Imam 'Ali invites us to view the world based on an inner understanding of the hidden structure of reality: outer differences are, from an inward dimension, viewed as divine tests. As human beings, we are free to respond to the outer or to conform to the inner. In other words, freedom can be understood, not in terms of the pursuit of personal gratification, but in terms of the opportunity it confers for spiritual growth.

Dealing more specifically with the matter of freedom, Imam 'Ali emphasizes that human freedom is limited by Divine fiat. In one passage, he states:

...Nobody can pass beyond the bounds of His Authority.[142]

---

[140] This view corresponds to the Qur'anic passages: "Do men count on being left in quiet if they say: 'We believe'? And that they will not be put to the test?" (*Surat Al-'Ankabut,* XXIX:2) and "And We shall test you by ill and by good in order to try you, and you will return to Us" (*Al*-Anbiya', XXI:35)

[141] Sermon 94 (*Khutba-e-Ashbah*), *Nahjul-Balagha,* Jafery. This appears as Sermon 90 in *Nahjul-Balagha,* Reza (*supra*).

[142] Sermon 191, *Nahjul-Balagha,* Jafery.

Freedom, in this sense, is equated with the conformance of an individual to his or her archetype. This is clarified in another sermon, where Imam 'Ali states as follows:

> For every one of you, Islam has fixed an ideal. Strive to achieve it. For all of you, there is a way-mark; try to be guided by it. Islam has its aim for each of you to aspire and to attain it. God has imposed certain duties and obligations upon you; discharge those duties and comply with those commands.[143]

The "way-mark" (or "sign") referred to in this passage is the human ideal or archetype corresponding to our *fitra* or primordial nature. The Arabic passage reads "...*wa-inna lakum 'alaman, fa-htadu bi'alamikum...*" The word *'alam*, which means "sign", denotes a metaphysical signification: all "signs" metaphysically point to God, whose reflection in humanity is the transcendent Intellect, whose content is Self-knowledge, *'ilm*. The "way-mark" is outwardly the Revelation, and inwardly the Intellect[144]. Both are pointers to Self-knowledge, that is to say, knowledge of one's original and universal nature, or *fitra*—"original" in that it relates us to our Origin, and "universal" in the sense of Shakespeare's "one touch of nature makes the whole world kin"[145]. Here again we find a correspondence between knowing and being: our deepest nature (the very core of our being) is a transcendent, divining nature, capable of intuiting the hierarchical order of the universe, and the essential connection between all things. This ontological "knowledge of essential connections" is the foundation of piety, the innate source of all moral wisdom. It is this wisdom, then, which defines the metaphysical boundaries of freedom.

As we see, freedom, in this sense, is not unbounded—rather, it is an ideal or archetype to be attained. In fact, it is incumbent upon all human beings to seek this "way-mark" and we can therefore see that freedom and obligation are correlatives: one is only truly free insofar

---

[143] Sermon 181, *Nahjul-Balagha*, Jafery. This is rendered by Reza in Sermon 175 in *Nahjul-Balagha*, Reza (*supra*) as: "...You have a sign. Take guidance from your sign. Islam has an objective. Proceed towards its objective..."

[144] Schuon remarks: "there are two poles for the manifestation of Divine Wisdom and they are: first, the Revelation 'above us' and, secondly, the Intellect 'within us'; the Revelation provides the symbols while the Intellect deciphers them and 'recollects their content, thereby again becoming conscious of its own substance. Revelation is a deployment and intellect a concentration; the descent is in accord with the ascent." (*Understanding Islam*, Frithjof Schuon, Unwin, *supra*, at page 57).

[145] William Shakespeare, *Troilus and Cressida*, iii.3.174.

as one is fulfilling one's divine obligation[146]. In other words, freedom is circumscribed by Truth or the obligation of veracity, which, when embodied, is piety or virtue. Any transgression of this boundary is therefore folly. In one passage, Imam 'Ali states that God detests most two kinds of people: the one who collects "half-truths" (in other words, the one who lacks veracity) and the one who "takes wrong advantage of the freedom and ease allowed to him by circumstances", failing to "realize that he is being given a long rope".[147] And in another passage, he states: "...the realization of one's limitations as well as obligations is the actual depth of knowledge and the height of under-standing".[148] The correlation of freedom and obligation derives from the metaphysical ideal of the "way-mark", and regulation and restraint can therefore be understood in terms of the need to conform to that ideal. Justice, as we have seen, is a matter of order and equilibrium. It is therefore a matter of properly observing limits, and not transgressing tendencies of presumptiveness (presumptiveness here being charac-terized by a failure to observe spiritually optimal boundaries).

Thus, human beings are called upon to master their desires (the easily-enticed human will) and to control their minds (the hubristic and over-reaching human intellect), as in this passage:

> O people! Fear God like a man who has mastered his emotions and desires and who has acquired complete control over his mind; fear God like a man who has developed his knowledge and wisdom and who has achieved command over his passions.[149]

It is only the human being who has achieved full mastery of self that truly understands his or her nothingness before God, and it is this understanding that is the foundation of the fear that saves.

From another perspective, the ontological guide of the "way-mark" or *fitra* is also an acknowledgment of the middle-way, the Straight Path or *al-Sirat al-Mustaqeem*. Thus in one of the *khutbas*, Imam 'Ali states:

---

[146] "Man's freedom is as real as himself. He ceases to be free in the sense of independent of the Divine Will to the extent that he ceases to be separated ontologically from God. At the same time, man is determined and not free to the extent that an ontological hiatus separates him from his Source and Origin, for only God is freedom" (Seyyed Hossein Nasr in *Knowledge and the Sacred, supra,* at page 146).

[147] Sermon 22, *Nahjul-Balagha,* Jafery.

[148] Sermon 94 (*Khutba-e-Ashbah*), *Nahjul-Balagha,* Jafery.

[149] Sermon 164, *Nahjul-Balagha,* Jafery. This appears as Sermon 160 in *Nahjul-Balagha,* Reza (*supra*).

> Remember! That extremes of right and left will lead you astray,
> moderation is the best course for you to adopt...along it is the correct
> route to liberation.[150]

This Straight Path represents the practical manifestation of the
balancing of the polarities within reality, bearing in mind that to
over-emphasize transcendence means to devalue immanence, and
vice versa. The apparent emphasis of one polarity over the other
may, however, be a legitimate corrective. Thus the rigor that evokes
reverential fear may be a necessary corrective to the gentleness of
the "spared rod", while in other instances the gentleness that evokes
mercy may be a necessary corrective to the excesses and constraints of
imposed strictures. Sometimes Justice is achieved through the "hardness" of rigor, at others through the "softness" of gentleness—all the
time bearing in mind that God's justice is compassionate, as is implied
by the *hadith* that God's Mercy precedes His Wrath. In practical
terms, this demands that each of us exercise a quality of moderation in
order to be true to our kardial nature. Such moderation—the criterion
for Justice—is founded on veracity, and constitutes "virtue", the outer
correspondence of the "way-mark" that is our innermost being.

To summarize, we have argued that Imam 'Ali's view of Justice
is premised on the "proper ordering" of things according to the metaphysical principles of Truth; that this ordering requires a deep and
"penetrating knowledge" of the hierarchical correspondence of structure and value; that such knowledge—as an ontological reality—is
the privilege only of those who have been able to embody Truth
through piety and have fully awakened within themselves a sense of
the sacred that perceives the world as a theophany; that, by virtue of
this privilege, such people have the moral authority to govern; that
Justice in terms of social governance is premised on reconciling tensions of freedom and restraint arising from the polarities within reality,
through a "synthesis of opposites", through conformity to one's inner
nature, the "way-mark" or *fitra* that is our primordial spiritual heritage.

Now that we have surveyed Imam 'Ali's metaphysically-based
conception of Truth and Justice, let us touch upon the significance of
this conception for the modern world.

---

[150] Sermon 21, *Nahjul-Balagha*, Jafery. This appears as a part of Sermon 16 in *Nahjul-
Balagha*, Reza (*supra*).

V. Implications for Modernity

A key question confronting humanity regarding Justice can be stated in these terms: "Who shall rule, God or man?" The answer for modern man—who denies or, at least, is skeptical of its transcendent origin and purpose—is to separate Church and State, which corresponds to the Augustinian separation between the City of God and the City of Man. In Islamic terms, this might be understood in terms of an attempt to separate *din* (religion or the spiritual realm) and *dunya* (politics or the temporal realm). For Imam 'Ali, the answer to the question that we have just formulated was clear: the ideals of human governance are rooted in a proper understanding of the metaphysical structure of reality, whose core and criterion is spiritual. As he reminded Governor Malik, "God is the supreme Lord over the Caliph".

Having concluded that government must be founded on a spiritual criterion of Truth and Justice, however, it is not at all clear that Imam 'Ali advocated a theocracy as the only legitimate form of government, though a theocracy is the prototypical state in Islam.[151] At the very least, he appreciated that human governance might embrace diverse forms of government, some of which might be benevolent and just, and others inequitable—and that he favored the former. For instance, remarking on the Kharijites' slogan "There is no order and law but that of God", Imam 'Ali stated:

> Yes! There can be no law and no order but that of God; but they (the Seceders) infer that none should be king or ruler over mankind but God.
>
> How is it possible? Necessarily there ought to be some form of government of man over man. There ought to be human agency as a ruler, and this may be either (transpire to be) a pious and benevolent ruler or an ungodly government.
>
> A benevolent and godly government is necessary so that, under its kind rule, Muslims and non-Muslims alike may prosper...[152]

The notion of "kind rule" for the benefit of "Muslims and non-Muslims" alike suggests that Imam 'Ali may have had in mind a

---

[151] Titus Burckhardt: "The prototypical Islamic state is theocratic, for in it spiritual power and temporal power are combined. Herein it differs from the traditional Christian state which, in Christ's words 'My kingdom is not of this world', can never be identified with the Church." (*Fez: City of Islam*, trans. by William Stoddart, Islamic Texts Society, Cambridge, 1992, at p.53).

[152] Sermon 45, *Nahjul-Balagha*, Jafery. This appears as Sermon 40 in *Nahjul-Balagha*, Reza (*supra*).

non-theocratic pluralistic government. Whether or not Imam 'Ali advocated theocratic rule, we may infer from his views that certain traditional bulwarks are necessary to enable a society to provide government consistent with the principles of Truth and Justice. Given the conditions of modernity—in particular, its much lamented loss of a sense of the sacred, there is no doubt a need to establish structures within society that rest on these traditional bulwarks, but it is beyond the scope of this paper to examine this issue in detail; suffice it to say that the multiplicity of viewpoints and interests regarding most issues of social governance among humankind suggests a solution rooted in a notion of "principled pluralism"[153] grounded in an objective and universal metaphysical perspective that is consistent with, yet transcends theology.

It is clear that, in Imam 'Ali's view, human governance and social justice were predicated on principles of divine governance rooted in such a metaphysical perspective, and premised on an ontological understanding of *tawhid*. Based on this view, there is no dimension of a theophany—no matter how we choose, from a human perspective, to compartmentalize, atomize or marginalize it—that can elude the sacred embrace of the Divine. All things are rooted in the spiritual dimension and must be referred back to their spiritual foundation. Without this "verticality", what is genuine and salvific in religion will atrophy, dissolving the moral basis of civilization[154]. A corollary of this

---

[153] The distinction between metaphysics and theology is that between the *din al-fitr* and the *din al-islam*. The exoteric component of any revealed tradition, while remaining vital to that tradition, is subordinated to its esoteric core, which is premised on a transcendent "principle" referred to, for example, in this passage from the *Divan: Muqatta'at* of Mansur al-Hallaj: "I have meditated on the different religions, endeavoring to understand them, and I have found that they stem from a single principle with numerous ramifications. Do not therefore ask a man to adopt a particular religion (rather than another), for this would separate him from the fundamental principle; it is this principle itself which must come to seek him; in it are all the heights and all the meanings elucidated; then he will understand them."

[154] Lamenting the loss of "verticality" in modernism, Gai Eaton remarks: "The horizontal depends upon the vertical, the outward depends upon the inward and, when the spiritual element is pushed into the background, then practical—down-to-earth—religious practice falls away. It no longer has any solid foundation in the transcendent reality which, by its very nature, gives all things under the sun their proper weight, no more and no less." (*Remembering God: Reflections on Islam*, Charles Le Gai Eaton, *supra*, at pages 129-130). Martin Lings observes that if man "is cut off from the spiritual plane, he will find a 'god' to worship at some lower level, thus endowing something relative with what belongs only to the Absolute. Hence the existence today of so many 'words to conjure with' like 'freedom', 'equality', 'literacy', 'science', 'civilization', words at the utterance of which a multitude of souls fall prostrate in

view is that there can be no opposition in metaphysics between *din* and *dunya*. By contrast, the modernist worldview, though it often includes a constitutional reference to God, is secular, based increasingly upon the privatization of religion. In part, this secularism is paradoxically often attributed to the desire to uphold the freedom of religion within a pluralistic society and thereby to avoid a theocracy based upon one particular theology. But religious views cannot be absented from the public sphere, however one might attempt to compartmentalize society into realms of the sacred and the secular.

Imam 'Ali's teachings clearly endorse a qualitative, spiritually devolutionary and sacred view of the world, where value descends from above to the domains below. This is the foundation of hierarchy and moral authority, an acceptance of a divinely ordained world in which freedoms are bounded by moral imperatives and rights by spiritual standards. By contrast, the modernist worldview is quantitative, materially evolutionary and secular, which celebrates freedom and equality without anchoring these in the objective and transcendent criteria of spiritual reality[155]. Its "authority" operates from below, not from top down, and is founded on subjective preferences or rationalized principles rather than on universal, transcendent, metaphysical principles grounded in the very structures of reality. Without a proper spiritual underpinning, its "freedom" is degenerative and overreaching[156], leeching from the soul the enriching and salvific elements of reverence, mystery and wonder which are required to sustain it, while its "equality" is homogenizing and weighed down by "political correctness", thereby inhibiting both legitimate authority and creative expression. The presumptive and laissez-faire modernist notions of "freedom" and the excessively rights-based modernist notions of "equality", which promote mediocrity by pandering to the 'lowest common denominator', are in marked contrast to Imam 'Ali's view

---

sub-mental adoration." (*Ancient Beliefs and Modern Superstitions*, by Martin Lings, Quinta Essentia, 1991, at page 45).

[155] Commenting on the modernist outlooks on freedom and equality, Martin Lings observes, "each in its own way is a revolt against hierarchy." (*Ancient Beliefs and Modern Superstitions*, by Martin Lings, *supra*, at page 45). He notes, "The desire for freedom is above all the desire for God, Absolute Freedom being an essential aspect of Divinity" (*ibid.*, at pages 45 and 46), and "The need for equality, which is part of the nostalgia in the soul of fallen man, is above all the need to be 'adequate' once more to the Divine Presence" (*ibid.*, at page 48).

[156] Emphasizing a universal traditional viewpoint, Schuon observes that "freedom consists much more in satisfaction with our particular situation than in the total absence of constraints, an absence scarcely realizable in the here-below, and which moreover is not always a guarantee of happiness" (*The Transfiguration of Man*, by

that true knowledge (*irfan*) and piety (*ihsan*) are the foundations of moral authority, and are hierarchical and therefore elevating. Genuine freedom vertically transcends horizontal limitations through detachment, while genuine equality is the intrinsic adequacy of the soul to compassion. The egoic individualism of the modernist cannot but degrade the soul, in contrast to the compassionate detachment of the faithful seeker that is ennobling. The Imam's caution is sadly true for our times: "The triumph of mediocre men brings down the elite"[157].

No doubt, the domains of the secular and the sacred may be opposed from a certain theological viewpoint, but, as we have seen, there exist metaphysical principles—rooted in the very structure of reality—that transcend even theology. This points to a crucial distinction between metaphysics and theology, and the primacy of the former over the latter. It is on the basis of this distinction, that the poet Jami could state:

> Be aware that justice and equity, not unbelief nor religion,
> Are needed for the maintenance of the kingdom.
> Justice without religion, for the next world,
> Is better than the tyranny of a religious Shah.[158]

Frithjof Schuon, World Wisdom Books, Bloomington, Indiana, 1995, at page 52).

[157] Quoted by Whitall N. Perry in *A Treasury of Traditional Wisdom, supra*, at page 968. This criticism of mediocrity and by implication of the centrifugal influence of societies that are governed primarily or purely on the basis of consensus rather than Principle, is also a criticism of a certain kind of democracy. Thus, Muhammad Iqbal wrote: "Democracy is a certain form of government in which men are counted but not weighed." Commenting on this in her essay, "The Development of Political Philosophy" (Chapter 6 of the anthology, *Iqbal: Poet-Philosopher of Pakistan*, Columbia University Press, NY and London, 1971 *Iqbal: Poet-Philosopher of Pakistan*, Columbia University Press, NY and London, 1971, edited by Hafeez Malik, at page 156), Riffat Hassan writes: "Iqbal's criticism that in a democracy persons are 'counted' not 'weighed' must be interpreted as an assertion that society takes note of 'individuality'—which is a material fact, but not of 'personality'—which is a spiritual fact." Though societies cannot always be governed by sages or "Philosopher-Kings" in the traditional utopian model outlined by Plato in his *Republic*, Imam 'Ali's cautionary words serve to remind us that all consensus (*ijma*) and personal striving for truth (*ijtihad*) have to be principled, that is, based on metaphysical principles (*usul*). Thus, certain kinds of democracies—namely, those that exclude any reference to the metaphysical roots of governance, that reflect rulership that is "sympathetic, humane and congenial" and tied to the principle of *noblesse oblige*—can in fact erode social values and undermine the bonds of affinity and love between the government and society that are vital to the fabric of a healthy society.

[158] Quoted at page 2 of *A Dictionary of Oriental Quotations*, edited by Claude Field, Swan Sonnenschien & Co., London, 1911. The passage, translated by Rehatsek, reads:

It is, therefore, essential that the criterion for Justice be rooted in a sound metaphysical view of reality that admits of the transcendent and operates out of a sense of the sacred. We have argued earlier that the Divine Quintessence—which is the Origin of the sacred—corresponds to Compassion or Mercy, the life-blood of creation and the dialectic of the *Nafas Rahmani*. It is this Quality, whose spirit constitutes our innermost being or *fitra* that is the true criterion of Justice. It is of this transcendent quality that Shakespeare writes:

> ...mercy is above the sceptered sway,
> It is enthroned in the hearts of kings,
> It is an attribute to God himself;
> And earthly power doth then show likest God's
> When mercy seasons justice.[159]

True Justice, in this sense, as we have argued, is only attainable through the "middle-path" of Imam 'Ali—a path that corresponds to the "way-mark" of our innermost being.

And here we come to two errors that are central to modern conceptions of Justice: the first is the error of premising Justice on a secular dogmatism[160] that devalues the transcendent by its anthropocentrism (man's way, not God's); and the second is the error of premising it on a religious dogmatism that devalues the immanent by its deracination of religion (following the letter, not the spirit). In the first case, the error is prone to manifest in the form of relativism—for instance, in the post-modernist tendency to subjectivism and permissive liberalism within society. In the second case, the error is prone to manifest in the form of reductionism—for instance, in the fundamentalist[161]

Adl wa insaf dan na kufr wa na din
Anche dar hifz-i-mulk dar kar ast
Adl be din nizam 'alam ra
Bihtar az zulm-i-Shah dindar ast.

[159] Act IV, scene i, *The Merchant of Venice*, William Shakespeare.

[160] Tage Lindbom writes: "Secularization...implies the loss by man of his capacity of objectivation, of his power to distinguish illusion from reality, falsehood from truth, the relative from the absolute. The deepest objective of secularism is precisely to 'liberate' man from the order by which he is submissive to his Creator, to 'emancipate' him from his existential source, to 'change' the system of truth in which he lives into a factual and mental relativity. Thus an inevitable consequence is, not an accrued perspicuity in the imaginative life of man, but on the contrary an ever growing opacity." (*The Tares and the Good Grain*, by Tage Lindbom, *supra*, at page 109).

[161] The term "fundamentalism" is a complex and nuanced term. We use this term to refer to the reductionist tendency in religions that sacrifices the "spirit" of religion to

tendency to reduce the vitality of spirituality to a mere abstraction and to reduce the life-blood of religion to mere blind adherence to prescribed formulae.[162]   Neither of these positions—relativism or reduction, secular dogmatism or fundamentalism—accord with Imam 'Ali's conception of the basis of a "just society". The Straight Path is the "middle path" that steers between these two errors.

Ultimately, as Imam 'Ali teaches, Justice is based on Truth, and Truth is a matter of recognizing spiritual realities and conforming to them. The criterion of judgment, both in the sense of self-regulation and of human governance, lies within our own selves (our *fitra*) and not in any constructed worldview (whether utopian, consensual, rational, or pragmatic) derived from outward things. Though the voice of this message may be dimmed in the ambience of modernity, its relevance remains vital for the salvation of human beings and human societies in all times. The truth of this message is universal, and we cite one example of its articulation, in a beautiful passage by Robert Browning, from the poem *Paracelsus*:

> Truth is within ourselves; it takes no rise
> From outward things, whate'er you may believe.
> There is an inmost center in us all,
> Where truth abides in fullness; and around,
> Wall upon wall, the gross flesh hems it in,
> This perfect, clear perception—which is Truth.
> A baffling and perverted carnal mesh
> Binds it, and makes all error: and to *know*
> Rather consists in opening out a way
> Whence the imprisoned splendor may escape,
> Than in effecting entry for a light
> Supposed to be without.

As the Imam taught, it is only by striving to know what we truly are, and to be what we truly know, that we can hope to fulfill the

---

the "letter" (though, we emphasize that we do not thereby equate "fundamentalism" with "exoterism") and is exclusivist to the point that it denies religious plurality premised in a transcendent unity (though, we emphasize that we do not thereby equate "fundamentalism" with "exclusivism"). For a discussion, see the Editorial, "'Fundamentalism': A Metaphysical Perspective", by M. Ali Lakhani, in *Sacred Web 7*, Vancouver, Canada, 2001, published in the anthology, *The Betrayal of Tradition: Essays on the Spiritual Crisis of Modernity*, edited by Harry Oldmeadow, World Wisdom Books, Bloomington, Indiana, USA, 2005, at p. 101.

[162] See the author's Editorial, "Pluralism and the Metaphysics of Morality", by M. Ali Lakhani, in *Sacred Web 3*, Vancouver, Canada, 1999.

conditions of Justice. For Justice is an attribute of Truth. We end with Imam 'Ali's cautionary words:

> Your cure is within you, but you do not know,
>   Your illness is from you, but you do not see.
> You are the "Clarifying Book"
>   Through whose letters becomes manifest the hidden.
> You suppose that you're a small body
>   But the greatest world unfolds within you.
> You would not need what is outside yourself
>   If you would reflect on 'self', but you do not reflect.[163]

---

[163] Cited by Sadr al-din Qunawi (d. 1274), a disciple of Ibn al-'Arabi, in his book, *Mir'at al-arifin fi multamas Zayn al-Abidin.* The citation from Qunawi is translated by William C. Chittick and quoted in his book, *Sufism: A Short Introduction, supra,* at page 84.

"'Ali slays a huge serpent which appears before him and his followers on their
way to confront the Benineccar tribe." From the Turkish manuscript *Siyer-i Nebī*,
volume VI, p. 90a,16th century. Istanbul, Topkapi Saray Museum. The serpent is
an emblem of the egoic self.

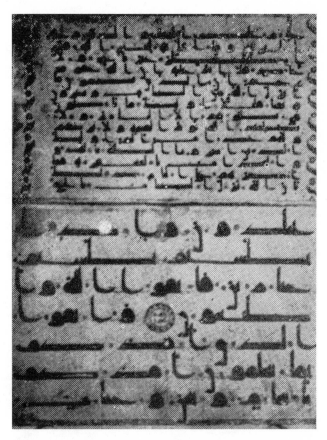

Page from a Qur'an kept in Istanbul and written by the third and fourth Caliphs; the upper fragment is in 'Ali's own hand; Qur'an 27: 59.

A SACRED CONCEPTION OF JUSTICE: IMAM 'ALI'S LETTER TO MALIK AL-ASHTAR[1]

Reza Shah-Kazemi

Introduction

This essay will offer some reflections upon the theme of justice in terms of the principles that determine the worldview of Imam 'Ali in general, and in relation to the letter written by the Imam to Malik al-Ashtar, appointing him as governor of Egypt, in particular. The aim here is to show that, according to this worldview, the orientation towards justice, conceived as the most fundamental of the virtues, is immeasurably deepened insofar as it is consciously linked to the spiritual precepts of the Islamic faith; and that it is correspondingly weaker insofar as it is separated from those precepts. The spirit underlying moral rules and ethical injunctions is strengthened by a commitment to transcendent principles, even though—or precisely because—these principles surpass the realm of action within which those rules and precepts operate. Contemplation and action are seen in this perspective as complementary, not contradictory; this complementarity goes to the very heart of the Islamic message of *tawhid*, of integral oneness, and it is embodied with dazzling evidence in the life of the Imam, as it is in the life of the Prophet. This harmony between the two principles—contemplation and action, being and doing, theory and practice, ideal and reality—also pervades the remarkable document that is the central focus of this essay.

As regards the epistle itself, it is found as number 52 in most editions of the *Nahj al-balagha*.[2] In broad historical terms, the letter has been a source of inspiration down through the centuries, being read as an ideal constitution for Islamic governance, complementing—through its relatively detailed description of the duties and rights of the ruler and the various functionaries of the state and the main classes of society—the more general framework of principles enshrined in the

---

[1] This is the revised text of a paper delivered at the International Conference on Imam 'Ali, Tehran, March 2001, organised by the Institute for Humanities and Cultural Studies.

[2] It is also found in numerous texts long predating the compiler of the *Nahj al-balagha*, al-Sharif al-Radi (d. 1013/404). See *Masadir Nahj al-balagha* ('Sources of the *Nahj al-balagha*'), 'Abd Allah Ni'mah (Beirut: Dar al-Huda, 1972), pp. 246-248.

famous 'Constitution of Medina' dictated by the Prophet.[3] As will be evident in what follows, however, the advice contained in the letter far exceeds the parameters conventionally set by political or legal texts dealing with governance. Despite being addressed in the first instance to the ruler or governor of the polity, much of the advice pertains in fact to universally applicable ethical principles and is therefore as relevant to those ruled as to those who rule. It is as much a statement of ethics as of politics—not a discursive 'system' or theory of ethics, to be sure, but an inspiring expression of the spiritual ethos which the Imam embodied and radiated; an ethos that flows directly from the sources of the Islamic revelation, and which therefore discloses the roots of virtue and ethics in a climate governed by the all-embracing principle of revelation.

It is possible, therefore, to read this document also as a commentary on that revelation, a commentary which in turn encourages the reader to delve more deeply into the meanings enshrined in the revealed texts. For the revelation, far from cutting short the operations of reason and imposing some unintelligible *diktat*, on the contrary presupposes the creative application of reason—those processes of reflection, assimilation, meditation and creative application for which the Imam is himself renowned; and which the Qur'an itself repeatedly calls for.[4] In this connection the following saying of the Imam is of fundamental importance, and is one of the many sayings which help explain why it is that in the discipline of exegesis, *tafsir*, he is so often referred to as the 'first interpreter' (after the Prophet himself, needless to say)[5]: 'The

[3] See S.H.M. Jafri, *Political and Moral Vision of Islam* (Lahore: Institute of Islamic Culture, 2000). In addition to discussing the Medina Constitution and the letter of the Imam to Malik—a full translation of which is also given—this book is a welcome addition to the scanty works in western scholarship that address the relevance of the intellectual legacy of the Imam to contemporary political and ethical discourse in Islam.

[4] See, for example, II:73; II:242; III:191; IV: 82; VI:151; VII:176; XVI:44; XXIII:68; XXXVIII:29 XLVII:24, *et passim*.

[5] In one saying attributed to 'Ali, there is a reference to the Prophet as the first of those who were taught by God the science of *ta'wil*, esoteric exegesis (literally: taking meanings back to 'the beginning', *al-awwal*, the source), and that he, the Prophet, in turn taught 'Ali this science. According to a hadith, 'Truly, 'Ali is with the Qur'an, and the Qur'an is with 'Ali.' In a famous saying, often quoted by Sufi commentators, 'Ali claimed to be able to load seventy camels with the pages of the commentary he could give on the opening chapter of the Qur'an, the *Fatiha*. Finally, it should be noted that Ibn 'Abbas, often also referred to as the 'first commentator', claims to have learnt the science of interpretation from 'Ali. For these four sayings and their sources, see Muhammad Muradi, '*Ravish-i tafsir-i Qur'an*' ('The Method of Qur'an

Qur'an consists of a book inscribed, between two covers; it speaks not with a tongue. It cannot do without an interpreter (*la budda lahu min tarjuman*).'[6] The reciprocity between revelation and the intellect is further underlined in this saying: 'The prophet of a man is the interpreter of his intellect (*rasul al-rajul tarjuman 'aqlihi*).'[7]

Thus, one of the purposes here is to show how the Imam's teachings can be read as creative interpretations of revelation, and to show also how these teachings so often presuppose an awareness of the spiritual precepts laid down in the Qur'an. In this perspective, the revealed text is not to be seen as some extraneous source, opposed to reason, but as the objective, outward expression of the very principles that the intellect itself yields to the 'inner prophet'—understanding by 'intellect' not simply the faculty of reason but the very source of consciousness articulating the human spirit. As will be seen below, this understanding of the intellect brings us close to what the Imam refers to as the 'heart', that inmost mode of perception that is capable of 'seeing' God.[8]

Commentary') in *Danish-nama-yi Imam 'Ali* (a 12-volume compendium of articles on 'Ali's life and thought), edited by 'Ali-Akbar Rashad (Tehran: Institute of Culture and Islamic Thought, 1380 Sh./2001), vol. 1, *Hikmat wa ma'rifat*, pp. 234, 235, 237-239.

[6] *Nahj*, p.144 (Sermon 125); *Peak*, p.278 (Sermon 124).

[7] *Ghurar al-hikam* ('The Finest of Aphorisms') (under the Persian title, *Guftar-i Amir al-mu'minin*), compiled by 'Abd al-Wahid Amidi (d. 1116/510), Persian edition and translation by Sayyid Husayn Shaykhul-Islami (Qom: Ansariyan Publications, 2000) p.595, no.2. The following saying attributed to Imam Musa al-Kazim expresses the harmony between intellect and revelation that characterises in large part the Shi'ite approach to this relationship: 'God did not send His messengers to His slaves except that they might use their intellect in regard to God (*li-ya'qilu 'an Allah*)'. Cited in Muhammad Baqir Sa'idi Rowshan, '*Wahy wa ma'rifat-i wahyani*' ('Revelation and revelatory knowledge'), in *Danish nama Imam 'Ali*, vol.1, p.149. Imam Musa al-Kazim also refers to the *'aql* as the 'inner proof' (*hujja batina*) that corresponds to the prophets and saints as the 'outer proof' (*hujja zahira*). See *Mizan al-hikma* ('The Scale of Wisdom'—a 10-volume compendium of Shi'ite *hadith*, thematically arranged) (Qom & Tehran: Maktab al-'Ilam al-Islami, 1983), vol.6, p.402, no. 13058.

[8] The word 'intellect' is preferred to 'reason' for the translation of *'aql*, in keeping with the original meaning of *intellectus* in Latin Christendom, and in accordance with the Patristic Greek meaning of *nous*. Reason, on the other hand, better translates the Latin *ratio* and the Greek *dianoia*. For whereas the *intellectus/nous* is capable of a direct contemplative vision of transcendent realities, reason is of an indirect, discursive nature; it works with logic and arrives at mental concepts, only, of those realities. With the intellect, then, one can effectively contemplate or 'see' the Real; with the reason, one can think about it. Losing sight of this distinction entails the reductive view of knowledge that has increasingly characterised western epistemology since the end of the Middle Ages. See S.H. Nasr, *Knowledge and the Sacred* (New York: Crossroad, 1981), for a profound exposition of the process whereby knowledge has drifted from its original moorings in the sacred, especially chapter 1, 'Knowledge

*****

Malik himself was a long-standing and dedicated follower of the Imam, and was referred to as one of his 'right-hand' men. The Imam's main antagonist in the civil war (657-661), Mu'awiya, was one person who referred to Malik thus, after hearing of the success of his mission to poison Malik before he was able to take up his post as governor in Egypt. He is reported by Tabari as remarking: "Ali b. Abi Talib had two right hands. One of them was cut at Siffin,[9] and the other today.'[10] For his part, the Imam's response to the news of Malik's assassination was reported as follows: 'Malik, and what was Malik! By God were he a mountain, he would be the solitary one [soaring above the others], and were he a rock, he would have been impenetrably solid. No horse could ascend it [such a mountain], no bird could fly up to it.'[11]

The letter takes on additional importance by being addressed to so prominent and trusted a companion. Before examining the letter itself, it might be helpful to situate the discussion in relation to some broader considerations, beginning with the most general 'definition'

and its Desacralization', pp.1-60. See also Mehdi Ha'iri Yazdi, *The Principles of Epistemology in Islamic Philosophy* (Albany: State University of New York, 1992), for a good account of traditional Islamic epistemology, in which knowledge is indissolubly wedded to the sacred. Finally, Rumi's famous line should be noted here, as it brings out well the importance of maintaining the distinction between reason and intellect: 'It is reason *('aql-i juz'i)* which has destroyed the reputation of the Intellect *('aql-i kulli)*' quoted by Nasr, 'Revelation, Intellect and Reason in the Qur'an' in *Sufi Essays* (London: George Allen & Unwin, 1972), p.55.

[9] 'Ammar was killed at the battle of Siffin by Mu'awiya's troops. This fact also dealt a heavy blow to the morale of Mu'awiya's army, given the well known prophecy of the Prophet that 'Ammar would be killed by ' a rebellious people'. See *Sahih Muslim*, (English translation), Chapter MCCV, pp 1508-1509, Traditions 6966-6970.

[10] Cited by Wilferd Madelung, *The Succession to Muhammad—A Study of the Early Caliphate* (Cambridge, 1997), p.266. The assassination took place in the year 658/38.

[11] *Nahj al-Balagha*, Tehran: Nahj al-Balagha Foundation, (edited by Shaykh 'Azizullah al-'Utardi), 1413 AH/1372 SH (1993). All translations of the Arabic text will be by the present writer, unless otherwise stated, and will be from this, the first critical edition of the work (hereafter referred to as *Nahj*). Reference will also be given to the best available complete translation, that of Sayed Ali Reza, *Peak of Eloquence* (New York: Tahrike Tarsile Qur'an, 1996) (hereafter referred to as *Peak*). In this translation the statement of the Imam is given as no. 452, pp. 668-669. In relation to the legacy of Malik, it is of interest to note that a tomb associated with him in Ba'labakk was described in the travelogue of 'Ali b. Abi Bakr al-Harawi (d.611/1215), *Kitab al-isharat ila ma'rifat al-ziyarat (*Damascus, 1953), p.9. See the translation by Josef Meri, *A Lonely Wayfarer's Guide to Pilgrimage* (Princeton, 2004).

of justice given by the Imam: 'Justice[12] puts everything in its right place.'[13] This evokes the famous definition of Plato: '...we have laid down, as a universal principle, that everyone ought to perform the one function in the community for which his nature best suited him ... that principle, or some form of it, is justice.'[14] There are indeed many remarkable parallels between Plato's *Republic* and the letter of the Imam to Malik. Although space does not permit us to enter here into a detailed comparison between the two works, we shall refer to some of the more obvious correspondences, and briefly refer, at the end of the essay, to the way in which the Imam's explicit spirituality sheds light on what is left implicit in Plato's philosophy.

What relates the Imam's definition of justice to the sacred is that the first and most important 'thing' to be put in its right place is one's relationship with God; everything else is derived from this spiritual imperative. This order of precedence is clearly established in the following important statement in the Imam's letter to Malik: 'Be just with God and be just with people [giving them what is their due] from yourself.'[15] The principle at work here emerges clearly from the following saying: 'Whoso establishes well-being between himself and God, God establishes well-being between him and mankind.'[16] Being

---

[12] The word used in this definition is *'adl*; other words used to denote justice, with slightly different connotations, but always containing the sense of equity and fairness, are *insaf* and *qist*. And for a comprehensive discussion of justice in theological context, see 'Allama Mutahhari, *'Adl-i ilahi* ('Divine Justice') (Tehran: Sadra Publications, 2001).

[13] *Nahj*, saying no.429, p.495. *Peak*, no.446, p.668.

[14] *The Republic of Plato*, Translation by F.M. Cornford (Oxford: The Clarendon Press, 1951), p.124. For the influence of Platonic and neo-Platonic conceptions of justice on the elaboration of ethical discourse in Islam, see M. Fakhry, *Ethical Theories of Islam* (Leiden: E.J. Brill, 1994), especially Part Three, 'Philosophical Ethics', pp. 61-147. Within this discourse, justice is not so much seen as one among several virtues, but as the perfection of the other virtues, especially the three principal Platonic virtues of temperance, courage and wisdom. These must characterise, respectively, the concupiscent, the irascible and the rational dimensions of the soul. When each such dimension is in its proper place, dictated by the virtue governing it, then can the soul as such be qualified as 'just'. See the essay by Bahram Kazemi, *'Bar resi-yi tatbiqi-yi mafhum-i 'idalat dar andishi-yi Imam 'Ali wa Aflatun'* ('A Comparative Analysis of the concept of justice in Imam 'Ali and Plato') in *Proceedings of the Congress on Imam 'Ali* (Persian articles), (Tehran: Institute for Humanities and Cultural Studies, 2001), ed. Mehdi Golshani, p. 170, for a saying of the Imam which closely parallels this Platonic view of justice.

[15] *Nahj*, p.368. *Peak*, p.535.

[16] *Nahj*, Saying no.86, p.420, *Peak*, Saying no. 89, p.589.

just with God means, among other things, conforming as best one can to His own nature, which is not only the source of justice but *is* justice: 'I bear witness', the Imam says in one of his sermons, 'that He is Justice (*'adl*) and He acts justly.'[17]

It might be objected here that, as between the divine reality of justice and the human expression of justice there is a radical disjuncture: in God, justice means that everything is in its right place, whereas for man justice entails the *effort* to put everything in its right place: an immutable metaphysical quality on the divine side, and a dynamic, volitive effort on the human side. One response to this is as follows: man's moral effort to act justly in the world herebelow—where things are not in their right place—is rooted in an innate spiritual predisposition to justice: just action thus expresses the principle of justice, which, in man as in God, is that immutable principle by which everything is in its right place. Just as God's action in creation, judgement, and other realms, is an expression of absolute justice, so, in man, just action is an expression, not only of a moral, volitive and intellectual effort to realize justice, but also of a spiritual affinity with the ultimate nature of reality—of things as they truly are, in God, and therefore as they ought to be, here on earth.

Applied to state and society, one of the most obvious consequences of this conception of justice is the necessity for piety and rectitude on the part of the rulers. As the Imam says in another of his sermons: 'The most momentous of the reciprocal rights that God has made obligatory is the right of the ruler over the subjects, and the right of the subjects over the ruler—a reciprocal obligation which God has ordained, each upon the other.'[18] He then makes the following point, which is altogether indispensable for any discourse on good governance in Islam: 'The subjects will not be righteous except through the righteousness of the rulers, and the rulers will not be righteous except through the uprightness of the subjects. So if the subjects render to the

---

[17] This is the beginning of Sermon no.205 in *Nahj*, p.248. In *Peak*, it is Sermon no.213, p.431. Sayed Ali Reza renders the sentence 'I stand witness that He is just', which is a possible rendering of *ashhadu annahu 'adl*. But the translation offered above brings out the strongly expressed theological principle of the Imam, namely, that the divine attributes are absolutely one with the divine essence, not superadded to it, as so many appendages. In the famous first sermon of the *Nahj al-balagha*, God is described as: 'He whose attribute has no bound limitation, no existing description, no fixed duration, no prolonged termination.' It is because His attribute is absolutely one with His essence that it acquires these properties. *Nahj*, p.7; *Peak*, p.91.

[18] *Nahj*, Sermon no. 207, p. 251; *Peak*, Sermon no. 215, p. 433.

ruler his rightful due, and he renders to them theirs, then will Right be honoured amongst them, the ways of religion will be upheld, and the banners of justice will be erected.' One of the main intentions of this essay is to reflect upon the ways in which the Imam tries to ensure that the ruler remains righteous and just; and, as will be clear from what follows, this involves much more than a simple exhortation to abide by the formal rules of Islamic Law.

The whole of the Imam's life can be seen as a quest for conforming as perfectly as possible to the divine nature, and to this quality of justice in particular. There are therefore too many aspects of this principle—social, economic, political, juridical—in connection with the Imam's life and teachings to address in the brief compass of this essay.[19] Rather, the concern here is with some of the key principles that emerge from the Imam's remarkable letter of instruction. The focus in the first part is on a particular dimension of justice, one which is political on the surface, ethical in its outward expression, but spiritual in depth: that is, the justice of the political ruler, justice conceived in relation to its more clearly definable diametrical opposite—injustice, tyranny, oppression and corruption. In the second part of the essay, it will be argued that a deep assimilation of the Imam's spirituality can bestow an existential power upon the moral effort to live according to just precepts, a power that is lacking when justice is conceived exclusively in terms of individual or horizontal values, that is, according to a secular 'moral philosophy', divorced from religious or spiritual principles. In the third part of the paper, the crucial role played by devotion and worship—formal and supra-formal—is discussed; it is proposed that contemplation of the divine reality is the fountain from which integral virtue flows spontaneously and ceaselessly. This point will be made clearer by means of a brief comparison with Plato's 'gazing' on the Sovereign Good, source of all virtue.

---

[19] See the volume of essays noted above, *Proceedings of the Congress on Imam Ali*, which address diverse aspects of the theme of justice in relation to the Imam's life and thought; the collection of legal judgements delivered by the Imam, *Qada' Amir al-mu'minin 'Ali ibn Abi Talib* ('The Legal Judgements of the Commander of the Faithful, 'Ali ibn Abi Talib'), compiled by 'Allama Shoushtari (Tehran: Institute for Humanities and Cultural Studies, 2001); the 27 essays devoted to the Imam in *Farhang—Quarterly Journal of Humanities and Cultural Studies*, vol.13, nos.33-36, Winter, 2001; and finally, one of the most important biographies of the Imam, the title of which brings out the centrality of the theme of justice in his life: *The Voice of Human Justice*, George Jordac (Tr. M. Fazal Haqq), (Qom: Ansariyan Publications, 1990).

The Imam's approach to justice on the part of a ruler or governor clearly transcends the boundaries of its historical context, and this will be made clear in what follows. For now, though, this point should be made emphatically: The letter is addressed to one of the Imam's closest and most trusted companions; so his warnings as regards injustice and oppression, in addition to expressing a universal theme, ought to be understood also in a very precise way. These warnings are applicable to all those who, while formally subject to Islam and its laws, and possessing, initially, all the right intentions, are nonetheless vulnerable to the temptations offered by political power, taking full cognisance of the unfortunate but proven truth expressed by the maxim, 'power corrupts'. Or, in the words of the Imam, 'He who rules, appropriates' (*man malaka ista'thara*).[20]

Going beyond the boundaries of Islam, the letter can be seen as addressing not only those who wish to rule according to just principles, but also all those who, while not having corrupt intentions at the outset, are nonetheless *corruptible*—this category embracing the overwhelming majority of mankind. The Imam's illumination of the principle of justice, then, although addressed in the first instance to a prospective governor of Egypt in the seventh century, is by no means outmoded. Whether one is operating in an avowedly Islamic or an overtly secular environment, whether the rule be autocratic or democratic, whether political institutions be strong or weak: wherever there are individuals vested with authority—and by that very token, subject to the temptations offered by power—the Imam's principles will not be irrelevant. For these principles do not presuppose any particular form of government, they address the universal theme of moral responsibility, but doing so in terms of that which transcends the level of morality, offering us insights derived from a direct vision of the ultimate spiritual realities. Being beyond politics, narrowly conceived, the principles are for that very reason capable of penetrating deeply and refashioning, from above, the moral substance of political consciousness. So although the Imam's perspective is particularly pertinent to the interface between spirituality, morality and governance within Islamic discourse and praxis, its relevance extends to all contexts wherein religious belief plays a part in the articulation of moral sensibility and the cultivation of political responsibility.

---

[20] *Nahj*, Saying no. 152, p. 438; *Peak*, Saying no. 160, p. 605.

What follows is an analysis of certain key sections of the letter, taking into account relevant points from other letters, sermons and sayings of the Imam; and citing sayings of the Prophet and verses of the Qur'an which illustrate or elucidate the themes raised in the letter.

Human Virtue and Divine Reality

A note of sombre realism resounds at the very outset of the letter. The potential for evil in man, when left to his own resources and deprived of divine grace, dominates the tone of the preamble—whence the stress on abiding by God's *wajibat*, the religious obligations binding on every Muslim. Malik is told to prefer obedience to God over all things, 'to abide by what He has commanded in His Book ... for no one prospers except through abiding by them, and no one is wretched except through repudiating and neglecting them'.[21] This preamble is introductory but by no means perfunctory: obedience to the Divine commands is not only to be seen, extrinsically, as legally binding, it is to be understood, intrinsically, as spiritually liberating. For this obedience plays a crucial part in liberating one from the tyranny of the 'soul which incites to evil' (*al-nafs al-ammara bi'l-su'*), to which the Imam refers, immediately after calling Malik to obedience: 'For truly the soul incites to evil, unless God has mercy'.[22] This sentence is almost identical to the words of the Prophet Joseph in the Qur'an (*Yusuf*, XII:53), and is of the utmost importance in setting the scene for the ethical injunctions and socio-political instructions to come. For the essential relationship that determines the spiritual substance of the soul, and *a fortiori*, its moral comportment, is the relationship between the human soul and divine grace. Without grace, the soul tends towards evil; but with the assistance of God, the soul is liberated from its own base inclinations and is guided back to its true, primordial nature, its *fitra*, to which the Qur'an refers in the following verse:

---

[21] *Nahj*, p.366; *Peak*, p.534.

[22] *Nahj*, p.367; *Peak*, p. 534. The Qur'an also refers to the 'upbraiding soul' (*al-nafs al-lawwama*) (*Al-Qiyama*, LXXV: 2), that is, the soul whose conscience is awakened, and thus blames or upbraids itself for its own transgressions; and to the 'soul at peace' (*al-nafs al-mutma'inna*) (*Al-Fajr*, LXXXIX: 27), the sanctified soul, no longer subject either to vice or self-reproach. For an explanation of these terms in the context of a discussion of Sufi psychology, see the article 'Sufi Science of the Soul', by M. Ajmal, in *Islamic Spirituality*, S.H. Nasr ed., vol.1, Foundations. London: Routledge and Kegan Paul, 1987, pp.294-307.

So set thy purpose for religion with unswerving devotion—the nature [framed] of God (fitrat Allah), according to which He hath created man. There is no altering God's creation. That is the right religion (al-din al-qayyim), but most men know not.

(Al-Rum, XXX: 30)[23]

The actual state of the fallen soul, then, is to give way to the ideal state of original human nature, an ideal state which is both origin and end of the human condition, but also the true substance of every human soul, and is thus always accessible in principle, even if, for the majority, it remains clouded by fallen human nature in practice.[24] In the quest for the revival of this primordial nature, one returns to the complementary functions of the human intellect and divine revelation. In the first sermon of the *Nahj*, cited above, the Imam tells us that God sent to mankind 'His messengers, dispatching prophets in succession, in order to claim from them [His creatures] the fulfilment of the covenant of His creation; to remind them of His forgotten graces; to remonstrate with them through communication [of His Revelation]; to unearth for them the buried treasures of the intellects (*dafa'in al-'uqul*).'

These 'buried treasures' can be identified with the original, God-given knowledge proper to the *fitra*. From this integral human nature, in complete harmony with the divine nature, all the essential virtues flow spontaneously and unhindered. 'Let your most beloved treasure be the treasure of virtuous acts'[25] the Imam writes. Now virtue will indeed be the 'most beloved treasure' for one who reverses the natural inclinations of the egoistic soul and establishes a supernatural orientation towards its own deepest nature, and, by that very token, towards the divine reality that furnishes the ontological foundations of all authentic virtue.[26]

The relationship between human virtue and divine reality is altogether indispensable in the Imam's perspective: on the one hand—in

---

[23] All translations of Qur'anic verses are from Pickthall, with occasional modifications.

[24] This state of fallen nature, together with the means of remedying it, are succinctly expressed in the chapter of the Qur'an called *The Time (al-'Asr): By the Time, truly man is in a state of loss, except those who believe and perform virtuous deeds, and exhort one another to truth and exhort one another to patience.* (CIII:1-3)

[25] *Nahj*, p.367; *Peak*, p.534.

[26] The divine reality, *al-Haqq*, does not simply constitute the foundation of virtue, but of every single positive quality, and, in the last analysis, every single existent entity. As the words in one of the most famous supplications attributed to the Imam put it: 'By Thy tremendousness (*'azmatika*), which has filled all things ... *by Thy Names which*

subjective terms—the practice of virtue attracts the corresponding divine quality; and on the other hand—in objective terms—the divine quality is the source and, in terms of true *tawhid*, the actual substance of all human virtue. That is to say, every positive quality, both in itself and in its manifestation, pertains to God, the One Who 'has no partner'. This mystical assimilation of the principle of *tawhid* can be seen as heavily implied in the verse of the Qur'an, *And thou threwest not when thou didst throw, but God it was Who threw.* (*Al-Anfal*, VIII:17). Not only must the individual be effaced before God in order to be truly virtuous, but also he must participate in and embody the very qualities he wishes God to manifest towards him; and his effort to do so is empowered in the measure that he grasps these same divine qualities—through intuition and contemplation, rather than simply rationally and theoretically. The relationship between intelligence and humility is to be underlined here: the intellectual perception of the divine qualities results in humility; and the effacement of the soul, in its turn, by eliminating egotism, displaces attention from the self and directs it to the transcendent Reality as source of all virtue and truth.

It is worthwhile dwelling a little on the notion of the 'soul which incites to evil', and on the Qur'anic story of Joseph within which this notion arises; for knowledge of this context would have been assumed by the Imam when he wrote this sentence, and he clearly intended that it be borne in mind by Malik and, by extension, any person reading this letter on governance.

Joseph gives this description of man's base inclinations after his innocence of all charges had been proven in the presence of the King. He says, though, *I do not exonerate myself*, this being explained by what comes next: *Truly the soul incites to evil, unless my Lord has mercy.* Indeed, on the two occasions when he was subjected to the seductive temptations of Zuleykha, it is made clear in the Qur'an that his successful resistance to her wiles was due not to his own moral and volitive resources but to the grace of God.[27]

---

have filled the foundations of all things, by Thy knowledge which encompasses all things, by the light of Thy face, through which all things are illumined...' *Du'a' Kumayl*, in *Supplications—Amir al-Mu'minin*, trans. W.C. Chittick (London: Muhammadi Trust, 1995), verses 4, 6, and 7 (emphasis added). From this point of view, every virtue must be considered the reflection on the human plane of a divine quality.

[27] At the first attempted seduction, this grace is implicitly present, through Joseph's 'vision' of the 'evidence' of his Lord. We read: *She desired him and he would have desired her, had he not seen the evidence of his Lord; thus it was, so that We might turn*

This theme of human helplessness in the face of attractive but immoral gratification should be seen as heavily implied in the Imam's repetition of the Qur'anic notion, *Truly the soul incites to evil, unless God has mercy.* These, then, are the two poles of attraction for the ordinary soul, that is, the soul not yet *at peace*[28]: its own base inclinations towards negative possibilities within the fleeting world of appearances; and the higher orientation towards the grace of God, attracting the soul back towards the pure positivity of ultimate reality. The very acuteness of the contrast contained within this powerful Qur'anic sentence galvanizes an awareness of the soul's absolute and unconditional need of God in all circumstances; it is thus a most fitting way to begin a letter of instruction to one who is being vested with authority over a vast and wealthy country where temptations aplenty lie in wait. It stands as a solemn reminder of the soul's susceptibility to seduction on all planes, gross and subtle, a susceptibility that can be neutralized and overcome, not by the soul itself, but only by the mercy and grace of God. However, going back to the words of Joseph (XII: 24), the 'vision of the evidence' of God implies active discernment and then, by way of moral consequence, resolute self-control. Thus, the human effort to avoid sin does not contradict the necessity of grace for the attainment of virtue, but rather expresses a grace already bestowed, already present within the conscientious soul: the very power of the human will to strive for virtue is to be seen as a 'grace', one which must however be rendered present, or actualised, through the very effort to avail oneself of this God-given power to strive for virtue.

The manner in which this grace is brought into the soul as a determinitive element of moral and spiritual life will be made clearer later on in the letter; but, for now, the negative side of the question needs further elaboration. For the ever-present temptation, on the part of the ruler, to abuse his power and to perpetrate injustice and tyranny needs to be given more than a passing reference. It might be argued that the question of how to refrain from injustice is much more difficult and subtle a problem than its positive counterpart—how to act

away from him evil and lewdness. (*Yusuf*, XII: 24) At the second attempt, when it was not just Zuleykha but also her invited guests who were trying to seduce him, the indispensability of God's grace is more explicitly articulated, by Joseph himself, when he makes the following utterance: *O my Lord ... unless Thou turn away their snare from me, I would feel inclined towards them ...*(*Yusuf*, XII: 33)

[28] As noted in note 16 above, this is *al-nafs al-mutma'inna*. In the Qur'an, God addresses this soul as follows: *O thou soul at peace, Return unto thy Lord, being content with Him and He with thee, Enter among my slaves, Enter my Paradise.* (*Al-Fajr*, LXXXIX: 27-30)

with justice. The positive rules of political governance are laid down by the Imam in a direct and straightforward manner;[29] but what is not so straightforward is the actual ability, on the part of any holder of political office, to maintain fidelity to these rules when confronted with the temptations offered by power. One might frame laws for punishing corruption, in other words, but what cannot be legislated is the *will or the capacity to remain incorruptible* in the face of the blandishments offered by political authority. This helps explain why the Imam's exhortations take on such a negative quality in the early part of the letter; for example, in the command to 'break the soul in the face of passionate desires', to 'dominate your inclination', to 'withhold yourself from that which is not lawful for you'.[30] It also explains why the ethical imperative of justice must be placed firmly within the context of a lived spirituality, failing which the injunctions to be fair, just and honest will lack that existential quality that transforms such injunctions from abstract postulates into unquestionable realities, and that transmutes formal obedience into spiritual affinity. Living according to just precepts no longer takes the form of compliance to outward rules but is the moral concomitant of one's inner being. In other words, an integral approach to justice leads to an *identification* with what is right, with *al-Haqq* as such, and not merely *doing* that which is right. There is a shift of consciousness from doing to being, or from action to contemplation, without this in any way implying that action is weakened or undermined. On the contrary, action comes to reflect, on its own plane, the divine object of contemplation, and thus becomes more, not less, effective; an orientation towards the Real imparts a deeper degree of reality to what one does in the realm of action, and to one's own mode of being. One *does* what is right insofar as one *is* real: this process of realization is expressed in the Islamic spiritual tradition as *tahqiq*, 'making real', and it applies on all levels, from the spiritual to the moral.

Overcoming Subtle Polytheism (*shirk*)
The Imam issues this stern warning: 'Do not set your soul up for war with God.' One might well ask what this means, what kind of actions or attitudes put the soul at war with God. It seems that the Imam is

---

[29] These rules, or rather counsels, are however punctuated by penetrating insights into human nature. It is these insights, together with the transcendent openings alluded to in the letter, that make this document so much more than just a treatise on governance.
[30] *Nahj*, p.367; *Peak*, p.534.

alluding to something rather more subtle than simply disobedience to God, manifested as so many violations of the religious obligations mentioned at the outset of the letter. While this is the most obvious meaning of 'fighting' against God, it does not exclude more subtle modes of opposition to divine reality, that is, attitudes that may accompany outward acts of obedience, but which contradict the spirit of those acts. One can take for example the cardinal vice of pride (*takabbur*) which the Imam repeatedly warns against: the ruler's pride constitutes a misappropriation of a divine quality, an arrogation to oneself of a greatness that belongs exclusively to God, He alone having the right to the quality of *takabbur*, He alone can be called, without insult, *al-Mutakabbir*, 'the Proud'. Vaunting oneself before people is tantamount to inwardly opposing the authority of God, and is thus an implicit denial of His unique and incomparable majesty; this denial of a concomitant of God's sovereignty can in turn be seen as a kind of 'war' with God. In other words, enmity with the transcendent reality is the invisible substance that pervades any pride or any act of arrogance or oppression by a ruler towards those beneath him.

The paradox here, that only a sense of spiritual values can reveal, is that an attitude of superiority towards those who are 'below' is in fact an attitude of rebellion towards that which is 'above': hence, an injustice towards creatures not only brings down upon its perpetrator the justice of the Creator, it also manifests, in and of itself, outright opposition to the Creator. Thus, an apparently horizontal vice—'horizontal' in the sense of relating to this world—is in reality a spiritual disorder, the outward immorality of corruption being but the symptom of an inner spiritual malaise, an implicit denial of the absoluteness—hence uniqueness—of the source of all power and authority, a forgetfulness of the reality expressed by the Qur'anic verse: *To whom belongeth the Dominion this day? To God, the One, the All-Conquering.*[31] The truth expressed by this verse should resound constantly in the ears of all rulers: 'this day' being understood as 'every day', and not just the Day of Judgement.

In the sermon known as *al-Qasi'a*—'the abasement', on account of its humiliation of the proud—Satan is described as being the first of those who 'competed with God' in respect of grandeur, and is thus the embodiment of the principle of pride and arrogance. When ordered to prostrate before Adam (*Sad*, XXXVIII: 71-74), Satan refused, because

---

[31] *Al-Mu'min*, XL: 16.

'vehement passion' overcame him, and he deemed himself superior to Adam because he was made of fire, whereas Adam was made of clay. Taking pride in this presumed superiority and thus rebelling against God's order, Satan is thus not only the first 'enemy of God' but also 'the leader of the bigots and the forerunner of the proud' (*imam al-muta'assibin wa salaf al-mustakbirin*).[32] The Imam warns his listeners: 'Beware lest he infect you with his disease', through his insinuations, whisperings and machinations. He urges them: 'Be resolute in placing self-abasement over your heads, casting self-glorification beneath your feet, and removing pride from your necks. And take up humility as the fortified watchtower between you and your enemy.'[33]

Humility, then, is the principal weapon in the war against Satan, whose key aim, inversely, is to inculcate pride, for pride is not only the worst of vices, but also the poison which infects and destroys all virtue. For virtue itself is converted to vice as soon as it is accompanied by pride: 'The sin that grieves you is better, in the sight of God, than the virtue that makes you proud.'[34] Also to be noted in this context is what the Imam writes, later on in the letter, about the dangers of excessive praise: Malik is told to beware of loving 'lavish praise', as this is among 'Satan's most reliable opportunities to efface the virtue of one who is virtuous.'[35]

It can be observed that, taken together, these statements constitute a commentary upon the Qur'anic account of Satan's disgrace, whereby a simple act of disobedience is grasped at its spiritual root, in a manner that brings home the ever present danger of falling prey to that 'hidden polytheism', to which the Prophet refers in the following saying: 'The creeping of *shirk* in my community is more hidden (*akhfa*) than the creeping of a black ant over a hard rock on a dark night.'[36]

The superficial notion of *shirk*—the worship of material idols—must be understood on a more subtle plane as false gods hidden within

---

[32] *Nahj*, p. 288; *Peak*, p. 384.

[33] *Nahj*, p. 290; *Peak*, p. 385.

[34] *Nahj*, no.43, p. 414; *Peak*, no.46, p. 581.

[35] *Nahj*, p. 382; *Peak*, p. 546.

[36] Cited by Sayyid Haydar Amuli in his commentary on *Yusuf*, XII: 106, And most of them believe not in God, except that they are polytheists (*illa wa hum mushrikun*). *Al-Muhit al-a'zam wa'l-bahr al-khidamm fi ta'wil kitab Allah al-'aziz al-muhkam* (Qom: Mu'assassa Farhangi wa Nashr Nur 'Ala Nur, 2001), vol. I, p. 284. The *hadith* is found in slightly differing versions in the *Masnad* of Ibn Hanbal, vol. 4 p. 403; *al-Mustadrak*, vol. 1, p. 113; and Tabarsi in his comment on verse VI: 108. These references are given by the editor of *Al-Muhit*, Muhsin al-Musawi al-Tabrizi, vol. I, p. 284, n. 54.

one's intentions, attitudes and orientations; as all elements of hidden pride, vanity, ostentation, pretentiousness. As the Imam says: 'Know that the slightest ostentatiousness (riya') is polytheism.'[37]

In this light, the meaning of Satan's act of disobedience can be plumbed in greater depth: it is the outward moral consequence of an inner spiritual malaise, a malaise which arises out of that pride which is 'hidden polytheism' and which brings in its wake disgraceful humiliation. Satan is disgraced because he disobeyed God; but he disobeyed God on account of pride. To be proud is therefore in and of itself a disgrace, a state of 'dis-grace'; it is not only that it carries within itself the seed of its own inexorable inversion. 'Do you not see how God humiliated him through his pride?',[38] the Imam asks. Being proud is in reality already a form of humiliation, for self-aggrandisement is tantamount to self-destruction.

Returning to the pride of those in power, the Imam expresses succinctly the train of thought that is set in motion within the mind of a ruler who is stepping on the slippery slope towards oppression: 'Do not say, "I have been given authority, I order and am obeyed", for this leads to corruption in the heart, and the erosion of religion.'[39] It should be noted that this self-glorification is seen as leading first to inner, spiritual corruption—that of the 'heart'—and then to the destruction of religion, this order of priority highlighting the fact that the outward prescriptions of religion require the right inward attitude if they are to be applied with integrity, and if they are to be maintained with stability. One might restate the Imam's idea thus: When power goes to the head, faith departs from the heart; and conversely, for faith to be properly manifested in the world, it must flow from a heart suffused with humility. This is another aspect of 'putting each thing in its proper place'.

The Imam continues: 'If the authority of your position engenders vanity and arrogance, then look at the grandeur of God's dominion above you ... this will calm your ambition, restrain you from your own vehemence, and restore to you what had strayed from your intellect.' The relationship between the intellect and humility should be carefully noted here: the part of the intellect that 'strays' when vanity and arrogance enter is precisely the part that is conscious of the absolute reality of God and the relative, derivative and ultimately

[37] *Nahj*, p. 83; *Peak*, p. 216.
[38] *Nahj*, p. 288; *Peak*, p. 384.
[39] *Nahj*, p.368; *Peak*, p.535.

illusory character of everything else. It is significant that the word for 'arrogance', *makhila*, is derived from the same root as the word for imagination, *khayal*, and is thus intimately connected with the realm of the imaginary, the fanciful, the illusory and the unreal. Arrogant pride is therefore an intense form of self-delusion, stemming from an intellectual defect; it manifests as a vice, but its cause goes deeper than the level of morality, for it involves not just an over-estimation of oneself, but also, and more fundamentally, an under-estimation of the Absolute. In this light, the overt egotism of the tyrant can be seen as an intensification of the congenital egocentricity that accompanies every person who has not realized the truth of the sole reality of God, and the ultimately illusory nature of all else. The sage alone assimilates fully the truth expressed by such verses as:

Everything is dying away except His countenance;[40]

Everything that is thereon is perishing; and there subsisteth but the Face of thy Lord, possessor of Glory and Bounty;[41]

The Truth has come and falsehood has passed away, indeed falsehood is ever passing away[42]

And only the sage draws from this truth the humility that dissolves all individualism and egocentricity—the roots of pride, vanity and arrogance that, in turn, are the life-blood of tyranny and oppression.

One can now better appreciate the Imam's warning: 'Beware of comparing [yourself] with God in greatness and likening [yourself] to Him in might, for God abases every tyrant and disgraces every braggart.'[43] One who does not act with justice towards God and His creatures, and instead tyrannizes them, will find that not only His creatures, but also God Himself will be his opponent: 'He remains at war with God until he desists and repents.'

This last point can be interpreted as follows: eventually, the tyrant will be forced to repent, even if this be only at the point of death and imminent judgement. Even if the tyrant appears to have successfully evaded the consequences of his tyranny in this life, he cannot evade

[40] *Al-Qasas*, XXVIII: 88.

[41] *Al-Rahman*, LV: 26-27

[42] *Bani Isra'il*, XVII: 81

[43] *Nahj*, p.368; *Peak*, p.535.

them in the Hereafter. But as regards the nature of the 'war' he wages with God in this world, prior to repentance or judgement—that is, his implicit opposition to ultimate reality, his violation of the deepest nature of things—this war takes various forms. One form of the war is constituted by the very persistence of tyranny on the part of the tyrant, for the longer the tyranny goes on, the more wretched becomes the soul of the tyrant,[44] the more firmly are the seeds of misery planted in his being, as is implied in the Qur'anic doctrine of *istidraj*—the drawing out of punishment by degrees:

> *Of those We have created are people who guide with truth and dispense justice therewith. But those who reject Our signs, We will lead them on by degrees [to punishment] from whence they know not. (Al-A'raf, VII:181-2)*

The punishment meted out 'by degrees' can take the form of an apparent success in worldly terms, as is clear from the following Qur'anic verse:

> *Let not their wealth nor their children please thee: God desireth only to punish them thereby in the world, that their souls shall pass away while they are disbelievers. (Al-Tawba, IX: 85).*

The tyrant or oppressor can be both a Muslim, in the formal sense, and at the same time be guilty of a mode of 'disbelief', taking the word *kafir* in the strictly etymological sense, that is, one who 'covers over' the truth, and its moral concomitants, by his being and by his actions.

---

[44] Plato's description of the utter misery of the tyrant's soul is apposite here: '... the despot's condition, my dear Glaucon, is supremely wretched ... Whatever people may think, the actual tyrant is really the most abject slave, a parasite of the vilest scoundrels. Never able to satisfy his desires, he is always in need, and, to an eye that sees a soul in its entirety, he will seem the poorest of the poor. His condition is like that of the country he governs, haunted throughout life by terrors and convulsed with anguish ... power is bound to exaggerate every fault and make him ever more envious, treacherous, unjust, friendless, impure, harbouring every vice in his bosom, and hence only less of a calamity to all about him than he is to himself.' *The Republic*, op. cit., p.299. Conversely, the happy man is the virtuous man: it is only in a life of virtue that true happiness can be attained. In the tradition of ethics stemming from Plato and Aristotle, man can only be happy when that which distinguishes him as man—his wisdom—is brought to fruition; and wisdom is only fully itself when it determines one's entire conduct, not when it is merely thought about. The Imam expresses this principle succinctly in his saying, 'Only he who acts according to what he knows, and whose knowledge harmonises with his action, can be called a true knower.' Cited by Ahmad Daylami, in '*Mabani wa nizam-i akhlaq*' ('The foundations and system of ethics'), in *Danish nama Imam 'Ali*, p.136.

This is connected with the contrast made in the verses quoted above (VII:181-2), that between those who dispense justice in accordance with the truth, and those who *reject Our signs*—the oppressors and tyrants, precisely.

Moral Conscience and Spiritual Consciousness

Another form taken by the 'enmity with God' is the inner war with one's own conscience. The voice of conscience—the very essence and sum total of secular ethics—can here be grasped in its plenary context, rather than simply as the somewhat hypertrophied foundation of individual morality to which it has been reduced in secular ethical discourse. This fuller context is the supra-individual or metaphysical source of individual conscience, the divine infusion of spiritual discernment within the soul; this infusion or inspiration serves as the basis of ethical discrimination; the divine quality of justice is thus translated, at the level of the morally responsible soul, into the voice of inner conscience:

> *And the soul and That which perfected it, inspiring it with* [consciousness of] *its wickedness and its righteousness. (Al-Shams,* XCI: 7-8)

The war against one's conscience—even if it be barely acknowledged by the oppressor—is in fact, and *a fortiori*, a war against God.

At a deeper level, then, this 'war against God' emerges with clarity as a war against the very reality that defines the soul as such, for the soul not only contains a moral conscience—an intrinsic and inalienable awareness of the difference between good and evil which has been instilled within it by God; it also contains an innate consciousness of the reality of the lordship of the divine, together with the corresponding slavehood of the creature. Spiritual consciousness is thus to be seen as the source of moral conscience. The Qur'an describes the immanence of this spiritual consciousness within each soul in terms which emphasise its supra-, or pre-personal nature; it does this by describing the degree of consciousness in question in terms of a 'moment' at the very dawn of creation; a 'moment' or ontological degree that precedes the human condition as such, but entering into the creative articulation of the human soul:

> *And when thy Lord brought forth from the children of Adam, from their loins, their seed, and made them testify against their souls* [saying], *Am I not your Lord? They said: Yes, verily, we testify.* [This was] *lest*

ye say on the Day of Resurrection: Truly, of this we were unaware.
(*Al-A'raf*, VII:172)

One observes here that the source of morality transcends the human level, even while forming part of the very definition of humanity. From this perspective, that which renders the human soul fully human is, precisely, the element of transcendence that goes infinitely beyond the soul, and yet mysteriously furnishes its own deepest being. In this light, the notions of tyranny and oppression take on a much more nuanced meaning, these vices being brought much closer to the lived reality of all souls, rather than being simply restricted to those possessing— and abusing—political power: the tyrant is he who violates, first and foremost, his own soul, allowing it to be dominated by the *nafs al-ammara*. Thus, the statement given by the Imam as epitomizing the attitude of one on his way to corrupting his own soul and becoming an oppressor—'I order and am obeyed'—is not just to be understood socially but also interpreted microcosmically. It thereby becomes the statement of the evil part of the soul, the *nafs al-ammara* which, literally 'orders' (*amara*) and is obeyed by the other elements of the soul, the intelligence, imagination, will, sentiment, sensibility, and so on.

The combat against one's own soul (*mujahadat al-nafs*) is often referred to by the Imam.[45] This necessity of struggling with and overcoming one's own faults is an essential aspect of justice in the sense defined earlier: putting each thing in its proper place means rectifying oneself before presuming to reform or rule over others: 'If your aspiration ascends to the reforming of the people, begin with yourself, for your pursuit of the reform of others, when your own soul is corrupt, is the greatest of faults.'[46] In his letter appointing Muhammad b. Abi Bakr governor of Egypt,[47] the Imam makes a strong connection

[45] This is what the Prophet referred to as *al-jihad al-akbar*, the greater war. See our article, "Recollecting the Spirit of Jihad", in *Sacred Web*, no.8, 2001, pp.137-155.

[46] *Ghurar*, vol.1, p.781, no.1. The following sayings of the Imam on the importance of spiritual struggle should be noted; translating the word *nafs* as 'ego' here brings out more clearly the nature of the struggle, which is not against the 'soul' in its entirety, but against its egotistic tendencies: 'The strongest people are those who are strongest against their own egos.' 'Truly, one who fights his own ego ... has the rank of the righteous martyr in God's eyes.' 'Struggling against the ego through knowledge—such is the mark of the intellect'. 'The ultimate battle is that of a man against his own ego.' 'He who knows his ego fights it.' 'No *jihad* is more excellent than the *jihad* against the ego.' Ibid., pp.208-211, nos.17, 8, 20, 23, 26, 28.

[47] The appointment was made in 657/36, that is, over a year before Malik was appointed to this post. See Madelung, *The Succession*, p.192.

between the bestowal of power and the need to oppose one's soul: 'And be aware, O Muhammad b. Abi Bakr, that I have appointed you as governor over the most immense of the forces at my disposal, the people of Egypt, *so you are obliged to oppose your soul and protect your religion*.'[48] (emphasis added) The relationship between the magnitude of power being placed at one's disposal and the spiritual responsibility resulting from this should be carefully noted. First it is in relation to one's own soul and its desires, and secondly, in regard to the religion that one must be on guard. The greater the power available, the greater is the obligation to control and restrain oneself: for if the soul yields to its own desires, gratifying them with the power at one's disposal, one ends up corrupting not just oneself, but also the religion which one is charged to uphold. Again one observes the ordering of priorities by an essentially spiritual principle: the outward form and application of religion depends for its integrity on the inward disposition of the soul of the Muslim. This is another expression of the principle of putting each thing in its proper place.

The commanding or ordering soul which arrogates to itself the right of autonomy and dominion is described succinctly by the Qurʾanic verse: *Truly man is rebellious, in that he deemeth himself independent.* (*Al-ʾAlaq*, XCVI: 6-7) Insofar as the soul pretends to be self-sufficient, and tries to detach itself from its total dependence upon God, it sets itself up as a god in its own right, and herein lies the true description of the tyrant, the one who, as the Qurʾan puts it *takes his own desire as his god.* (*Al-Jathiya*, XLV: 23) Knowledge of one's nothingness before God, and, consequently, of one's unconditional need of God, might be taken here as the principal means of loosening the grip of the 'soul which commands to evil'; for only that soul which already commands itself to evil commands others to evil, and only the soul which is lowly before God will be humble, compassionate and just in its dealings with people.

This principle emerges clearly from the following words of the Imam: 'And let the most beloved of affairs to you be those most centred upon Right[49] the most comprehensive in justice, the most inclusive of popular approval, for the disapproval of the common folk undermines the approval of the elite...'[50] This stress on the importance of the

[48] *Nahj*, p. 329; *Peak*, p,487.

[49] *Awsatuha fiʾl-haqq*. One has here a good expression of the principle expressed by the Aristotelian term 'the golden mean'.

[50] *Nahj*, p. 368; *Peak*, p. 535.

common people is not only sound practical advice for the smooth and fair administration of the state; it can also be seen as reflecting the spiritual imperative of realizing the actual lowliness of man in relation to God, and thus as a way of encouraging the ruler to identify with the poor, rather than the rich, on the principle, *O mankind, ye are the poor before God, and God, He is the Rich, the absolutely Praiseworthy.*[51]

The Imam's own poverty and rigorous austerity was indeed proverbial. That this was far from a shunning of the world for its own sake is made clear in the following exchange between the Imam and an ascetic, 'Asim b. Ziyad. The Imam tells him to think of his family, and not to cut himself from the good things (*al-tayyibat*) that God has permitted. 'Asim retorts: 'O Commander of the Faithful, and here you are, in your rough clothes and your coarse food!' The Imam replies: 'Woe to you, I am not like you. God the exalted has made it incumbent on true leaders that they proportion themselves to the weakest among the people (*yaqaddiru anfusahum bi-da'fati'l-nas*), so that the poverty of the poor will not engender covetousness.'[52] Here we have a rigorous expression of the need for equality between the most powerful and the most powerless. But this does not imply a levelling of all classes, it should be noted: it is only incumbent on the rulers to live like the poor, not the whole of society. This is a psychologically effective way of ensuring that the inevitable inequalities in society will not generate envy among the have-nots, while eschewing the unrealistic aim of establishing, totalitarian-fashion, a quasi-absolute equality between all classes.

The Compassion of Justice

This identification with the poor also enhances the ruler's awareness of his own perpetual need of God, thus helping him to live more fully on the mercy of God, in hope and trust; the natural concomitant of such a life is the bestowal of mercy and compassion upon one's fellow human beings. The capacity to act with compassion in no way conflicts with the demands of justice; rather, it is an intrinsic aspect of justice, conceived ontologically. To act with compassion accords with justice not only in the sense of putting things in their right place—one must extend compassion wherever one can, without overlooking the necessity of condign punishment, where this is unavoidable; compassion also and above all else conforms to justice in being at one

---

[51] *al-Mala'ika*, XXXV: 15.
[52] *Nahj*, pp. 243-4; *Peak*, pp. 419-420.

with the true nature of things, with the intrinsic character of the Real. It is thus that at the head of every chapter of the Qur'an (except one) the name *Allah* is followed by *the infinitely Compassionate, the ever-Merciful*. Put differently, the capacity to act with compassion stems not so much from personal sentiment as from an innate affinity with the very nature of divine reality, that higher reality in which, as the Qur'an tells us, *My mercy encompasseth all things*;[53] a reality in which *thy Lord has prescribed for Himself mercy*;[54] a reality whose essential character is determined by the principle 'My mercy takes precedence over My wrath'.[55] Thus one finds the following sayings of the Imam on the necessity of showing mercy: 'The dispensing of mercy brings down [divine] mercy.'[56] 'As you grant mercy, so will you be granted mercy.'[57] 'I am astounded by the person who hopes for mercy from One above him, while he is not merciful to those beneath him.'[58]

The wrathful side of the nature of things is not denied here, but it is clearly subordinated to the higher ontological principle of mercy; there is, in other words, no common measure between the relativities that are subject, accidentally, to wrath and punishment, and the realities, intrinsically beatific, to which mercy and compassion give access. One is therefore more 'real' insofar as mercy predominates over wrath, spiritually, within one's own soul and morally, in one's conduct; and it is in the very nature of justice, conceived in this sacred manner, to tend towards compassion wherever possible, even though there must also be a place for rigorous application of corrective penalty where this is unavoidable. Indeed, later in the letter, the Imam instructs Malik to inflict corporal punishment upon any executive officer found guilty of misappropriation of public funds. [59] The Imam's counsels and letters are replete with stern warnings of swift and severe retribution to his governors, the severity of his warnings being in the measure of his unflinching fidelity to the requirements of fairnesss and honesty in the administering of public revenues. For example, he writes to Ziyad b. Abihi, deputy governor of 'Ali's cousin, 'Abd Allah b. al-Abbas:

---

[53] *al-A'raf*, VII: 156.

[54] *al-An'am*, VI: 54.

[55] This is a *hadith qudsi*, a divine saying uttered through the Prophet. See Wensinck et al, *Concordance et indices de la tradition musulmane*, Leiden: E.J. Brill 1936-1969, 2:239.

[56] *Ghurar*, vol. 1, p. 580, no.1.

[57] Ibid., p. 581, no. 9.

[58] Ibid., p. 581, no.4.

[59] *Nahj*, p. 374-5; *Peak*, p. 540.

'I swear by God an oath in all sincerity: if news reaches me that you have misappropriated the revenue of the Muslims—whether a small or large amount—I shall inflict a severe punishment upon you, one which will lighten your wealth, burden your back, and degrade your affair.'[60]

The Imam was also severe in relation to his own relatives, if there was even a hint of a request for favours that required the abuse of public funds. In one sermon he refers to an incident when his blind brother, 'Aqil b. Abi Talib, made such a request.[61] 'He thought I would sell my religion for him', the Imam says, but he responded by taking a red-hot piece of iron near his brother's body, causing him to cry out in pain. He told his brother that, by making such a request, he was urging him to enter into a much more intense fire.[62]

Similarly, when he was informed of the misappropriation of funds by his cousin and long-standing ally, 'Abd Allah b. al-Abbas,[63] his response was a thundering remonstrance. The Imam orders his cousin: 'Fear God and return their property to these people. If you do not, and God gives me authority over you, I excuse myself before God in regard to you [and your wrong-doing], and I shall indeed strike you with my sword—with which whomever I have struck enters the fire. By God, even if Hasan and Husayn had done the like of what you have done, they would not have been granted any leniency by me ...'[64]

The mention of the Prophet's grandsons is significant here: however close be the relationship between oneself and a wrong-doer, however exalted their status be, the principle of justice demands absolute equality of treatment; there are to be no favours for any of one's favourites. Not only does this attitude express the very opposite of that nepotism that undermined the administration of the Imam's predecessor,[65] it is also precisely what the Qur'an instructs: *O ye who*

---

[60] *Nahj*, p. 322 (letter no. 20); *Peak*, p. 481.

[61] See Madelung, *The Succession*, p. 264, for the context of this request and the consequences of its refusal.

[62] *Nahj*, p.264; *Peak*, p. 444.

[63] This letter, no.41 in most editions, is simply addressed to 'one of his [i.e. 'Ali's] administrators', and refers to the recipient of the letter only as his cousin. Some historians and commentators doubt whether the cousin in question is indeed Ibn al-Abbas. See al-Khu'i's *Minhaj al-bara'a fi sharh Nahj al-balagha*, vol.20, pp.75-76, for a brief discussion of this letter, and Madelung, *The Succession*, pp. 271-278, for details of the angry exchange of letters between the two, based on the historical sources.

[64] *Nahj*, p. 355; *Peak*, p. 511.

[65] See Madelung, *The Succession*, pp. 81-113 for a balanced, non-partisan appraisal of

believe, be staunch in justice, witnesses of God, even though it be against yourselves, your parents or your near of kin ... (Al-Nisa', IV: 135)

Returning to the theme of mercy, the following passage is remarkable in placing the necessity of compassion in a universal context, and is one of the most important expressions by the Imam on the unity of the human race and the equality of all human beings. It stands forth as a corrective to all forms of prejudice, particularism and communitarianism that would apply justice or compassion only to members of one's own 'group' however defined:

> 'Infuse your heart with mercy for the subjects, love for them, and kindness towards them. Be not like a ravenous beast of prey above them, seeking to devour them. For they are of two types: either your brother in religion or your like in creation. Mistakes slip from them, defects emerge from them, deliberately or accidentally. So bestow upon them your forgiveness and your pardon, just as you would have God bestow upon you His forgiveness and pardon; for you are above them, and the one who appointed you as governor is above you, and God is above him who appointed you ... and through them He tests you.'[66]

The universal applicability of compassion is here allied to a reminder of the absolute sovereignty of God: no man—whether the governor or the ruler appointing the governor—is anything but a slave of God, utterly dependent upon His mercy. Thus, each person who finds himself in a position of relative superiority over others must constantly remember his own inferiority vis-à-vis the Absolute, and this awareness both leads to compassion on his part towards those beneath him, and attracts to himself the compassion of God above him. One might cite here an incident which demonstrates well the Imam's compassionate implementation of justice, and which also serves as an expression of the principle referred to earlier: all people are 'your like in creation'. The Imam came across an old, blind beggar, and inquired about him. He was told that the beggar was a Christian. He told those around him: 'You have employed him to the point where he is old and infirm, and now you refuse to help him. Give him maintenance from the public funds (*bayt al-mal*).'[67] In addition, this sentence contains the

---

the injustices that came to characterise 'Uthman's government, the grievances against him as caliph, and the rebellion that led to his being killed.

[66] *Nahj*, p. 367; *Peak*, p. 534-5.

[67] Cited by Shaykh Husayn Nuri Hamadani in '*Usul wa mabani-yi hukumat-i Islami*

seed of an entire programme of social welfare, based on the principle of redistributive justice, and on a policy of strict non-discrimination between Muslims and others. Social justice and religious equality flow forth, in this perspective, from compassion conceived not as a sentiment only, but as an intrinsic dimension of the Real.

Before turning to the second part of the essay, it should be noted that the final sentence of the passage cited earlier, warning the governor that he should regard his power over his subjects not simply as a privilege, but more as a trial from God, clearly expresses the Imam's own attitude to rulership. In the famous sermon, *al-Shiqshiqiyya*, he says that he accepted power as an unavoidable duty: 'Had God not taken from the learned [a promise] that they would not acquiesce in the rapacity of the tyrant nor in the hunger of the oppressed ... I would truly have flung its rope [that of the caliphate] back upon its withers ... and you would indeed have discovered that this world of yours is as insignificant to me as that which drips from the nose of a goat.'[68] In this, we see a striking exemplification of Plato's ideal attitude to power, that possessed by the true 'philosopher', he who acts as ruler only for the sake of the people, 'not regarding it as a distinction, but as an unavoidable task ... caring only for the right and the honours to be gained from that, and above all for justice as the one indispensable thing in whose service and maintenance they will reorganize their own state.'[69]

The principle underlying this approach to the question of authority and governance is clearly that of *noblesse oblige*: if one has been granted the grace, the blessing or the privilege of knowledge, together with a clear sense of justice, a correspondingly greater obligation is created. One's duty to God increases in proportion to the graces bestowed. This is expressed as follows in one of the sermons of the Imam, after he had been praised by one of his supporters: 'The blessings of God upon a person do not become tremendous without the right of God over him becoming tremendous.'[70]

Having a 'Good Opinion of God'

We now come to a subtle point in the Imam's letter, one which can all too easily be overlooked, given the extreme conciseness with

---

az manzar-i Imam 'Ali' ('Principles and Foundations of Islamic government from the perspective of Imam 'Ali'), in *Proceedings of the Congress on Imam 'Ali*, p.8.

[68] *Nahj*, p. 16; *Peak*, p. 106.

[69] *The Republic of Plato*, op. cit., p. 256.

[70] *Nahj*, p. 252; *Peak*, p. 434.

which it is expressed, and given the fact that its logical and positive concomitant is not explicitly stated by the Imam here. It comes when he is instructing Malik on the kinds of advisers he should have close to him. He tells him to avoid misers and cowards, adding 'Truly, miserliness and cowardice and avarice are so many diverse inclinations comprised within a bad opinion of God.'[71] The phrase 'a bad opinion' of God (*su' al-zann*) evokes the idea of a misunderstanding of the divine nature, arising out of a series of misconceptions of the qualities of God. From this point of view, all human vices arise out of an intellectual dysfunction, which in turn is the consequence of weak faith—or even outright atheism, since disbelief in God is a denial of God's reality, thus, a kind of 'bad opinion' in regard to Him. The converse of this follows logically: a strong and deep faith generates a 'good opinion' of God—an accurate intellectual and contemplative perception of the divine Reality—and this good opinion in turn leads to the soul being 'im-pressed' (and not simply 'impressed') by the divine qualities comprised within that Reality. These qualities must be understood not only as transcendent, being absolutely one with the divine Essence, and thus utterly beyond the purview of the human soul; they are also to be grasped as models, exemplars, patterns or perfections for the soul to emulate, in the measure of its possibilities. This is the very opposite, it should be noted, of 'comparing oneself with God in greatness': one must be as much 'like' God as possible, but this spiritual development unfolds within the unalterable context of one's slavehood to Him. In other words, one must be generous, for God is *al-Karim*; kind, for He is *al-Latif*, and so on. But one must also be lowly, humble and effaced, even if there is no divine quality that can be posited as the exemplar of this virtue. All such virtues as lowliness, humility and effacement are modes of expressing the absolute dependence of man upon God, or as manifesting the incommensurability between the relative and the Absolute. Thus, as between the human and the divine, there is both positive and inverse analogy: in terms of the first, 'He who shows not mercy will not have mercy shown to him';[72] and in terms of the second, *O mankind, ye are the poor before God, and God, He is the Rich, the absolutely Praiseworthy.*[73] There must therefore be a synthesis between the active human virtues—as positive reflections of the divine qualities—and the spiritual consciousness of one's nothingness before

---

[71] *Nahj*, p. 369; *Peak*, p. 536.

[72] This is a famous saying of the Prophet. See *Mizan al-hikma*, (1403 AH) vol.4, p.69, *hadith* no.6963.

[73] *al-Mala'ika*, XXXV: 15.

the divine reality—the inverted reflection, on the human plane, of the divine transcendence; one is both slave and representative of God, *'abdu'Llah* and *khalifatu'Llah*. A consciousness of one's slavehood ensures that one does not slip from representing God to competing with Him, albeit unconsciously, in grandeur; and active commitment to representing God ensures that the consciousness of slavehood does not slip into a mode of paralysis or the neglect of one's duty towards the world. The equilibrium between these two dimensions of human existence is another aspect of spiritual justice, of putting things in their right place; and it also attunes the quality of moral action to the harmony of pure being.

State and Society

The Imam proceeds with a description of the different classes of people within state and society: the army, the scribes, the judiciary, executive officers, tax-collectors, merchants and artisans, and, finally, the destitute—each class having its particular rights and duties. The instructions that are given in this part of the letter can be regarded as the expressing the cutting-edge of justice in actual practice, within the exigencies of social and political life. The governor is to regard each of the classes under his authority as having rights and obligations, but the essential feature of the governor's relationship to society as a whole is, again, determined by his primary duty to God, for it is God who has 'prescribed to each [class] its share and has ordained—as a binding covenant (*'ahdan*) with us from Him—for each its limits and its duties, according to His Book or the *Sunna* of the Prophet.'[74]

The governor's duty to society, then, is part of the universal covenant between man and God, the *'ahd* that is so frequently encountered in the Qur'an. Again here, one feels that by using this Qur'anic term to reinforce the obligation of acting justly towards all classes of society, the Imam knows that the impact of his words would be deepened immeasurably through their resonance with such verses as the following:

> *Is one who knoweth that what is revealed to thee from thy Lord is the Truth like one who is blind? But only men of substance take heed/ Those who abide by the covenant* ('ahd) *of God, and break not the tryst* (mithaq). *(al-Ra'd, XIII: 19-20)*

[74] *Nahj*, p. 371; *Peak*, p. 537.

> *Approach not the wealth of the orphan except with that which is more right, until he attain maturity; and abide by the convenant—truly, the covenant will be asked about. (Bani Isra'il, XVII: 34)*

It is also significant that, immediately prior to this passage in the letter, the Imam advises Malik to study much with the 'scholars' (*al-'ulama'*) and to hold much discourse with the 'sages' (*al-hukama'*). This should be done so as to 'consolidate that which brings well-being to your lands, and to further entrench that which has already been established by your predecessors.'[75] The distinction here between the scholars and the sages is important. It appears to be hinting at the distinction between formal rules as established in the Qur'an and the Sunna, and the spirit behind them—the spirit of wisdom, that is, without which the rules cannot be applied with care and sensitivity.

There follows a passage in which the interdependence of each class or element of society is succinctly described. It begins with the underpinning of the state by the soldiers, and ends with the governor himself as the hub around which the different elements revolve. But this horizontal centre is nothing without the vertical axis that connects it, and thereby the whole of the society, with the Real. The soldiers are described as the 'fortresses' of the subjects; and the governor is told, at the end of this passage, that he cannot accomplish what God requires of him without resolute determination and seeking of assistance from Him (*al-ihtimam* and *al-isti'ana*). This crucial point will be reinforced later in the letter, when the needs of the poor are addressed.

As regards the instructions pertaining to the different elements of state and society, it suffices for our purposes here to draw attention to a few salient points. First, as regards the commander of the troops, Malik is told to select for this position the person who is 'the most sincere in relation to God, the Prophet and your Imam, the purest of heart, the one most excellent in forbearance (*hilm*), from among those who are slow to anger, glad to pardon, kind to the weak, severe with the strong; one who is neither moved by violence, nor held back by weakness.'[76]

This description of the ideal warrior, needless to say, reflects the Imam's own character. What is to be noted is the importance placed on kindness, gentleness and forbearance—qualities not usually associated with fighting men. One observes a spiritually refined attitude towards

---

[75] *Nahj*, p. 370; *Peak*, p. 537.
[76] *Nahj*, p. 372; *Peak*, p.538.

an activity which, left to its own devices, runs riot with the norms of
decency and propriety. Again, one cannot help noticing the similarity
between the Imam's description of the perfect warrior and Plato's
description of the 'guardian', the protector of the ideal state. Plato
defines the problem attendant upon the formation of forces for the
protection and defence of the city as follows: how to ensure that
men whose natural disposition is 'spirited' and courageous are 'to
be kept from behaving pugnaciously to one another and to the rest
of their countrymen?' For 'they must be gentle to their own people
and dangerous only to their enemies.'[77] This echoes the Qur'anic
description of those who are with the Prophet as being *severe against
the disbelievers, compassionate amongst themselves* (*Al-Fath*, XLVIII:
29). Whence the Imam's emphasis placed on the gentle qualities
requisite in a warrior as the complement to the martial virtues.

Turning to the next category, the judges, the Imam refers to the
following as key virtues that must be present in those who are to
dispense legal justice: they must not be confused by complexities, or
angered by litigants; they must be unflinching in the face of the truth,
free from greed, dissatisfied with superficial solutions, consequential
in argumentation, steadfast in the search for the truth of all matters,
immune to praise and temptations. 'Such people', the Imam adds, 'are
indeed rare.'[78] He also recommends that the judges be paid generously,
for 'this will remove from him deficiency and thus diminish his need for
help from people'—a key requisite for maintaining the incorruptibility
of any judiciary.

As regards administrators, Malik is told to test their honesty
before employing them, being careful not to allow any partiality or
favouritism to intervene in his choice. He is to continue to check and
investigate their actions. As noted earlier, stringent punishments are
to be administered if there is evidence of any abuse of privilege, and
appropriation of public funds.

In relation to those tilling the soil, and from whom the land tax is
collected, the Imam dispenses this wise maxim: 'Let your concern with
the cultivation of the land outweigh your concern with the collection
of the tax; for no tax will be collected if there be no cultivation. And
whoever exacts the tax, without cultivating the land, ruins the land

---

[77] The answer is that the 'spirited' disposition, for which 'gymnastic' was necessary,
must be tempered by 'music'—all those arts over which the Muses presided: music,
art, letters, culture and philosophy. See Chapter IX, pp. 65-99.
[78] *Nahj*, p. 374; *Peak*, p. 539.

and destroys the people.'[79] The Imam's further exhortations to be attentive to the needs of the tillers of the soil, and to be fair to all those who seek redress of wrongs, are concluded with the following warning:

> 'The devastation of the land only comes about through the destitution of its inhabitants; and the destitution of its inhabitants only comes about when the desire to amass wealth controls the souls of the governors, when they have doubts about what endures, and when they profit little from exemplary teachings.'[80]

As regards the meaning of the phrase 'having doubts about what endures' (*su' zannihim bi'l-baqa'*), the commentators write that it could mean either that the governors think that they will endure forever, forgetting that they will die and be judged in the Hereafter; or that they doubt that their position will endure for long, and hence exploit the opportunities available to them while they can. For our part, the first explanation is the more likely, given the extent to which it echoes the following Qur'anic verses—which can be taken as one such 'exemplary teaching' (*'ibra*) the Imam mentioned at the very end of the sentence:

> *Woe be to every slandering backbiter/Who amasseth wealth and counteth it./ He thinketh that his wealth will render him immortal./ Nay, but he will be flung to the all-consuming Fire. (al-Humaza, CIV: 1-4)*

The Imam uses the same word, *jama'a*, for the amassing of wealth that is found in this verse. The lesson is clear: greed is a symptom of spiritual myopia. Forgetfulness of what truly endures leads to differing degrees of greed, understood here as desire for a false material richness to take the place of a true spiritual plenitude; and this, in turn, engenders exploitation and oppression. Again one observes how, in the Imam's perspective, the vice of injustice not only leads to corruption but is itself also the product of a chain of causes rooted in a basic inversion of spiritual values, a failure to discern the true nature of things.

The advice given as regards the appointment of scribes likewise is sealed with a spiritual message. Malik is told that he must avoid the temptation to appoint only those persons who have shown their best

---

[79] *Nahj*, p. 375; *Peak*, pp. 540-541.
[80] *Nahj*, p. 375-6; *Peak*, p.541.

side to him; he must examine their previous record, together with the impression left by them on the common people, and then appoint only those well-known for their trustworthiness. Doing all of this is described as 'proof of your sincerity towards God.'[81]

Merchants and craftsmen are then described by the Imam as being those who bring diverse benefits to society, and must therefore we treated well. On the whole they are peaceable, and should be left in peace to their trades, but their vices must be checked: hoarding, miserliness, cheating.

The Poor: those 'most in need of justice'

The Imam now comes to a point in the letter to which he wants Malik to pay special attention. He begins the passage with the exclamation, 'Allah, Allah' to stress its urgency. The instruction here pertains to those who have no resources at all—the destitute, the crippled, the orphans, the elderly—those who are 'most in need of justice from you' and should be treated in a manner such that 'God may excuse you on the day you meet Him'.[82] All of these, and others who are in need, but refuse to beg, should be helped by the governor, and he should appoint an officer with the specific task of bringing to light the needs of the most destitute and to provide for them. Then he adds the following crucial words: 'This is onerous for the governors, and [the fulfilment of] all rights is onerous, but God makes it light for those who aspire to the Hereafter, who restrain their souls in patience, and trust in the truth of that which is promised them by God.'

What needs to be highlighted here is that the spiritual element is what makes practicable an ideal that otherwise would be a heavy 'burden'; the divine assistance is assured for those whose attention is not confined to this world alone, but whose aspirations extend beyond it to the Hereafter. Paradoxically, it is only when this world is seen through to the next, that a fully just attitude towards this world emerges. Those, on the other hand, whose *talab*, or aspiration, does not go beyond this world will be more likely to fall prey to the easy option of neglecting the destitute—for, in the horizontal scales of political evaluation, the costs to the ruler in pursuing a policy of charity towards the poverty-stricken may outweigh the benefits to him. This is where an ethical policy tied to a this-worldly appraisal, to pragmatic politics or to personal interest, reveals certain inherent flaws:

---

[81] *Nahj*, p. 376; *Peak*, p. 541.
[82] *Nahj*, p. 377; *Peak*, p. 542-3.

but when the notion of right in regard to the poor is suffused with aspiration for the Hereafter, and impregnated with firm faith in God's inexorable justice and infinite compassion, an attitude of unflinching fidelity to the needs of the destitute in society will be generated and re-generated ever anew. Such an attitude, which goes far beyond the conventional notions of charity or generosity, will not be susceptible to any contrary suggestion stemming from pragmatism or individualism, and still less from indifference or wilfulness. With this attitude firmly in place, the next quality mentioned by the Imam, that of patience, flows naturally. For, in the light of a concrete and not merely notional presentiment of the absolute values in question, patience can be indefinitely extended, no longer dependent on personal will alone, but sustained by the empowering grace that flows from heartfelt faith. The Imam finishes the above point with reference to those with the right aspirations having, as a consequence, confidence in the truth of God's promise: if the promise of God's reward, of His unfailing justice and His infinite compassion be true, then the governor's effort to extend mercy to and to deal justly with the poor will, again, be immeasurably but palpably relieved. The 'burden' of having to help those who are weak and helpless—and from assisting whom, no political benefit is derived—is transformed into an inescapable duty concomitant upon one's spiritual conviction. This conviction is grounded in the certitude that not only is such charity something good, right and proper, but that this goodness, rectitude and propriety are in harmony with the true and inalienable substance of ultimate reality.

These aspects of spiritual reality are veiled from worldly rulers by their covert prejudices, at best, and their overt vices, at worst. Such rulers are oblivious not only to the truth of God's promise, relating to ultimate felicity, but also to His warnings and threats of punishment. This brings us to the question of the role played by the Hereafter within the ethical framework of the Imam's worldview. While it is undoubtedly true that the notion of the Hereafter figures prominently in the Imam's spiritual conception of justice, there is a deeper side to this seemingly simple utilization of the ethical impact of divine threats and promises on human action.

The Imam frequently echoes, implicitly if not explicitly, the Qur'anic principle that the *Hereafter is better and more lasting.* (*Al-A'la*, LXXXVII:17) The Hereafter is not only the 'time' when divine threats and promises are consummated: it is also the 'space' within which all positive qualities—spiritual, angelic, divine—are manifested in their plenary nature, those qualities that are glimpsed on earth as reflections of the higher realities, and which encompass and subtly penetrate the entire sphere of terrestrial existence. The Qur'an, more so than any other scripture, it should be noted, affords to the imagination numerous and complex descriptions of paradisal bliss; one of the key functions of which is alluded to in the Qur'an itself: the mere thought of Paradise is itself a purification of the mind and heart,[83] a means of averting from the soul the ever-present temptation to seek its ultimate happiness and well-being in this world alone. On the contrary, one's well-being in the herebelow, in regard to action lies in the performance of good deeds; and such well-being is proportioned to the depth of one's belief that *whatever good you send before for your souls, you will find it with God, better and more tremendous as reward.* (*Al-Muzzammil*, LXXIII: 20)

Thus, a profound orientation towards the Hereafter translates itself into a perception of heavenly beatitude already in the herebelow, in the form, precisely, of those acts and attitudes which, being good, are of one and the same nature as that felicity to which they lead; in this light, morally good actions and noble intentions are grasped by one who sees beyond the veil of this world as vivid prefigurations of heavenly realities, and not just as ethical prerequisites for salvation. Goodness, in other words, does not just lead to a heavenly reward: it already *is* something of this reward: *Is the reward of goodness aught but goodness?* (*Al-Rahman*, LV: 60) It is for this reason that the Imam describes himself as belonging to a group whose degree of spirituality is such that 'their hearts are in the Gardens [of Paradise] while their bodies are at work.'[84] Their outward actions in the world belie their inward transcendence of all action; they act, but are not bound by the fruits of their action, to borrow a concept from the *Bhagavad Gita*. In other words, the very fact that their inmost consciousness is attuned to a higher reality than that of the world ensures that their worldly activity will manifest something of that higher reality; and conversely, it implies that the turmoil and tribulations of the world cannot disturb that inner state of tranquillity, cannot take their 'hearts' out of the 'Gardens', even if their 'bodies' are in this world, and subject to its exigencies. It is only their outward being that is subject to outward things; their inner realities remain in imperturbable serenity.

---

[83] *Assuredly We purified them with a pure quality—remembrance of the Abode* [of the Hereafter]. (*Sad*, XXXVIII: 46)
[84] *Nahj*, p. 302; *Peak*, p. 394.

Realization of Intention

These considerations can be elaborated further by bringing in the altogether crucial issue of intention. Even if the effort of the just man to live according to justice is frustrated by the imponderables of terrestrial life, nonetheless, the right intentions that motivate him, together with his awareness of the immutable divine qualities as models or principles guiding his endeavour, produce a real inward 'taste' of the grace that furnishes the spiritual foundation of his moral life. If God's promise is true, and one is absolutely certain of this truth, then the impact of that truth on the soul of the sincere believer transforms a personal ethic into an incontrovertible reality, a desirable value into an unconditional imperative; morality is thus deepened by (and into) spirituality, an existential and all-encompassing mode of being within which the burden of individual 'duty' is not only lightened immeasurably, it is transformed into an accompaniment of one's 'taste' of spiritual reality: one then acts justly out of a sense of gratitude for what one has already received and not only out of hope for something as yet unattained. The Qur'an speaks of the paradisal reward as something already granted; thus the future has already come to pass, for one whose certainty of Paradise is absolute: *We have given you* [the paradisal fountain of] *al-Kawthar: so pray to your Lord and sacrifice...* (*Al-Kawthar*, CVIII: 1-2). Worshipping God as a consequence of the certainty of the beatitude to come—and which has thus, in one respect, already come—is well expressed by the following saying of the Imam: 'Indeed there is a group who worship God out of desire [for something not yet attained]; and this is the worship of the merchants. And there is a group who worship God out of fear, and this is the worship of the slaves. And there is a group who worship God out of gratitude, and this is the worship of the free.' [85]

Furthermore, the just man is liberated from the material consequences of his actions in the measure of the rectitude and sincerity of his intentions; actions being evaluated in the Islamic perspective not according to consequences but intentions. One's intention is to be just, not for the sake of some earthly reward, or some tangible consequence in the world, but purely for the sake of justice itself, and this essence or principle of justice is in turn inseparable from the divine nature. For justice is at one with God not simply because that which God commands is just: rather, God commands just acts precisely *because* they are just, and because this justice is one with His own nature,[86] as we noted at the outset: 'I bear witness that He is Justice and He acts justly.' If God acts justly as a result of His very nature, which is pure justice, the spiritual man will act justly out of a desire to conform to God's nature, and not simply out of obedience to God's commands, and never out of desire for any earthly reward. As the Qur'an says:

> The most pious will be far removed from it [the punishment of Hell], he who gives of his wealth to purify himself; and nobody possesses, in the sight of such a person, any favour that might be bestowed on him as reward [for his generosity]—[His action is performed] only seeking only the Countenance of his transcendent Lord, and he will be content. (Al-Layl, XCII: 17-21)

The same principle is expressed in the description of the righteous, the *abrar*. The commentators of the Qur'an are agreed that the occasion for the revelation (*sabab*) of the following verses was when the Imam and his family went for three consecutive days without food. At the end of each day, just when they were about to break their fast, someone more in need than they asked for food. The Qur'an relates this as follows:

> They feed, out of love for God, the needy, the orphan and the prisoner, saying: We feed you only for the sake of God; we desire from you neither reward nor thanks. (Al-Insan, LXXVI: 8-9)

In the very measure that good action is performed for the sake of that absolute goodness which God is, the performer of the action is imperturbably content, untouched by the blame or praise of others; and neither deflated or dejected by any outward adversity that thwarts his good actions, nor inflated or elated by the successful consequences of his good actions.

Again, one observes the difference between a secular ethic of justice and a spiritual conception of justice: whereas a secular ethic stands or falls according to the degree of success in realizing outwardly its ideal of justice, a spiritual conception already sees the fulfilment of its ideal in the sincere intention to be just. Now while this may

---

[86] One is touching here upon that oft-debated theological question: is an injunction just because God enjoins it, or does He enjoin it because it is just? While Ash'ari theology tends towards the former, the adherents of the 'Adliyya school—Shi'ite and Mu'tazila alike—affirm the latter of the two positions.

seem on the surface to condone the failure to achieve justice in society, and is thus easily exploitable as a subterfuge by which actual injustice is legitimated by appealing to good but thwarted intentions—the very opposite is in fact the case: for the fulfilment of a spiritual ideal of justice essentially requires an unyielding struggle to achieve it— failing which the intention is shown to be lacking sincerity. To hold an intention with sincerity essentially implies striving diligently and ceaselessly in pursuit of its realization. Thus, however formidable the obstacles, however compelling the arguments of pragmatism may be, however much one's strenuous efforts are brought to nothing due to unavoidable exigencies of outward life, the just man never despairs, he never abandons the effort to achieve justice, *precisely* because the achievement of justice in this world is not the sum total of his aims. The just person knows that the intention is already, in an invisible but spiritually palpable way, its own fulfilment; and he knows, with a sense of sober realism, that the outward realization of all intentions depend upon circumstances beyond his control, and, ultimately, on the grace of God.

So, far from implying any lack of resolve on the part of one motivated by a sacred conception of justice, the efforts of such a person will, on the contrary, be as ceaseless and unyielding as the reward in which one fervently believes is eternal and unfailing; such efforts will also be sustained by the consciousness of the subtle continuity between just intentions and the divine quality of justice, and thereby the divine nature itself. An inalienable sense of the sacred, then, sustains the just man in his pursuit of justice. The secular ideal, on the other hand, is all too likely to disintegrate under pressure, because of its quasi-absolute dependence upon two relativities: the relativity of the individual soul, susceptible to a range of compromising factors, outward and inward; and the relativity of the outward world itself, to which the secular ideal is inextricably tied and by which its validity will be judged. One need not advance the dogmatic claim that all secular conceptions of justice are bound to fail in practice, only that, in comparison with a sacred conception of justice, it will lack those immeasurable and inexhaustible spiritual resources that are nourished by sincere faith. 'With men this is impossible, but with God all things are possible', as Jesus says, according to the Gospel. Put into the present context, one might formulate this truth as follows: When justice is conceived in a secular framework, personal idealism hangs by the thread of social contingency; in a sacred conception of justice, by contrast, divine grace supports the incorruptible ideal of justice, which is thus held high above the frailties and vicissitudes to which the human soul and human society are both subject. The salience of this ideal is clearly to be seen in the Imam's own experience as caliph: a continuous series of bloody conflicts, against foes that professed Islam, prevented him outwardly from putting into effect many of the principles and policies that flowed from his conception of sacred truth and justice—but none of this resulted in dejection, despair or cynicism, or in even a slight diminution in his efforts to achieve justice whenever and wherever possible,[87] as is amply demonstrated in the nature of his own administration, and in the stream of letters and counsels to his officers and governors, including the one now being considered.

The Virtue of Worship

We now come to what is arguably the lynchpin of the entire epistle, the most important means by which the sacred substance of all the virtues is assimilated by the ruler, namely, prayer. We saw at the beginning of the letter how the Imam began with a counsel to observe the obligatory prayers. At this point, after stressing the need to perform all administrative tasks in their appropriate times, the Imam instructs Malik to set apart the 'most excellent' of his available time for 'what is between you and God',[88] that is, acts of worship and devotion. Malik is urged to pay special attention to the obligatory prayers as the means by which he 'purifies' his religion for God, or renders sincere his devotion to God. Now this instruction is not to be taken only as an exhortation to perform the formal prayers; it must also, and above all, be understood in the light of the deeper meaning of 'purifying one's religion for God', that is, purifying the substance of the relationship between the soul and God; for it is the depth of this relationship that will determine the quality of all human virtue. As the Imam says elsewhere: 'Know that your every act is dependent upon your prayer.'[89] It is not simply the physical performance of the prayer that matters, but the inward quality that accompanies it and enlivens

---

[87] 'No act is negligible if it is accompanied by piety.' *Nahj* (Tehran, 1378, Ed. and Tr. Sayyed Ja'far Shaheedy), Saying no.95, p. 376; *Peak*, Saying no. 95, p. 590.

[88] *Nahj*, pp. 378-9 *Peak*, p. 543.

[89] From the letter to Muhammad ibn Abi Bakr, in which he was appointed governor of Egypt by the Imam, *Nahj*, p. 330; *Peak*, p. 487. We translate the word *taba'* as 'dependent', but the word also connotes the ideas of 'consequence', 'following on from', and 'as a result of'. The import is clear: the quality of one's action is determined by the quality of one's prayer.

it from within.[90] The sincerity, intensity, and frequency of prayer are essential to its efficacy. The Imam continues: 'Give unto God of your body [i.e. your vital energy] in your nights and your days, and perform fully that by which you draw near to God, doing so perfectly, without becoming dull or deficient, taking your body to its limits (*balighan min badanika ma balagha*).'

All the stress here should be on the word *taqarrub,* 'drawing near': one attains the divine nearness most directly through deep devotion, offered up alone, in the dead of the night, with all one's heart.[91] This nearness being realized, all of one's other actions in the world are imbued with something of the spiritual quality gained through the divine proximity. Thus can all action be assimilated to 'devotion' in this wider sense, all outward actions being truly governed by the sincere intention to give oneself to God: if one's inner life is dominated by prayer, then prayer comes to penetrate one's outer life also. Hence, as the Imam said, just after telling Malik to set apart the best of his times for God, 'all times [and actions performed therein] are for God if the intention underlying them is good, and if your subjects derive security therefrom.' In other words, all the actions of the ruler will partake of the sacred, in the measure that his devotion truly enters into the source of the sacred. Then one can envisage an overflow, as it were, from the fountain of formal and supererogatory prayer, into the outward domain of action. This subtle truth is beautifully expressed in the famous *hadith qudsi,* often referred to as the hadith of *taqarrub*: 'My slave draws near to Me through nothing I love more than that which I have made obligatory for him. My slave never ceases to draw near to Me through supererogatory acts until I love him. And when I love him, I am his hearing by which he hears, his sight by which he sees, his hand by which he grasps, and his foot by which he walks.'[92] To thus 'see' and act through God can be understood, at one level at least, to mean 'seeing things as they really are',[93] and then acting

---

[90] When someone mentioned in the presence of the Imam that a certain Kharijite was known for his long prayers at night, he said: 'A sleep with certainty is better than a prayer in doubt'. *Nahj,* saying no.93, p. 422; *Peak,* saying no.97, p. 591.

[91] See the eloquent and spiritually moving description of the pious given by the Imam in response to the request by Hammam, who, it is said, fell into a swoon and died after hearing it. *Nahj,* Sermon no.184; *Peak,* Sermon no.192.

[92] *Sahih al-Bukhari* (Summarized) Riyadh: Maktaba Dar-us-Salam, 1996/1417, no. 2117, p. 992.

[93] 'Our Lord, show us things as they really are' (*hadith*). This prayer might be said to sum up the relationship between faith and objectivity, two key foundations of sacred justice.

upon that vision; in other words, it implies perfect justice, putting each thing in its place. It is important to note in the above *hadith qudsi* the distinction between the obligatory and the supererogatory acts of devotion—both are means of 'drawing near' but it is only through the latter that the slave comes to perceive and act through the divine.

It is also important to note the phrase, 'taking your body to its limits'. Strenuous effort is called for here, it is far from sufficient to perform the prayers and devotions in a mechanical or perfunctory manner; it must be done with all one's being. As noted earlier, the sincerity (*ikhlas*) demanded by the Imam's conception of the oneness of God calls for the totality of the soul; and it is in prayer that the deepest dimension of one's soul is expressed. Hence, the prayer must be accomplished not just with one's tongue, or one's body, but all one's heart: 'He who prays without making an effort is like one who shoots arrows without a bow.'[94]

Elsewhere, the Imam refers to the key (supererogatory) practice by which this spiritual station is attained. He does this in a commentary upon the following words of a Qur'anic verse: ... *men whom neither commerce nor trade diverts from the remembrance of God* (XXIV:36). 'Truly God has made remembrance (*al-dhikr*) a polish for the hearts, by which they hear after suffering from deafness, and see after being dim-sighted ... There have always been slaves of God ... with whom He held intimate discourse through their thoughts, and spoke with them through the essence of their intellects. They diffused illumination through the awakened light in their hearing and their seeing and their hearts, calling unto the remembrance of the days of God.'[95] The importance of the *dhikr*, both as a principle of awareness of ultimate reality, and as a concrete means of attaining this awareness, is clearly of the utmost importance in the Imam's perspective. There is much evidence to indicate that the Imam does imply, by the word *dhikr*, a methodical practice of invoking the (or a) divine name, as well as a principle of permanent awareness of God embracing all modes of worship, meditation and reflection. Again, these sayings can be read as commentary upon such Qur'anic verses as the following:

And invoke thy Lord within yourself, in humility and awe, and beneath thy breath, in the morning and in the night. (Al-'Araf, VII: 205)

[94] *Peak*, no.347.
[95] *Nahj*, Sermon no.213, p.260, *Peak*, Sermon no.220, p.440.

O ye who believe! Invoke God with much invocation. (*Al-Ahzab*, XXXIII: 42)

And invoke the Name of thy Lord, devoting yourself to it with utter devotion. (*Al-Muzzammil*, LXXIII: 8)

And invoke the Name of thy Lord morning and evening. (*Al-Insan*, LXXVI: 25)

Glorify the Name of thy Lord, the Exalted. (*Al-A'la*, LXXXVII:1)

The following saying of the Imam is a key to understanding the reason for invoking God's Name: 'He who loves a thing dedicates himself fervently to its invocation.' (*man ahabba shay'an lahija bi-dhikrihi*)[96] It is thus that the lover of God should devote himself utterly to the invocation of the Name of God, to give himself to it in abundance (*kathiran*). The combination between the words *lahija* and *dhikr*, clearly indicating the constant, verbal repetition of the invocation, figures also in the Imam's famous *Du'a' Kumayl*, here with an additional, explicit reference to the tongue: '... my tongue has devoted itself to thy remembrance/invocation (*lahija bihi lisani min dhikrik*); he implores God: 'make my times in the night and the day inhabited by Thy remembrance'; and 'make my tongue remember/invoke Thee with utter dedication' (*ij'al lisani bi-dhikrika lahijan*). The invocation as a practice is clearly alluded to in the verse which says: 'O He whose Name is a remedy, and whose invocation is the cure (*ya man ismuhu dawa' wa dhikruhu shafa'*).'[97] Finally, the following verse relationship between the practice of the *dhikr* and the 'drawing near', *taqarrub*, which the Imam mentions in his advice to Malik: the *dhikr* is referred to as that by which 'I attain nearness to Thee' (*ataqarrabu ilayk*).[98]

---

[96] *Ghurar*, no. 8528, p.690.

[97] *Supplications*, Tr. W. Chittick, p.28, verse 63; p.36, verse 132; p.38, verse 148; p.40, verse 156 (we have slightly modified Chittick's translation). Cf. the description of the 'man of substance' (*dhu lubb*): 'renunciation has curbed his desires, and invocation quickens his tongue (*awjafa al-dhikr bi-lisanihi*).' *Nahj al-balagha*, op. cit., p.77; *Peak of Eloquence*, op. cit. p.210. In connection with the healing power of the invocation, the following image of the Prophet is to be noted: '[He was like] a physician roving with his medicine, having fortified his remedies, and heated up his implements, ready to place them at the disposal of those who need them: hearts which are blind, ears that are deaf, tongues that are dumb. With his medicines he seeks out the domains of heedlessness (*ghafla*) and the homelands of perplexity.' *Nahj*, p.120; *Peak*, p.251-2.

[98] *Supplications*, Tr. Chittick, p. 28.

In case one might be wondering whether this is not becoming too remote from the social or outward dimensions of justice, it is useful to continue with the above sermon, where the Imam describes in detail the qualities of the slaves illumined by the invocation. 'Truly there are people who belong to the *dhikr*, they have adopted it in place of the world, such that *neither commerce nor trade* distracts them from it; they spend the days of their life in it ... they instruct people in justice, and themselves are steadfast therein.'[99]

It is necessary to underline that, just as earlier it was seen that the sincerity of a good intention was proven by the effort to realize it, so it is clear now that, in regard to prayer, its sincerity is likewise proven, and rendered efficacious, through sustained effort to prolong and intensify it 'taking your body to its limits'.[100] What this has to do with justice should be clear: if justice is grasped as a quality rooted in the Real, (*al-Haqq*), then one's nearness to the Real cannot but draw one nearer to justice, and to all positive qualities, spiritual, intellectual and moral. Thus, the relationship between worship and justice must be firmly established if the conception of justice is to be qualified as 'sacred'. From this perspective, justice is both cause and consequence of worship: on the one hand, justice requires us to put everything in its place, thus, God must be given His due, and this entails, sacramentally, worship and prayer; on the other hand, justice emerges, ethically, as a consequence of this worship, as do all the virtues, this, in the measure of the 'nearness' granted by God to His worshipper.

Gazing on the Good

We have made occasional references above to some similarities between ideas in the Imam's letter and those discussed in Plato's *Republic*; and we would like to conclude this essay by suggesting that what we are given by the Imam in this stress on prayer—together with its essence, the remembrance of God—is a devotional principle which complements the philosophical position of Plato, and might be seen as rendering explicit in spiritual terms what is implied in Plato's pedagogy. After discussing the question of justice at great length, Plato comes, in chapter 23 of *The Republic*, to address the crux of the matter: the

---

[99] Cf. 'He who invokes God, glorified be He, God enlivens his heart and illuminates his inner substance (*lubb*).' *Ghurar*, no. 9545, p.764.

[100] The Qur'an informs us of the night vigils of the Prophet and a group (*ta'ifa*) with him: *Truly thy Lord knoweth that thou standst in prayer for almost two-thirds of the night, and half of it, and a third of it—as doth a group from those with thee.* (LXXIII: 20)

nature of the Sovereign Good, which most concerns the ideal ruler, the 'guardian', whose moral and intellectual education is at the heart of the practical dimension of the book. '... the highest object of knowledge is the essential nature of the Good, from which everything that is good and right derives its value for us... I need not tell you that, without that knowledge, to know everything else, however well, would be of no value to us ...'[101] But Socrates does not respond to the entreaties of Glaucon to describe the nature of this Good, offering instead to speak of its 'offspring'. This leads him to make an analogy between the Good and the sun: what the sun is to visibility, the Good is to intelligibility and being. He proceeds with the famous allegory of the cave and then describes the educational programme that would turn the attention of his prospective rulers (the guardians) from the world of shadows to the world of real objects; a programme comprising mathematics, arithmetic, geometry, solid geometry, astronomy, harmonics and dialectic. Having successfully passed through all stages of their education, 'when they are fifty, those who have come safely through and proved the best at all points in action and in study must be brought at last to the goal. They must lift up the eye of the soul to gaze on that which sheds light on all things; and when they have seen the Good itself, take it as a pattern for the right ordering of the state and of the individual, themselves included.'[102] But Plato does not anywhere state what this 'gazing' actually means, nor how it is to be achieved, by what means, intellective, contemplative or methodic.

At an important point in the *Republic* Glaucon presses Socrates on the definition of the Sovereign Good: 'But, Socrates, what is your account of the Good? Is it knowledge, or pleasure, or something else?' Socrates refuses to give an account, saying, after some further dialogue, 'I am afraid it is beyond my powers; with the best will in the world I should only disgrace myself and be laughed at.'[103] It is interesting to note that Dhi'lib al-Yamani, very much after the manner of Glaucon, provocatively asked the Imam whether he had seen the object of his devotion. To this the Imam replied: 'I would not be worshipping a lord whom I have not seen.' Dhi'lib then asked: 'O Commander of the Faithful! How didst thou see Him?' The Imam replied: 'O Dhi'lib! Eyes see Him not through sight's observation, but hearts see Him through the verities of faith.'[104]

---

[101] *The Republic*, op. cit., p. 210.

[102] Ibid., p. 256.

[103] *The Republic*, op. cit., p.211.

[104] We have followed William Chittick's translation; this is from his *A Shi'ite Anthology*

He then proceeds with a series of paradoxical allusions to the indefinable reality that he has, nonetheless, witnessed by the eye of the purified heart. We are reminded here of the 'polishing' of the heart effected by remembrance; and this very word evokes the essence of Plato's approach to knowledge as 'recollection', *anamnesis*.[105] But, as noted above, Plato does not, in any of his dialogues, make a direct reference to the devotional, methodical or contemplative counterpart to his educational, ethical and intellective endeavour. While speculation may abound as to whether there was any spiritual method in Plato's teaching, and if there was, why he did not divulge it. One answer can be gauged from a statement in Plato's famous 7th letter, where he denies that any exposition can be given of the true reality of philosophy, and points instead to the 'disciplined way of life', and rigorous 'daily routine' which the subject demands if philosophy in the deepest sense is to be realized. 'No treatise by me concerning it exists or ever will exist. It is not something that can be put into words like other branches of learning; only after long partnership in a common life devoted to this very thing does truth flash upon the soul, like a flame kindled by a leaping spark, and once it is born there, it nourishes itself thereafter.' [106]

This brings us back to the importance of active spirituality for the practice of authentic virtue. If the Real—indefinable in its essence—is the foundation of all good, the means of assimilating the Real, at all

---

(London, 1980), pp.38-39.

[105] See, for the most explicit exposition of this doctrine, the dialogue entitled *Meno*, in *Protagoras and Meno*, Tr. W.K.C. Guthrie, London: Penguin, 1979.

[106] *Phaedrus and Letters VII and VIII*, Tr. W. Hamilton (London: Penguin, 1978), p.136. This statement contradicts the judgement of Plato made by Peter Kingsley in an important recent book. He argues that Plato marks a shift in the Pythagorean/Orphic tradition, away from the intensely practical, mystical and magical concerns of his philosophical forebears, towards a more cerebral approach to philosophy: with Plato and Aristotle, he writes, 'the philosophical life as an integrated combination of practice and perception fell apart at the seams, and another ideal came to predominate instead: 'a new type of man, the unworldly and withdrawn student and scholar' [quoting Jaeger]". *Ancient Philosophy, Mystery and Magic: Empedocles and Pythagorean Tradition*, Oxford: Clarendon Press, 1995, p.158. While this 'new type of man' does appear to reflect Aristotle's kind of philosopher, it seems to be rather wide of the mark in respect of Plato; and it certainly does not conform to the image of Plato in the Islamic tradition of mystical philosophy, and it ignores the sub-text or hidden references ('spiritual switches') to attitudes, practices, and orientations that are presupposed by the text. See on this subject Sara Rappe, *Reading Neoplatonism: Non-discursive Thinking in the Texts of Plotinus, Proclus, and Damascius* (Cambridge: Cambridge University Press, 2000). The outstanding work by Algis Uždavinys, *Philosophy as a Rite of Rebirth* (London, 2006, forthcoming), demonstrates beyond any

levels, and not just mentally, cannot be disdained. Plato's philosophical approach to the Good can be complemented and deepened by an appreciation of the Imam's means of 'drawing near' to the Real, wherein intellectual comprehension and spiritual devotion go hand in hand. Integral, deep-rooted justice emerges as one of the fruits of this 'drawing near', just as, for Plato, gazing on 'that which sheds light on all things ... the Good itself' results in the capacity to take the Good 'as a pattern for the right ordering of the state and of the individual'.

****

In this essay we have attempted to sketch the outlines of a spiritual approach to the theme of justice, such as this presents itself in, principally, the letter of the Imam to Malik al-Ashtar. We are fully aware that we have only skimmed the surface of this important subject, but hope nonetheless to have at least indicated, firstly, that this is a subject of relevance to any political discourse worthy of being qualified as 'Islamic'; secondly, that the Imam's letters and discourses are a vast and largely untapped source of inspired ideas that can illuminate the role of spiritual principles in formulating ethical values and determining the quality of political practice; and finally, that there can be no fully authentic 'Islamic' approach to politics, society or the individual without taking into account the requirements and the fruits of worship, taking this in its widest sense. Sincere worship transforms the notion of the Absolute into a concrete reality that imparts to the soul an existential impetus, a spiritual resource, which buttresses, stabilizes, and deepens one's moral life. What is derived from the consciousness of divine reality is not so much a philosophy of ethics as a 'spiritual morality', an ethical orientation that is both the consequence of a lived spirituality and the cause of continuous, dynamic and ever-deepening realization of spiritual truth. Virtue, in such a perspective, becomes 'moral truth' or 'moral realism', understanding by realism an assimilation of spiritual reality; and ethical behaviour translates that truth into action, on all planes, individual, social and political.

If it be objected that this perspective is hopelessly utopian, the harsh exigencies of politics and the sublime ideals of spirituality being poles apart, we would respond: if no effort is made to comprehend

doubt the mystical discipline, or spiritual praxis, underlying the Platonic approach to knowledge; philosophical 'discourse' is but the tip of an iceberg, an outward expression of that spiritual transformation which Uždavinys aptly refers to as a 'rebirth'

the deeper aspects of Islamic piety and spirituality, the result of any ostensibly 'Islamic' discourse—whether in politics, sociology, ethics or any other field—will be reduced to an outer shell, deprived of the inner life that gives its all its meaning and, more importantly, its trans-formative power. For Islamic concepts to be grasped aright they must, on pain of abstraction, be assimilated not simply by the mind but by the heart. For, as the Imam stresses, it is the heart—the inmost point of one's consciousness—that 'sees' the true nature of things.

This leads us back to the devotional practices that are all too often regarded as the preserve of a minority—seen as mystical or misguided, depending on one's standpoint—instead of being grasped as a God-given means of reducing the gap between what one aspires to and what one is, of moving from the actual to the ideal, of making concrete what otherwise would remain abstract, of living that which is thought about, and of rendering existentially galvanising what otherwise might perhaps only be theoretically compelling. Nothing could be further removed from this perspective than 'de-contextualizing' it, if this means ignoring—as so much unnecessary 'superstructure'—the Imam's repeated, insistent and uncompromising emphasis upon the devotional dimensions of Islam. The principle of justice requires that all the elements of one's life—spirituality, worship, ethics, action—be bound together in a harmonious, indissoluble and interconnected whole, in accordance with the ideal of *tawhid.* There can be no question of detaching the domain of the virtues from that of spirituality, for, in the Imam's perspective, the only true virtue is one that is rooted in, sustained by, and oriented towards the divine reality. Thus one must conclude that justice, together with all the other virtues, can only be brought to fruition in a soul—and a society—permeated and penetrated by spirituality. In other words, the remembrance of God—in its most profound sense—is the inalienable spiritual substance of all human virtue.[107]

---

[107] See our forthcoming work, *Justice and Remembrance — Introducing the Spirituality of Imam 'Ali b. Abi Talib* (London, 2006), where a longer version of this chapter will appear, together with an essay on the Imam's elucidation of the meaning and the practice of the 'remembrance of God.'

"Muhammad peforms the ritual prayer with Khadija and 'Ali, as Gabriel taught him." From the Turkish manuscript *Siyer-i Nebī, volume II, p. 283b,* 16th century. Istanbul, Topkapi Saray Museum

'ALI IBN ABI TALIB'S ETHICS OF MERCY IN THE MIRROR OF THE PERSIAN SUFI TRADITION

Leonard Lewisohn

Prologue

Both venerated as a saint and violently detested by the aristocratic clans and classes of the nascent Arab Islamic state, 'Ali ibn Abi Talib in his lifetime was famed for his piety, lauded for his justice, and revered for his erudition in matters theological and spiritual. He was the cousin, and later, son-in-law of the Prophet Muhammad, marrying his daughter Fatima. As a young man, he was the Prophet's first male convert to Islam and his staunchest ally. After the Prophet's death in 11/632, 'Ali played a muted political role in the early Islamic state established by the first three caliphs, this in marked contrast to his important activity during the Prophet's life-time, and then as caliph himself, from 35-40/656-661.[1] Amongst his 'partisans' – the Shi'ites – 'Ali is renowned today as 'the Leader' or First Imam, and a key member the Prophet's 'holy family' (*ahl al-bayt*, consisting of the Prophet, 'Ali, Fatima, and their two sons: al-Hasan and al-Husayn). Amongst the 'followers of the Prophet's traditions', or Sunnis, he is still venerated as the fourth Caliph, worthy successor of the reigns of Abu Bakr, 'Umar and 'Uthman.

His own period of rulership over the young Islamic Empire, which began after the assassination of 'Uthman, was brief – just five years in length, as noted above. Although he acquiesced to the first Caliph Abu Bakr's leadership of the community, he had serious differences with, and, in fact, turned down all offers of position and public office under the two subsequent Caliphs: 'Umar and 'Uthman.[2]

His differences in opinion and outlook with the latter two caliphs became even further accentuated during his own caliphate, when he was forced to fight two major battles. From the moment of his

---

[1] For a general account of 'Ali's early years before the death of the Prophet, see Martin Lings, *Muhammad, his life based on the earliest sources* (London: Unwin Hyman 1988)

[2] Syed Husain Mohammad Jafri, *The Origins and Development of Shi'ite Islam* (Oxford: OUP 2000), p. 64.

accession, 'Ali was confronted by a civil war spawned by conflicts and rivalries between the early Muslim elite and Arab tribal powers.[3] The *casus belli* of this conflict was the implication of many of his supporters in the ranks of the early Muslim ascetics and the *Ansar* ('Helpers' of the Prophet during his exile in Medina) in the assassination of 'Uthman. 'Ali's two sons, Hasan (d. 50/670) and Husayn (d. 61/680) had failed to stop an angry mob from murdering the Caliph, and 'Ali proved incapable of successfully apprehending his killers. His entire rule was thus taken up in battling against a panoply of powerful vested interests.

'Ali's first war was waged against 'A'isha bint Abi Bakr, the daughter of Abu Bakr and the favourite wife of the Prophet, who, early on, had dissented from his leaderMisbahp and crying vengeance for the blood of 'Uthman, challenged his rule. Although she and her allies, Talha and al-Zubayr, were soon defeated at the Battle of the Camel (36/656) and she was put under house arrest in Medina,[4] 'Ali was immediately confronted by a much more dangerous enemy, the governor of Syria, 'Uthman's cousin Mu'awiya, who was now also seeking vengence for 'Uthman's murder.[5] 'Ali fought Mu'awiya at the Battle of Siffin on the banks of the upper Euphrates in 37/657, his army being commanded by al-Malik al-Ashtar, but after months of confrontation and stalemate, followed by fruitless negotiations, 'Ali decided to accept an arbitrated solution to the conflict.

The settlement that was eventually reached was violently rejected on religious principles by the Khawarij, an early Islamic terrorist group who believed themselves to be the only true Muslims, and in 21/661, one of their more fanatical members, 'Abd al-Rahman b. al-Muljam, assassinated 'Ali with a poisoned sword in the mosque of Kufa in Iraq.[6]

This is a brief outline of the main external events of 'Ali's adult lifetime. They are not, however, the concern of this study, which is devoted, like the rest of the chapters of this book, to the intellectual and spiritual dimension of 'Ali's thought, as recorded in his aphorisms, sermons, and letters noted down by his followers. Rather than the events of tribal politics and social history, the focus is on 'Ali's

---

[3] Ira Lapidus, *A History of Islamic Societies* (Cambridge: CUP 1988), pp. 56-58.

[4] H.A.R. Gibb, "'Ali b. Abi Talib," EI², I, p. 383.

[5] Jafri, *op. cit.,* p. 90.

[6] M.G.S. Hodgson, *The Venture of Islam*, vol. 1: *The Classical Age of Islam* (University of Chicago Press 1977 rpt.), pp. 212ff.

moral theology, and in particular on his impact on the Sufi tradition as viewed through the writings of the some key classical Persian Sufi Sunni writers. The political life of 'Ali, the course of his negotiations with Mu'awiya, his life as a warrior and military strategist, are obviously less of an issue here.

It might be mentioned that Sufis have rarely been Shi'ite except in Persia,[7] and that Shi'ite beliefs about the metaphysical nature of 'Ali's Imamate usually were not widely held, or at least not universally stressed, by Sufis in Persia until after the rise of the extremist Shi'ite *(ghulat) Mujtahid* cult[8] in Safavid Iran in the late 16th century. Khwaja 'Abdullah Ansari of Herat (d. 481/1089), author of the *Manazil al-sa'irin,* and the first Persian translation-adaptation of Sulami's *Tabaqat al-sufiyya* and many other works in Persian and Arabic, declared, for example, that of the two thousand Sufi masters he was acquainted with, only two were Shi'ites.[9] Since abstract theosophical debates about 'Ali's sainthood or *wilayat* as conceived by various Shi'ite[10]—whether Sevener (Isma'ili) or Twelver—sects, have already been treated by a number of other sources,[11] little attention will be paid to them here. Speculations about his role as 'Imam', understood in either the social, cosomological or soteriological senses of the word, and Isma'ili beliefs about him, such as those advocated by Al-Qadi al-Nu'man (d. 363/974), the founder of Isma'ili jurisprudence, are also outside the

---

[7] J.S. Trimingham, *The Sufi Orders in Islam* (Oxford: OUP 1998 rprt.), p. 136. Nasrollah Pourjavady points out that "Sufism developed basically as a form of Sunnism, whence it follows that the Shi'ites were opposed and at times even hostile to the Sufis." "Opposition to Sufism in Twelver Shiism," in Frederick de Jong, Bernd Radtke (eds.), *Islamic Mysticism Contested: Thirteen Centuries of Controversies and Polemics* (Leiden: Brill 1999), p. 614.

[8] An overview of the origins of this cult of clerics can be found in my "Sufism and the School of Isfahan: *Tasawwuf* and *'Irfan* in Late Safavid Iran ('Abd al-Razzaq Lahiji and Fayd-i Kashani on the Relation of *Tasawwuf, Hikmat* and *'Irfan,"* in L. Lewisohn & David Morgan, eds., *The Heritage of Sufism: Late Classical Persianate Sufism: the Safavid and Mughal Period,* III, Oxford: Oneworld 1999), pp. 63-134; also cf. R. Savory, "Some Reflections on Totalitarian Tendencies in the Safavid State," *Der Islam,* 52 (1976), pp. 226-41.

[9] Ibid., p. 137.

[10] Once of the best surveys of the Sufi understanding of 'Ali's sainthood, both from the Akbarian, Sunni and Shi'ite perspectives, can be found in Ma'sum 'Ali Shah Shirazi, *Tara'iq al-haqa'iq,* ed. M.J. Mahjub, (Tehran: Kitabkhana-yi Barani 1345 A.Hsh. /1966), I, pp. 503-33.

[11] A good survey can be found in Amir-Moezzi's *The Divine Guide in Early Shi'ism: the Sources of Esotericism in Islam,* tr. D. Streight, (Albany: SUNY 1994).

scope of the present essay.[12] Likewise, discussion of Nusayri doctrines in which 'Ali is held to be the incarnation of the Universal Soul and an emanation of God, cannot be entered into here.

The chronological range of this study runs from the mid-7th to the late 15th centuries, the emphasis being on the views of the great classical masters of the mainstream Sunni Sufi tradition about 'Ali. His role as founder of the later Sufi Orders and as exemplar of Sufi practices are commented on briefly, as well as Sufi doctrines of spiritual poverty and renunciation based on his *dicta* and *exempla*. His contribution to the development of Sufi ethics from a comparative Christian-Islamic perspective is presented, and his place in the Islamic chivalric tradition is discussed in considerable detail. Lastly, there is an overview of some of 'Ali's ecstatic sayings, many of which feature as fundamental reference points in later Sufi Apophatic Theology.

I. 'Ali, the Founding Father of Sufism

'Ali ibn Abi Talib's fundamental place as the founding father and originator of the Sufi Orders (*turuq* or *tara'iq*) in Islam, from whom derive most all the initiatic chains *(silsila)*, is reiterated in nearly every classical Sufi manual.[13] According to one of the earliest Arabic

---

[12] Al-Qadi al-Nu'man held the Prophet responsible for bringing the exoteric revelation *(tanzil)* of the *Shari'a*, while viewing 'Ali as a repository of knowledge, responsible for providing its esoteric interpretation *(ta'wil)*, and considering him to be "infallible *(ma'sum)*" and divinely guided. See E. Kohlberg, "'Ali b. Abi Taleb." ii. 'Ali as Seen by the Community: Among Sufis" in *Encyclopedia Iranica*, I, pp. 843-45.

[13] A good overview of the impact of 'Ali on the later Sufi tradition is given by E. Kohlberg, "'Ali b. Abi Taleb." ii. 'Ali as Seen by the Community: Among Sufis" in *Encyclopedia Iranica*, I, pp. 846-47; while a detailed discussion of the impact of 'Ali on the later Sufi tradition is provided by Kamil Mustafa al-Shaibi, *Sufism and Shi'ism* (Surrey: LAAM Publications 1991), p. 17ff. S.H. Nasr [*Sufi Essays* (Albany: SUNY Press 1991, 2nd ed.), p. 113] points out that the *Nahj al-balagha*, compiled by Sayyid Sharif Radi but ascribed by all Shi'ites to 'Ali, along with other early Shi'ite works such as the *Sahifa al-sajjadiyya* and the *Usul al-kafi* (by Imam Zayn al-'Abidin and al-Kulayni respectively) "outline a complete exposition of Islamic gnosis and have served in fact as a basis for many later gnostic and Sufi commentaries." Although I will be examining Ali's place and importance among the mainstream Sunni Sufis down to around the beginning of the 14th century, discussion of the later developments of the proto-Shi'ite Kubravi school of Sufis—such as the thought of authors such as 'Ala' al-Dawla Simnani (d. 736/1326), who believed that 'Ali was superior to the other three caliphs, or the theories of Sayyid 'Ali Hamadani (d. 1385) who made veneration of 'Ali a fundamental article of faith and viewed him as an epiphany of the uncreated divine Essence (see Lloyd Ridgeon, *'Aziz Nasafi* [London: Curzon Press 1998], p. 195) is beyond the scope of this study. By the same token, I shall not be entering into the

manuals of Sufism: *Al-Ta'arruf li-madhhab ahl al-tasawwuf,* by Abu Bakr Muhammad Kalabadhi (of Bukhara, d. 380/990), the five initial 'founding fathers of Sufism' are given as 'Ali, followed by his four descendents (the succeeding Shi'ite "Imams"): al-Hasan (d. 50/670), al-Husayn (d. 61/680), 'Ali ibn Husayn Zayn al-'Abidin (al-Sajjad, d. 95/712) and Muhammad al-Baqir (d. 114/732).[14] A century later, in a Persian commentary on the same work, entitled *Sharh-i Kitab al-ta'arruf li-madhhab ahl al-tasawwuf,* written by Abu Ibrahim Mustamli Bukhari (d. 434/1042-43), 'Ali's pivotal place in Sufism is celebrated as follows:

> 'Ali b. Abi Talib, may God beautify his profile, is the secret mystery of the gnostics *(sirr-i 'arifan)* and the whole Muslim Community agree that 'Ali b. Abi Talib represents the breaths of inspiration of all the prophets (*anfas-i payghambar-ast; Ali puer Abi Talib spiritus prophetorum tenet*). He has sayings the like of which no one prior to him ever uttered and after him the like of which no one has expressed."[15]

Writing only a century after Kalabadhi, in his *Kashf al-mahjub* (the first Persian manual of Sufism), 'Ali Hujwiri (d. 464/ 1071-2) further magnifies 'Ali's rank:

> Among them [i..e the Sufis] is the son of Muhammad's uncle: he who drowned in the ocean of affliction *(ghariq-i bahr-i bala),* consumed by the fire of love *(hariq-i nar-i wala),* the leader of all the saints and pure apostles *(muqtada-yi awliya va asfiya).* In this (Sufi) Path he holds a grand rank and a high degree *(andarin tariqat sha'ni 'azim va darajati rafi'),* and enjoyed a comprehensive gift in being able to express himself with exact expressions and explain the principles of Divine truth. Junayd said,

thought of Persian theosophers who can be classified as specifically Shi'ite thinkers, such as Haydar Amuli (d. after 1385) who believed that 'Ali was the *Khatm al-walaya* (Seal of Sainthood), Ibn Abi Jumhur Ahsa'i (d. after 901/1496) or Mulla Sadra (d. 1050/1640). The views of these figures about the role of 'Ali in Islamic thought would require separate studies and should not be conflated with the study of 'Ali in classical Sufism.

[14] See Kalabadhi's *Kitab al-ta'arruf li-madhhab ahl al-tasawwuf,* tr. A.J. Arberry, *The Doctrine of the Sufis* (Cambridge: CUP 1989 rprt.), p. 12.

[15] See Abu Ibrahim Isma'il ibn Muhammad Mustamli Bukhari, *Sharh-i Ta'arruf li-Madhhab al-tasawwuf,* ed. M. Rawshan (Tehran: Intisharat-i Asatir 1363 A.Hsh./1984), I, p. 199.

"'Ali-yi Murtada is our master as regards the principles and the endurance of affliction *(shaykhina fi 'l-usul wa 'l-bala)*."

That is to say, he is the Imam of this Spiritual Path as regards both knowledge *('ilm;* i.e. theory) and practice *(mu'amala)*—may God be content with him. The reason for this is that adepts of this way call the intellectual theory *('ilm)* of this Path its 'principles', while its practice consists entirely in the endurance of affliction.[16]

Junayd's foregoing remark that "'Ali is our shaykh as regards the principles and the endurance of affliction," demonstrates the intimate relationship between the classical masters' definitions of Sufism and the martial virtues of endurance and perseverance. The definition of the practice of Sufism as consisting "entirely in the endurance of affliction,"[17] which Hujwiri describes during his retelling of the life of 'Ali, was the probable inspiration behind Rumi's later, quite similar, opinion that "Sufism is finding delight at the descent of affliction."[18]

In his *Memoirs of the Saints,* composed in the succeeding (12th) century, Farid al-Din 'Attar echoes Junayd's pronouncement about 'Ali's pivotal place in Sufism exactly, but makes one significant addition, affirming 'Ali to be "our master as regards the principles *and derivatives* (of Sufism) and in the endurance of affliction."[19] Here, 'Attar reaffirms that the Sufis trace not only their *Tariqa* affiliation back to 'Ali, but also derive their juridical practice and application of *Shari'a* Law from 'Ali. 'Attar goes on to quote Junayd: "In his endurance of war and combat, things are related of 'Ali that no one can bear to hear, for he was a prince to whom God gave much knowledge and wisdom. "[20]

As we can see from the above quotations from these key early Persian Sufi masters—Kalabadhi, Bukhari, Hujwiri, 'Attar—'Ali does indeed hold a pivotal place among the founding fathers of Sufi doctrine.[21]

---

[16] *Kashf al-mahjub,* ed. V.A. Zhukovskii, (St. Petersburg 1899. Reprinted Leningrad 1926), p. 84.

[17] Ibid.

[18] *Mathnawi-yi ma'nawi,* ed. R.A. Nicholson (Rprt.: Tehran: Amir Kabir 1984, bi-sa'-yi Nasru'llah Purjavadi), III: 3261. In his commentary on this Arabic verse, Nicholson admitted not knowing "to whom this definition of *tasawwuf* is due."

[19] 'Attar, *Tadhkirat al-awliya',* ed. Muhammad Isti'lami. (3rd ed., Tehran: Zawwar: 1365/1986), p. 420.

[20] Ibid.

[21] 'Ali's role as originator of Sufism is also constantly reiterated by other key Persian Sufic texts, such as Husayn Wa'iz-i Kashifi Sabziwari, *Futuwwat-nama-yi sultani,* ed.

Furthermore, in addition to being an exemplar of all that is stalwart and steadfast in their mystical discipline, 'Ali is portrayed in Persian Sufi texts as the originator of the ascetic movement in Islam. He is famed as a special advocate of the poor, nicknamed 'the Father of Dust' (Abu Turab) because of his unkempt and often soiled appearance. Much of the teaching of the early Sufis concerning renunciation (*zuhd*) and doctrines on eschewing the ways and wiles of the world are often buttressed by citations of 'Ali's insights and admonitions.[22] Hujwiri, who was amongst the earliest Sufis to write in Persian, thus cites this key ascetic saying ascribed to 'Ali: "Do not make your wife and children your chief cares and occupation. If your wife and children are friends of God, well, God will take care of His friends, while if they are enemies of God, why worry yourself about the enemies of God?" This admonition, he comments, concerns the issue of severing the attachment of the heart from all things but God.[23]

'Ali was asked to describe the purest kind of occupation *(pakiza-tarin-i kasbha chist?)*, Hujwiri tells us. He replied that it is "making the heart rich in God," upon which, Hujwiri comments that "any heart which is made strong through God will not be made poor by worldly losses and deprivations nor be made glad by worldly gains and goods. The reality of this matter relates to the issue of poverty and purity *(faqr u safwat)*."[24] This saying is paraphrased in verse by 'Attar in his *Musibat-nama*.[25]

Such sentiments are echoed in most of the later Persian mystical texts as well. In his mediæval Persian manual of Sufism, the *Misbah al-hidaya*, 'Izz al-Din Mahmud Kashani (d. 735/1334) devotes a

Ja'far Mahjub (Tehran: Bunyad-i farhang-i Iran 1350 A.Hsh./1971), p. 61. A large number of Shi'ite theological authorities testify to this as well, amongst which can be mentioned Hasan b. Yusuf al-Hilli, in his *Kashf al-yaqin fi fada'il Amir al-Mu'minin*, Persian translation by Hamid Rida Azhir (Tehran 1329 A.Hsh./1950), p. 93. I am grateful to Dr. Shahram Pazuki's reference to this in his excellent article on "'Alid Sufism" which is entirely devoted to this topic: "Tasawwuf-i 'Alawi: Guftari dar bab-i intisab-i silasil-i Sufiyya bih Hadrat-i 'Ali (unpublished lecture text, delivered at the conference on Imam 'Ali [Shiraz 1379 A.Hsh./ 2000], p. 86.

[22] For instance, 'Ammar ibn Yasir (d. 37/657), one of the first converts to Islam and a pious companion of the Prophet, addressed 'Ali, saying, "May God give you the love of the poor, so that He would make you accept them as followers, and make them accept you as their leader." Abu Nu'aym Isfahani, *Hilyat al-awliya'*, I, p. 71; cited by Kamil Mustafa al-Shaibi, *Sufism and Shi'ism*, p. 35.

[23] *Kashf al-mahjub*, ed. V.A. Zhukovskii, p. 84.

[24] *Kashf al-mahjub*, ed. V.A. Zhukovskii, p. 85.

[25] *Musibat-nama*, ed. Nurani Visal (Tehran: Intisharat-i Zuwwar 1976), p. 212 supra.

lengthy chapter to the classes of ascetics and mystics whose varied spiritual characters are expressed through their divergent attire. He delineates eight types of religious people, each of which dress in a different manner to express their spiritual condition. In his description of the sixth type, devotees who are retired and possess leisure, he writes that "they are very zealous about maintenance of freedom of thought and keeping the purity of contemplative moments untarnished, not wishing to occupy their time in anything but God... For this reason, they abandon frivolities and excesses and content themselves with the bare necessities. In this context it is related that 'Ali ibn Abi Talib, peace be on him, bought a shirt for three dirhams, and its sleeves were so long that it went over his fingers."[26]

It is not only the "ascetic spirit"[27] and moral character of 'Ali which later Sufis took as their model, but also his staunch piety and god-fearing nature.[28] For this reason, the sayings of 'Ali are a constant source of reference amongst Sufis in their elaboration of doctrines of 'spiritual poverty (*faqr*)' in Sufism.[29] This is especially true when one considers such classical Persian works as the *Silk al-suluk* by the Chishti Sufi master Diya al-Din Nakhshabi (d. 751/1350), one of the most beautifully written manuals of Sufism in mediæval India. In this text, the author devotes several chapters to the theme of poverty, suitably illustrated by tales about and maxims ascribed to 'Ali.[30]

Likewise, 'Ali serves as role-model and exemplar of particular Sufi rituals and customs, an advocate of specific key practices and humane ideals of Sufism. He often seems to exemplify the ideal 'free spirit' of the later Persian Sufis – as a votary of music and song – customs not usually identified with ascetic ideals. Examples from the life of 'Ali are cited by several eminent Sufis, for instance, in defence of the doctrine of audition to music or *Sama'*. Ahmad b. Muhammad al-Tusi (writing circa 646/1248) relates several stories portraying the Prophet and 'Ali as the central figures, standing by or commenting upon the singing

[26] Kashani, *Misbah al-hidaya,* ed. Jalal al-Din Huma'i (Tehran: Kitabkhana Sana'i, n.d., 2nd ed.), p. 278.

[27] See al-Shaibi, *Sufism and Shi'ism,* p. 12.

[28] In his discussion of ritual prayer, Hujwiri notes that 'Ali used to tremble and his hair stood on end when he rose to pray, and he remarked: "The time has arrived to fufill that trust which the heavens and earth were impotent to bear." *Kashf al-mahjub,* ed. V.A. Zhukovskii, pp. 386-87.

[29] See Javad Nurbakhsh, *Spiritual Poverty in Sufism,* trans. Leonard Lewisohn (London: Khaniqahi Nimatullahi Publications 1984).

[30] Nakhshabi, *Silk al-suluk,* ed. Ghulam 'Ali Arya (Tehran: Zawwar 1369 A.Hsh./1990), see esp. pp. 39, 112.

or dancing of certain eminent Companions of the Prophet, and cites the names of some them such as Zayd ibn Haritha, 'Abd Allah Ja'far (the brother of 'Ali who was later killed in the battle of Mu'ta), who practised or participated in ceremonies resembling *Sama'* to buttress his arguments in favour of this fundamental Sufi practice.[31]

Perhaps the most interesting story (from the *Musnad* of Ahmad Hanbal) is one which emphasizes the canonicity of dancing *(raqs)* in Islam! Zayd ibn Haritha, Muhammad's adopted son, along with 'Ali and his brother Ja'far, stand in the Prophet's presence. The Prophet compliments each of them in turn, causing them to leap with joy. Since leaping (the Arabic word is *hajala)* is part of dancing *(raqs),* then all of dancing must be considered allowable the author argues. Abu Hamid Muhammad al-Ghazali (d. 505/1111) also uses the same tradition as a point of departure to justify the legality of dancing in the last part of his tract on the 'Etiquette of *Sama'* and Ecstasy' of his *Ihya' 'ulum al-din,* his monumental attempt to revive Islamic faith and piety on the basis of Sufism.[32] The same stories are repeated by Abu Najib al-Suhrawardi (d. 564/1168) in his *Adab al-muridin.*[33]

II. 'Ali's Ethics of Mercy in Persian Spiritual Chivalry

'Ali ibn Abi Talib is traditionally known among Shi'ite jurists and theologians as the stern and militant warrior. He is dubbed the "Commander of the Faithful (Amir al-Mu'mimin)." Yet in the Islamic chivalric tradition he is celebrated as being an incarnation of God's attributes of mercy, tolerance, forgiveness, and generosity. In fact, these qualities ascribed to 'Ali in the Persian chivalric tradition offer us a virtual Muslim parallel to the ethics of the 'Sermon on the Mount' in the Christian Gospels (Matthew V: 39), which is a prime source for quotations of Christ among the Sufis.[34]

---

[31] Ahmad b. Muhammad al-Tusi, *Bawariq al-ilma',* Arabic text with English trans. in James Robson, *Tracts on Listening to Music* (London: RAS, Oriental Translation Fund, vol. 34 NS, 1938), pp. 133ff.

[32] Ghazali, *Ihya' 'ulum al-din,* (Damascus: n.d.), II, p. 267.

[33] *Adab al-muridin,* Arabic text with Persian translation by 'Umar ibn Muhammad ibn Ahmad Shirakan, ed. N. Mayil Haravi (Tehran: Intisharat-i Mulla 1984), p. 61. See my "The Sacred Music of Islam: *Sama'* in the Persian Sufi Tradition" in *the British Journal of Ethnomusicology,* VI, 1997: 1-33.

[34] Tor Andrae, *In the Garden of Myrtles: Studies in Early Islamic Mysticism,* tr. B. Sharpe (Albany: State University of New York 1987), p. 27, notes that "approximately half of all the New Testament sayings quoted in these (Sufi) sources are taken [from the Sermon on the Mount]."

In the later Islamic tradition, there were two groups who staunchly upheld the Qur'anic ethics of divine mercy and advocated high moral standards of forgiveness and tolerance in Islam. The first and foremost of these groups were the Sufis, the second were the *Ahl-i Futuwwa* or people of chivalry. Nearly all the Persian Sufis, regardless of their religious sect and juridical school *(madhhab),* regarded 'Ali as the supreme chevalier, the prototype of the ideal Muslim knight in the chivalric tradition *(futuwwat)* of Islam.[35] He is always the *Sayyid al-Fityan,* who is the epitome of courage, generosity and selflessness.[36] Sufi authors in this context often cite a statement supposedly made by Muhammad to 'Ali: "O 'Ali! The chevalier is truthful, faithful, trustworthy, compassionate, a patron of the poor, extremely charitable and hospitable, a doer of good works and of modest demeanour."[37]

The Prophet's encomium of 'Ali here reflects the nature of the Qur'an itself, in which God's names relating to love and compassion are mentioned ten times more often than names related to wrath and severity. The image of 'Ali portrayed by Persian texts on chivalry reflects this predominance of mercy over wrath in the Muslim scripture,[38] where men and women are enjoined not to "despair of God's mercy! Surely, God forgives all sins." (XXXIX: 53). As Reza Shah-Kazemi in his chapter on 'Ali's notion of justice in this volume points out, "The capacity to act with compassion in no way conflicts with the demands of justice; rather, it is an intrinsic aspect of justice, conceived ontologically." This is because the divine reality itself *is* compassion and mercy, which "embraces all things," according to the Qur'anic dictum (VII: 156; XL: 7). "My mercy precedes My wrath" (as the celebrated Sacred Tradition informs us).

[35] Cf. Jalal al-Din Rumi's *Kulliyat-i Shams ya Divan-i Kabir,* ed. B. Furuzanfar (Tehran: Amir Kabir 1976), I, 155: 1770-73.

[36] "This view was associated with the saying *La fata illa 'Ali,* which had allegedly been uttered by a divine voice during the battle of Uhud." See E. Kohlberg, "'Ali b. Abi Taleb." ii. 'Ali as Seen by the Community," in *Encyclopedia Iranica,* I, p. 846. "The reality of chivalry is confined to two moral traits," writes Wa'iz-i Kashifi Sabziwari, both derived from 'Ali, "the first of these is to be of benefit and use to one's friends, which is realized through generosity *(sakhawat),* and the second is protect them from being harmed by their enemies, and that is found through courage *(shuja'at)* ... and verily, the perfection of both these traits could be found in 'Ali, for which reason he is the leader of the chevaliers of this community." *Futuwwat-nama-yi sultani,* p. 22.

[37] Cited by Rashid al-Din Maybudi, *Kashf al-asrar wa 'uddat al-abrar,* ed. 'Ali Asghar Hikmat (Tehran: Intisharat-i Danishgahi, 1952-60), V, p. 668.

[38] See Daud Rahbar's analysis of some 90 different concepts of divine Forgiveness in Qur'an: *God of Justice: A Study in the Ethical Doctrine of the Qur'an* (Leiden: E.J. Brill 1960).

The vast diffusion of the Islamic chivalric orders—or guilds supported by chevaliers—was an inseparable aspect of the socio-cultural history of classical Sufism throughout the Middle East. In the thirteenth century, centres of the *futuwwat* movement appeared all through Asia Minor such that, in the words of Ibn Battuta in his celebrated travelogue, "every city, oasis and village in Rum has its own group of *javanmardan* under the control of a superior called the *akhi*... The leader of each group has his own *zawiya* fully furnished with rugs, lighting and the other domestic necessities."[39] Although these leaders were usually from the artisan classes, their centres caused their doctrines to gain popularity, attracting the notables throughout Anatolia to join their company.[40]

During the twelfth and thirteenth centuries such fraternities of chivalry *(futuwwat)* with their own institutional structure seemed suddenly to proliferate throughout Anatolia and Persia. When the Abbasid Caliph al-Nasir li-Din Allah (577/1181-620/1223) attempted to establish a "pan-Islamic *futuwwa*" throughout the entire Muslim East, he was helped to implement his policies by the famous Sufi Shaykh Shihab al-Din Abu Hafs 'Umar Suhrawardi (d. 632/1234), who composed two *Treatises on Chivalry* in Persian.[41] In these treatises, passages from which are discussed below, Suhrawardi completely incorporated the ethics of Sufism into those of chivalry, thus becoming "the first of a series of writers in Persian to inaugurate a literary category which, in Irano-Turkish territories (and also in Egypt during the Ottoman period) was to continue until the beginning of modern times."[42]

The Caliph's invitation to neighbouring princedoms in the Middle East to join his *futuwwat* organization gave it the stamp of official State recognition and has, in fact, been termed "the most important historical event in Islamic chivalry. The most important by-product of this political movement was the tradition of Sufi chivalry *(futuwwat-i sufiya),*" espoused by Suhrawardi.[43] In accord with both

---

[39]Cited by M. Kiyani, *Tarikh-i khanaqah dar Iran* (Tehran: Kitabkhana Tahuri, 1369 A.H.sh./1990), p. 483. In fact, Ibn Batutta's entire stay in Anatolia was spent in either the *zawiya*s of the *Fati*s or the *Khanaqah*s of the Sufis.

[40]See Sadiq Gawharin, "Maktab-i fatiyan," in *A'in-i javamardi ya futuwwat* (New York: Bibliotheca Persica Press 2000), pp. 218-19

[41]Ed. M. Sarraf, in *Rasa'il-i javamardan,* French introduction and synopsis by H. Corbin (Tehran: French-Iran Institute, 1973), pp. 89-166.

[42]C. Cahen, s.v. *Futuwwa,* in EI². Also see H. Corbin's introduction to the *Rasa'il-i javamardan.*

[43]Ibid. An excellent overview of the history of *futuwwat* and its relation to Sufism is

Shi'ite and Sunni Islamic tradition, Caliph Nasir issued a proclamation *(manshur)* that 'Ali should be considered the 'supreme chevalier' or *Sayyid al-Fityan,* the Lord of the Chevaliers, "since all of the virtues and meritorious modes of conduct practised in chivalry derive from him."[44]

Classical chivalry was thus clearly and directly modelled on the practice of the companions of the Prophet, and in particular based on the conduct and character of 'Ali.[45] In fact, in a number of important Persian Sufi texts on chivalry he is often given the title of the 'Supreme Pole of the Chevaliers' *(qutb al-aqtab-i javanmardan).*[46] Innumerable stories in the Muslim chivalric tradition portray 'Ali as an expert in conflict resolution,[47] whose efforts to defuse conflict which could lead to permanent injury to any of the accused parties are constant and unrelenting. Although there was a significant difference of opinion in matters of jurisprudence between the chevaliers and the legalists (as between the Sufis and jurists), especially with respect to the application of the law of retribution *(qisas),* spiritual chivalry functioned as a kind of standard-bearer of a Sufi-'Alid Islamic morality based on tolerance, compassion and forgiveness. Even if the code of chivalry was to all appearances exoterically subservient to the canon Law of Islam *(Shari'a),* it was strictly differentiated from this Law by its predominately relaxed attitude towards exacting punishment for crimes, for which retaliation or punishment, legally speaking, could be due. Suhrawardi in one of his treatises clarifies this important distinction as follows:

> Although there are many things which are permissible according to the *Shari'a,* but forbidden according to humaneness *(murawwa)* and

also given by S.H. Nasr, "Spiritual Chivalry," in S.H. Nasr (ed.), *Islamic Spirituality,* II; *Manifestations* (New York: Crossroad 1991), pp. 304-15.

[44] Muhammad Ja'far Mahjub, *A'in-i javamardi ya futuwwat,* p. 62.

[45] The Prophet once referred to 'Ali as "the son and brother of the chevaliers," Wa'iz-i Kashifi Sabziwari relates. So 'Ali asked him, "Then who are my father and my brother amongst the chevaliers?" The Prophet informed him, "Your father was Abraham, and I am your brother. My chivalry derives from that of Abraham, while yours comes from me." *Futuwwat-nama-yi Sultani,* pp. 19-20.

[46] E.g. Kashani, *Tuhfat al-ikhwan fi khasa'is al-fityan,* ed. Sayyid Muhammad Damadi (Tehran: Intisharat-i 'ilmi u farhangi 1369 A.Hsh./1990), p. 260; and Kamal al-Din Husayn b. 'Ali Wa'iz-i Kashifi's (d. 910/1504) *Futuwwat-nama-yi Sultani,* ed. Ja'far Mahjub (Tehran: Bunyad-i farhang-i Iran 1350 A.Hsh./1971), p. 6. Also cf. Henry Corbin, *En Islam iranien: Aspects spirituels et philosophiques* (Paris: Éditions Gallimard 1971), IV, p. 413, 415-16.

[47] 'Ali thus remarked (Wa'iz-i Kashifi Sabziwari, *Futuwwat-nama,* p. 10) that "chivalry

chivalry *(futuwwa)*, this does not mean that chivalry and the *Shari'a* are opposed to each other. However, the character of the adherents of chivalry is that if someone does ill to them, they do something good to that person in response, while according to the *Shari'a*, one requites evil with evil.[48]

...It is true that there are several moral traits *(khislat)* which the Law approves of and condones but which chivalry forbids. Chivalry's disapproval of these moral traits is positively pleasing *(pasandida-ast)*, for they all relate to sacrificing one's own self-interest and personal share for the sake of another's comfort and convenience. ...Thus, adherents of chivalry believe that if someone insults you, you should pray for him; if someone deprives you of something, give him something when he is in need; if someone severs his ties with you, adhere to him faithfully and never desert him. If someone hits you, gouges out your eye or breaks your tooth, forgive him. This is the [true] chivalry and humaneness *(muruwwat)* and the essence of God's Word, the Qur'an, for forgiveness stems from divine Mercy *(rahmat)* while [seeking to exact] justice belongs to the Law *(shari'at)*.[49]

Here, the moral standpoint of spiritual chivalry appears to be for all practical purposes identical to the spirit of the words of Christ: "Love your enemies, bless them that curse you, do good to them that hate you, and pray for them which despitefully use you, and persecute you."[50] Christ's dictum is repeated almost verbatim in two anecdotes ascribed to the Prophet, the last of which is narrated on the authority of 'Ali[51] in the following Persian text on Sufi chivalry:

The Prophet once asked (his companions): "Can any of you behave like Abu Damdam?"

"Why? What was the conduct of Abu Damdam?" they asked.

"Every morning," he replied, Abu Damdam used to say, "O God, I have given away my name and reputation as alms to the one who has treated me unjustly. The one who strikes me, I will not strike back, and the one who blames me I will not blame, and I'll do no ill to the one who harms and treats me unjustly.

is that you have no enemies, whether in this world or the next."

[48] *Rasa'il javanmardan*, p. 105.

[49] *Rasa'il javanmardan*, p. 106.

[50] Matthew V: 44

[51] A special homology between the person of Christ and that of 'Ali is often found in Sufi texts, as Henry Corbin points out, *En Islam iranien*, I, pp. 282-83.

And Amir al-Mu'minin 'Ali declared that once when the Prophet was asked about the meaning of good humour and character *(husn-i khulq),* he replied that it is that one "act with generosity towards anyone who hinders you; adhere to anyone who severs their ties with you, and forgive anyone who does you ill."

Now, the perfection of chivalry is comprised by these moral traits, insofar as in the Qur'an (XLI: 34) it is related: "The fair and foul deed are not alike. Parry the foul deed with what is fairer, and then behold, the one between whom and yourself was enmity will become an intimate friend."[52]

By means of a tale concerning the comportment of the 'Ali who was ordered to investigate a charge of unlawful sexual behaviour brought before the Prophet by one of his followers, Suhrawardi successfully illustrates 'Ali's incarnation of the precedence of the virtue of mercy and forgiveness in Islam over application of the letter of the Law through the following tale:

In the time of the Prophet — may the blessings of God be upon him — a person came to him and said, "O Prophet of God! I saw a strange man with my wife in my house doing such and such a thing, so I closed the door of my house and have come here to ask for justice from the Prophet."

The Prophet—peace be upon him—turned away from the man and said nothing. The man repeated his entreaty a second time… Again the Prophet kept his silence. But again the man reiterated his complaint, "O Prophet of God, the circumstances are just as stated. I demand justice!"

The Prophet looked furiously at the man and said, "Have you seen it with your own eyes?"

"Yes." he said. "I have witnessed it myself."

The Prophet turned to the Prince of the Faithful, 'Ali and said, "Go, O 'Ali, enter this burgher's house and look *correctly.*"

A question here arises: Why did the Prophet send 'Ali and not someone else? Although he commanded Bilal to perform certain tasks, why did he especially designate 'Ali to attend to this task? The answer is that if he had sent other people, they would not have had the same knowledge to which 'Ali had access, for they would have gone into the house and have given witness to exactly what they saw there. 'Ali, on the other hand, was wiser than all of them, more famed for his chivalry than anyone else, and for this the Prophet

---

[52] Kashani, *Tuhfat al-ikhwan fi khasa'is al-fityan,* p. 277.

himself stated, "There is no *fata* (chevalier) but 'Ali; there is no sword but *dhu'l-faqar.*"[53]

Now, one part of chivalry consists in the concealment of faults *(sitari)*. Therefore, the Prophet sent 'Ali, knowing that he would go to the house and return, with a testimony based on reason, such that both his testimony would be correct, while demonstrating the other man's testimony to be false.

The purpose of all this is that the adultery remain concealed, for God is the Concealer of faults and the Forgiver of sins.

So 'Ali went to the door of that house, opened it and went inside. Closing his eyes tightly, he walked around inside the house, then returned to the door and left the house with his eyes still shut. He returned to the Prophet and said, "I swear by God that I saw no one at all in that house."

– Now 'Ali spoke truthfully, for he had closed his eyes, so that he indeed saw no one and it is for that reason that the Prophet said, "I am the city of knowledge and 'Ali is its gate."[54]

This story, retold a century later in another Persian work on Sufi chivalry[55] by the Suhrawardi Sufi Shaykh 'Abd al-Razzaq Kashani, (d. 792/1329), author of many important Arabic and Persian Sufi theosophical works, forms an exact Muslim parallel to Jesus' maxim, "Judge not, and ye shall not be judged; contemn not, and ye shall not be contemned: forgive, and ye shall be forgiven,"[56] which Alexander Pope in his Universal Prayer paraphrased thus in verse:

Teach me to feel another's woe,
To hide the fault I see;
That mercy I to others show,
That mercy show to me.

This tale also neatly parallels another parable of Jesus, that of the unjust servant, in which a foreman is punished for harshly judging his underling for the very fault that he has displayed himself (Matt. XVIII: 22-35). 'Ali's apparent excess in mercy, his outward injustice in fulfilling the letter of the *Shari'a* law[57] is practised in the name of

---

[53] On the interior hermeneutical senses of this sentence in the context of Persian chivalry, see Corbin, *En Islam iranien,* IV, p. 416; 427

[54] *Rasa'il javanmardan,* pp. 108-9.

[55] Kashani, *Tuhfat al-ikhwan fi khasa'is al-fityan,* , p. 230.

[56] Luke, VI: 37

[57] There are those who would interpret these tales of 'Ali's tolerance of sexual misconduct, his willingness to cast the veil of divine forgiveness over the face of

a compassion[58] that is actually 'higher' than the mere letter of that law, a tolerance and mercy identical to that of the father in the Gospel parable of the Prodigal Son (Luke XV: 11-32), and one and the same with Jesus's forgiveness of the woman taken in adultery (John VIII: 1-11). The English mystical poet William Blake's verses in defence of Jesus's teaching on forgiveness, celebrating his failure to fulfil the law and command of Moses regarding stoning the woman taken "in the very act" of adultery, capture the spirit of 'Ali in the above story exactly:

> Mutual Forgiveness of each Vice,
> Such are the Gates of Paradise.
> Against the Accuser's chief desire,
> Who walk'd among the Stones of Fire,
> Jehovah's Finger Wrote the Law:

human sin, as idle indulgence. But this is to miss the point of these stories altogether. Righteousness consists in beholding one's *own* sin, not in exposing the sins of one's neighbour, as several of the Prophet's pronouncements affirm, *viz.* "If a person conceals the weakness of another in this world, God will conceal such a one's weakness in the Hereafter," (Ghazali, *Kitab Adab al-suhbah wa'l-mu'asharah ma'ah asnaf al-khalq*, ed. M.S. al-Mu'ini [Baghdad: Matba'at al-'ani 1984], p. 344); and "Do not harm Muslims, and do not revile them, and do not pursue their imperfections [which might also be translated: 'do not seek to divulge their genitalia' or 'do not seek to bare their privates']. For indeed, whosoever persecutes and hounds a brother for his defects (private parts, genitalia), shall have his own imperfections hounded by God." (cited by Muhammad Asad, *Principles of State and Government in Islam* [Berkeley: University of California Press 1966], p. 85; Mohammad Hashim Kamali, *Freedom of Expression in Islam* [Cambridge: Islamic Texts Society 1997], p. 124)

Furthermore, there are two powerful legal impediments to reporting adultery in Islam: (1) the *shari'a* stipulates that four witnesses are required to establish the guilt of both parties; and (2) as a deterrent to calumny and compromising the integrity of the innocent, the *shari'a* applies a maximum penalty of 80 lashes for false accusation and libel *(iftira')* to anyone who accuses a man or woman of adultery, yet cannot produce four witnesses to validate his or her testimony. (see Kamali, *Freedom of Expression in Islam*, p. 175). Numerous stories highlight the fact that 'Ali understood both the legal impediments and moral restraints which must be exercised regarding such delicate cases. It is related that once 'Umar b. al-Khattab was patrolling Medina at night and saw a man and woman committing adultery. The following day he summoned the other Companions, and asked them if he should enforce the required penalty for adultery on the basis of what he had witnessed during the night. 'Ali pointed out to him that the law required four witnesses to prove an accusation of adultery, and as caliph, he was legally bound to honour this stipulation as much as any private citizen. In his citation of this story, Ghazali notes that "this is strong evidence that the *Shari'a* demands the concealment of sins (*satr al-fawahish*); it also discourages spying on or reporting the private affairs of others." (Ghazali, *Kitab Adab al-Suhbah,* pp. 345-46, cited by Kamali, *Freedom of Expression,* p. 125).

[58] Compassion for sinners, and concealment of sin is a leitmotif of the sayings and sermons of 'Ali collected in the *Nahj al-balagha;* e.g. his adage: "Do not hurry to expose

Then Wept! Then rose in Zeal & Awe,
And in the midst of Sinai's heat
Hid it beneath his Mercy Seat.[59]

Here 'Ali's chivalric conduct, which is commended by the Prophet
as a kind of 'true lie' that is ethically higher than the 'false truth' of
those Puritan divines who pharisaically advocate the legal punishment
for adultery and lechery,[60] also recalls this advice of St. Paul: "Brethren,
if a man be overtaken by a fault, ye which are spiritual, restore such
an one in the spirit of meekness; considering thyself, lest thou also be
tempted. Bear ye one another's burdens, and so fulfil the law of Christ.
For if a man think himself to be something, when he is nothing, he
deceiveth himself" (Galatians, VI, 1-3)

the fault and reveal the sin of anyone, for perhaps they may be forgiven..." (*Nahj
al-balagha*, Arabic text with Persian translation by Ja'far Shahidi, [Tehran: Intisharat-i
'ilmi u farhangi 1368 A.Hsh./ 1999], p. 137).

[59] *Blake: Complete Writings*, ed. G. Keynes (London: OUP 1972), p. 761.

[60] Another story told by Suhrawardi about 'Ali's attitude towards forgiveness of sexual
sin illustrates that this was the case even more vividly:

"...One day, the Commander of the Faithful ('Ali) said to the Prophet: "O Prophet
of God, certain people came to visit you today, bringing with them another Muslim.
On encountering me, they offered their salutations and stopped. I asked after their
business. They told me they were on their way to see you. Again I asked them their
business.

"A man and a woman have committed adultery. We are going to testify against
them to the Prophet of God, so that they can be stoned—so that the legal penalty
may be properly administered." they declared

"Begone," I said, "forsake your testimony! Busy yourselves in some other occupation which gives you some merit in this world and some benefit in the hereafter. What
sort of business is it anyway, which you intend?"

"But," they contested, "the command of God is that the adulterer/adulteress
should be scourged by the lash." [as per the Qur'an XXIV: 2: "The adulterer and
adulteress, scourge each one of them (with) a hundred stripes. And do not let pity for
the twain withhold you from obedience to God, if you believe in God and the Last
Day. And let a party of believer witness their punishment."]

I said, "Yes, I believe in the word of God and I verify the word of the Prophet,
but if you shut your eyes and turn a blind eye to this, and withdraw your testimony,
the spiritual reward will be much greater." In this manner I discouraged them, and
would not allow them access to the Prophet.

When I had related all of this to the Prophet, he commented: "Your behaviour
in this matter was delightful to God and myself who am his Prophet. You will receive
your just reward for this deed both in the world and in the hereafter on the Plain of
the Day of Resurrection when all humankind is denuded [before God]. Because you
covered over the sins of those two Muslims, and refused to rend their veil, you will
be garbed in the robes of paradise." (*Rasa'il javanmardan*, pp. 114-5.)

Perhaps it is not irrelevant to note here that in Shi'ite Islam, 'Ali is traditionally
celebrated for his incredible sexual potency (see Shahla Haeri, *Law of Desire: Tem-*

In the debate between heartless severity and boundless mercy, between blind adherence to legal premises and empathetic intuition of spiritual facts, between pharisaic virtue which is in truth no virtue, and clemency and forbearance which the exercise of love awards the pure in heart, few authors speak with greater authority than Walter Pater. In an essay devoted to *Measure for Measure*, Shakespeare's play where the same moral dilemma confronted by 'Ali in the foregoing tale is faced by a hypocritical jurist who presides over a case of apparent adultery, abiding by the norms and laws of human justice while assuming the infallible position of the supreme Judge, Pater writes:

> The idea of justice involves the idea of rights. But at bottom rights are equivalent to that which really is, to facts; and the recognition of his rights therefore, the justice he requires of our hands, or our thoughts, is the recognition of that which the person, in his inmost nature, really is; and as sympathy alone can discover that which really is in matters of feeling and thought, true justice is in its essence a finer knowledge through love. It is for this finer justice, a justice based on a more delicate appreciation of the true conditions of men and things, a true respect of persons in our estimate of actions that the people in *Measure for Measure* cry out for as they pass before our eyes..."[61]

'Ali's conduct reflects precisely this "finer justice" based on love which refuses to confound morality with outward righteousness and will not regard only the observances of the law as real virtue, disdaining to prefer the niceties of ritual over the spirit of righteousness. The outward commissions and omissions of the law cannot amount to virtue according to 'Ali, for all morality begins and ends in the rendering of "the deeds of mercy" as "we do prey for mercy."[62] 'Ali's own "deeds of mercy" and his willingness to forgive rather than punish offenders when faced with apparent cases of adultery and theft, is consistently

porary Marriage in Islam [Syracuse: Syracuse University Press 1989], p. 170), having fathered fourteen sons and nineteen daughters by nine wives and several concubines (H.A.R. Gibb, "'Ali b. Abi Talib," EI², I, p. 385).

[61] Walter Pater, "Measure for Measure" in idem, *Appreciations: with an Essay on Style* (London: 1890), pp. 176-91, cited in George L. Geckle (ed.), *Measure for Measure: 1783-1920*, (London: Athlone Press 2001), pp. 166-67

[62] Shakespeare, Merchant of Venice, IV: i, 197-98.

[63] See Amir Sijzi, *Fawa'id al-fu'ad,* trans. B.B. Lawrence, *Nizam ad-Din Awliya: Morals for the Heart,* (New York: Paulist Press 1992), pp. 301, 358.

[64] H.A.R. Gibb, "'Ali b. Abi Talib," EI², I, p. 385.

stressed by a number of Persianate Sufi masters, among whom the great Chishti saint Nizam al-Din Awliya' (d. 725/1325) may be counted. [63]

Although scholars such as H.A.R. Gibb, distracted by their exclusive focus on the political aspect of 'Ali b. Abi Talib's career, mistakenly judge that a mere outward "obedience to the divine Law was the keynote of his conduct" and assert that "his ideas were governed by an excessive rigorism,"[64] a closer examination of his ethics reveals exactly the contrary: the predominance of mercy and forgiveness in his thought. Analysing the famous letter from 'Ali to Malik al-Ashtar (also subject of Reza Shah-Kazemi's chapter on 'Ali's 'justice' in this volume), Abdulaziz Sachedina reveals that the so-called 'eye for an eye' doctrine of retribution *(qisas)* described in Qur'an II: 179, which dictates that "the law of fair retribution is a source of life," has been interpreted by most Muslim jurists as meaning "retributive justice as a process of rehabilitation rather than as a cycle of violence of the sort common in the pre-Islamic tribal culture of revenge." Therefore,

> Reconciliation flows from forgiveness and willingness on the part of the victim to forego retribution as an end in itself. From the Koranic admonition to forgive and accept compensation, it seems retributive punishment is worth pursuing only to the extent that it leads to reconciling (*shifa' al-sudur* = 'healing of the heart') the victim and the wrongdoer, and rehabilitating the latter after his or her acknowledgement of responsibility.[65]

'Ali 's understanding of retribution or retaliation as just such a 'healing of the heart' rather than lust for punishment and quest for revenge appears clearly in the following set of anecdotes related by Suhrawardi:

> In the same manner, the word of God declares, "Retaliation is prescribed for you in the matter of the murdered: freeman for freeman, slave for slave, female for female [Koran I 178]." Thus, in the era of the Prince of the Believers, 'Ali—may God be content with him—a man who had unjustly slain another man, was brought by some people before 'Ali. 'Ali said, "You tell me that the punishment of 'retaliation... in the matter of the murdered' is necessary to be meted out to him as commanded by the word of God. But you

[65] Abdulaziz Sachedina, *The Islamic Roots of Democratic Pluralism* (Oxford: OUP 2001), pp. 111-12.

[66] *Rasa'il-i javamardan,* p. 106.

[67] *Rasa'il-i javamardan,* pp. 106-08.

could have interceded for him yourselves, saying, 'Do not take him to task for this crime. This man's destiny was so ordained: in Pre-eternity the Divine Pen had written down this deed; it was the hand of Fate. The Angel of Death arrived, and mounted this person on the horse of ignorance [so that he perform this deed]. Forgive him and let me atone for the blood he has spilled.' 'Ali himself went to great lengths to intercede for the man, such that if the wounded party refused to accept his intercession, he would offer to pay his blood-money in order to satisfy them … In the end, he made peace between all the opposing parties and resolved the problem.[66]

And if a person had committed theft and was brought before the Commander of the Faithful, with proof of his theft, he would first order that his hand be cut off according to the text of the Word of God: 'As for the thief, both male and female, cut off the hands of both. It is the recompense of their own deeds, an exemplary punish-ment from Allah.' (Qur'an V 38). Then he would say:

"It is correct that his hand be cut off, but [let us not cut off his hand] and forgive him for my sake anyway. Let me atone for his crime, for this thing that he stole was not your divinely allotted portion. This poor man has been afflicted by the tides of fate and destiny did him a bad turn. Satan tempted him and drove him from the straight path of piety. I myself will pay you back for all the goods he has stolen."[67]

'Ali's 'justice beyond the letter of the law' in this context functions as a bold precursor to later Sufi antinomianism; his attitude here is in fact the guiding spirit behind later Muslim mystics' indifference towards "forbidding wrong,"[68] and their view that such matters reflect "a desiccated pietism which is irrelevant to the inner values of Sufism."[69] 'Ali's tolerance—always prepared to plead the cause of mercy against the rigors of the law and to cast out the beam in his own eye before beholding the mote in his brother's[70]—also anticipates the radical moral theology of his direct heir in the Sufi tradition, Hasan al-Basri (d. 110/728).[71] Inspiration drawn from 'Ali's conduct in such

---

[68] Michael Cook points out that "an inspection of the tables of contents of the classical handbooks of Sufism rapidly reveals that forbidding wrong is just not a Sufi topic." *Commanding Right and Forbidding Wrong in Islamic Thought* (Cambridge: CUP 2000), p. 460.

[69] Ibid., p. 465.

[70] Matthew, vii: 3.

[71] Cf. The following two sayings of Hasan:

"O son of Adam, you will never realize the reality of faith *(iman)* until you abandon reproaching other men for faults that you yourself possess and begin to rectify them these defects within yourself. Therefore, first rectify these imperfections in yourself!

anecdotes pervades the piety of the mediæval Qalandari dervishes and the *qalandariyya* genre of Persian poetry as well.[72] His teachings can be seen reflected in a verse by the *qalandar* Persian Sufi poet 'Iraqi (d. 688/1289), which serves as a poetic apologia for 'Ali's deliberate merciful 'shutting of the eye':

> In my wallet as long as cash
> of 'good' or 'evil' can be found
> On the street of the people of chivalry
> I'll never have any circulation.[73]

In sum, the main virtues of 'Ali's *shari'a,* upon which the code of Islamic *Futuwwa* was later founded, constitute an antithesis to all forms of militant fanaticism that not only reduce the religion of Islam to its legal dimensions alone, but also applies this legalistically defined religion in the most literalist manner.[74] Such forms of Islam, playing

---

If you attend to your own faults, you will find yourself too preoccupied to busy yourself with others." From Ghazali's *Ihya',* cited in Javad Nurbakhsh, *Hasan Basri: pir-i payravan-i tariqat u rahnama-yi javanmardan* (London: Khanaqah-i Ni'matu'llahi 1375 A.Hsh / 1996), pp. 173-74.

"Do not summon people to God until you have first purified yourself. Satan desires nothing more than for us to vainly ornament our hearts with the bare letter of this mission, and so close the door to 'enjoining righteousness and eschewing evil' to our own souls." ('Attar, *Tadhkirat al-awliya',* p. 34)

[72] 'Ali is a key figure in the antinominian Sufi theologies of the Abdals of Rum and the Haydari qalandars of 15th century Anatolia (see Ahmet Karamustafa, *God's Unruly Friends: Dervish Groups in the Islamic Later Middle Period, 1200-1550* [Salt Lake City: University of Utah Press 1994], pp. 46, 67-71; see pp. 32ff. for a good discussion of the ethics of the qalandar in Persian thought and literature). 'Ali also plays a central role in Bektashi Sufi doctrine: see John Birge, *The Bektashi Order of Dervishes* (London: Luzac & Co. 1937), pp. 134-40. Among the Qalandars, 'Ali is celebrated with the sobriquet: the 'King of Lamps' *(Shah-chiragh):* see Abu Talib Mir-'abidini & Mihran Afshari, *Ayin-i Qalandari, mushtamal bar Chahar risala dar bab-i qalandari, khaksari, firqa-yi 'ajam u sukhanvari* (Tehran: Intisharat-i Fararavan 1374 A.Hsh/1995), p. 37. Although the role of 'Ali in the Shi'ite Sufi tradition has not been covered in this essay, it is worth drawing attention to a lengthy *Futuwwat-nama-yi Amir al-Mu'minin ('Ali's Book of Chivalry),* included in an anonymous Sufi treatise on the Qalandar Path (published in *ibid.,* pp. 142-46), composed in 1079, where the *qalandari* rites of shaving the scalp are traced back to ceremonies conducted by the Prophet and 'Ali *(ibid.,* pp. 145-46)

[73] *Divan-i 'Iraqi,* ed. M. Darvish (Tehran: Javidan, n.d.), p. 132.

[74] As can be seen from the above stories, 'Ali's *shari'a* is the exact opposite of contemporary theories of criminal law preached and inspired by Wahhabi theologians, who have often been referred to by mainstream Muslim jurists as the modern-day ideological successors of Khawarij who assassinated 'Ali: see Khaled Abou El Fadl *et al., The Place of Tolerance in Islam* (Boston: Beacon Press 2002), pp. 8-9.

the role of the stern *Censor morum*, have bound the spiritual desires of mystical Islam with the briars of nomocentric prejudice and bias, mutilating the Sufis' 'religion of love' *(madhhab-i 'ishq)* into a severe creed which is all observance of the Sabbath and total ignorance of the needs of man. The image of 'Ali in the Persian Sufi tradition is that of a mystic who preached turning the other cheek, seeing and hearing no evil, patience under affliction, acting with good conduct and cheer to harsh and unfair treatment.

The spiritual and ethical teachings of 'Ali as viewed from *within* the Islamic Sufi tradition have so far been the focus of this study. At this juncture it will be useful to consider the relevance that his teachings have in a significant extra-Islamic context, namely in the ongoing metaphysical dialogue shared historically between Platonic, Islamic and Christian mystical theologies.[75]

In his chapter on the explicitly 'sacral' nature of 'Ali's teachings in his letter to Malik al-Ashtar, Reza Shah-Kazemi rightly contrasts the horizontal human morality, and purely individual conception of justice, "according to a secular 'moral philosophy'," (p. 67) with the vertical (Platonic) conception of justice in which man contemplates the divine reality from which all virtue flows. Since, as Shah-Kazemi notes, so many of 'Ali's pronouncements are placed effectively "beyond religion," transcending "the level of morality, offering us insights derived from a direct vision of the ultimate spiritual realities" (p. 68), they are also "beyond politics," as it is narrowly conceived and for this reason they can actually help refashion the "moral substance of political consciousness." The teachings of 'Ali, particularly those teachings adopted by the Persian Sufi chivalric tradition described above, thus seem to serve as a Muslim counterpart to the sort of universal morality eulogized by Alexander Pope's (d. 1744) verses:

> For Modes of Faith, let graceless zealots fight;
> His can't be wrong whose life is in the right:
> In Faith and Hope the world will disagree
> But all Mankind's concern is Charity:

---

[75] For a preliminary study of which, see my "The Esoteric Christianity of Islam: Interiorisation of Christian Imagery in Medieval Persian Sufi Poetry," in Lloyd Ridgeon, ed. *Muslim Interpretations of Christianity* (London: Curzon Press 2000): 127-56.

[76] Essay on Man, IV, 307-09

[77] Cf. William Chittick, *Faith and Practice of Islam: three Thirteenth Century Sufi Texts* (Albany: SUNY 1992), p. 13.

> All must be false that thwart that One great End
> And all of God, that bless Mankind and mend.[76]

No doubt, the actual socio-political context of 'Ali's teachings is exclusively *Islamic* – insofar as they presuppose obedience to *Shari'a* commands – but the actual conception of *virtue* on which they are based is *a priori* innate in the soul, accessible to all human beings, and inclusively capable of being *felt* and *tasted* (as in Pope's verses cited *infra*) by all, regardless of their outward religious affiliation or sectarian denomination. ("Spiritual consciousness is thus to be seen as the source of moral conscience" as Shah-Kazemi writes).

'Ali's doctrine in this sense transcends the dichotomy of separative religious identities. Indeed, the notion of felicity or bliss (*sa'adat*) in Islam[77] parallels the doctrine of 'benevolence' or 'virtue' in Christianity. Pope's verses on the metaphysical source of 'virtue' in this regard merit citation:

> Know then this truth (enough for Man to know)
> 'Virtue alone is happiness below'.
> The only point where human bliss stands still,
> And tastes the good without the fall to ill,
> Where only Merit constant pay receives,
> Is blest in what it takes and what it gives,
> The joy unequal'd, if its end it gain,
> And if it lose, attended with no pain:
> Without satiety, tho' ever so blest,
> And but more relish'd as the more distress'd.
> The broadest mirth unfeeling folly wears,
> Less pleasing far than Virtue's very tears.
> Good, from each object, from each place acquir'd,
> For ever exercised, yet never tir'd,
> Never elated, while one man's oppressed;
> Never dejected, while another's bless'd...[78]

The dichotomy between the secular and sacred conceptions of justice underscored by Dr. Shah-Kazemi in his chapter is not meant to dogmatically invalidate all non-religious moral codes, nor to reject self-validating intuitive ethical knowledge independent of divine revelation,

[78] Pope, *Essay on Man*, IV: 309-24
[79] The well-known hadith states: 'Actions will be judged according to their subtle intentions'.
[80] See Majid Fakhry, *Ethical Theories in Islam* (Leiden: Brill 1994), p. 78ff. Later

but simply to emphasize the fundamental commonplace premise of a Sufi moral theology, that every action is always weighed in the balance of the actor's intention, according the Prophet's word.[79] The intentional theory of action of course did not originate with Muhammad. It had been enunciated in ancient Greece by Aristotle in his *Nichomachean Ethics* (9.8.7): "The conferring of a benefit where a return is not sought is morally acceptable, and the value of a gift is not to be judged by its intrinsic worth but by the spirit of the giver."[80]

The emphasis in most pre-modern ethical theory, whether Christian or Islamic, is on the interior attitude of the doer, held to be of paramount importance in one's performance of charitable deeds— more important than the actual deed in fact. If 'Ali's doctrine of justice is extracted from the "highly emotional and violent"[81] hothouse sectarian milieu of early Medina and Kufa, where he ruled, and put within a more universal context of religious moral theory, it comes quite close to later Muslim Sufis' moral intuition of a universal 'religion of love' (*madhhab-i 'ishq*), which, as Rumi put it, is "beyond all formal religious denominations".[82] Incidentally, this same doctrine of justice appeared amongst the Cambridge Platonists, such as Henry More (1614-87),[83] whom Alexander Pope paraphrases (in lines following those just cited), when he exhorts his reader to

> See! the sole bliss which Heav'n could on all bestow;
> Which who but feels can taste, but thinks can know:
> Yet poor with fortune, and with learning blind,
> The bad must miss; the good, untaught, will find;
> Slave to no sect, who takes no private road,
> But looks thro' Nature, up to Nature's God;
> Pursues that Chain which links th' immense design,
> Joins heav'n and earth, and mortal and divine;
> Sees, that no being any bliss can know,
> But touches some above, some below;
> Learns, from this Union of the rising Whole,
> The first, last purpose of the human soul;

translated into Arabic by Ishaq Ibn Hunayn (d. 911), this work had a tremendous impact on the development of later Islamic philosophical and Sufi ethics.

[81] Syed Husain Mohammad Jafri, *The Origins and Development of Shi'ite Islam*, p. 94.

[82] *Mathnawi*, ed. Nicholson, II: 1770.

[83] Cf. Henry More, "On Liberty of Conscience," in David George Mullan (ed.), *Religious Pluralism in the West* (Oxford: Blackwell 1998), pp. 159-65.

[84] Pope, Essay on Man, IV: 327-340

[85] See Khwaja Nasir al-Din Tusi, *Akhlaq-i Nasiri* [I: 3] (Tehran: Intisharat-i Khwarazmi

And knows where Faith, Law, Morals, all began,
And end, in LOVE of GOD, and LOVE of MAN.[84]

That pivotal point "where human bliss stands still," described by Pope above, corresponds in Islamic philosophical ethics to what later Muslim philosophers such as Nasir al-Din Tusi (d. 672/1273),[85] Jalal al-Din Dawwani (d. 907/1501)[86] as well as Akbarian Sufi sages like Shaykh Mahmud Shabistari (d. after 741/1340) [87] and Muhammad Lahiji (d. 912/1507)[88] propounded as 'perfect Justice *('adalat)'* and 'sound equilibrium (*i'tidal*)' – which are the 'perfection' (the Aristotlean 'golden mean')[89] and the fulfilment of the three Platonic virtues of wisdom, courage, and temperance, resulting from the perfect harmony of the three faculties (rational, irascible, concupiscent) of the Soul.[90] In his essay in this volume, M. Ali Lakhani describes this same pivotal point of human virtue "where bliss stands still" as constituting the 'proper place' where Truth and Justice are found, being a spiritual centre that lies simultaneously at the deepest level of Being and in the depths of one's own being. This same "Union of the rising Whole,/ The first, last purpose of the human soul" (in Pope's lines cited above)

1360 A.Hsh./ 1981), p. 109.

[86] See Dawwani's *Akhlaq-i Jalali* (Lucknow: lithograph edition, n.d.), pp. 48-50.

[87] See his *Gulshan-i raz* in Samad Muwahhid (ed.), *Majmu'a-i athar-i Shaykh Mahmud Shabistari,* (Tehran: Kitabkhana-i Tahuri 1365 A.Hsh./1986), vv. 594-606. Pope (vv. 311-12) seems to actually paraphrase Shabistari's verse 607: "The appearance of Goodness (*niku'i*) is in 'sound equilibrim' (*i'tidal*)'. The summit of physical perfection lies in 'Justice or equipoise (*'idalat*)'."

[88] Muhammad Lahiji, *Mafatih al-i'jaz fi sharh-i Gulshan-i raz,* ed. Muhammad Rida Barzgar Khaliqi and 'Iffat Karbasi, (Tehran: Zawwar 1371 A.Hsh./1992), p. 401, commenting on v. 607 (ibid.) notes that "justice (*'idalat*) is constituted by harmonious equipoise (*masawat*), and that cannot be obtained without unity (*wahdat*) ... which unity itself *is* Justice."

[89] The doctrine of the golden mean also appears in this saying of 'Ali: "The best actions are those pertaining to the intermediate course *(al-namat al-awsat)."* In Fakhry, *op. cit,* p. 160, n. 8.

[90] Fakhry, *Ethical Theories in Islam,* pp. 111ff. Fazlur Rahman ("Aklaq," *Encyclopedia Iranica,* I, p. 722.) underscores the metaphysical nature of Tusi's concept of justice: "From Tusi onward, the Muslim ethical writers begin to stress the virtue of justice. One reason for this is that, since the essence of all virtue is the 'mean' between extremes, justice itself constitutes the essence of all 'means'. Thus a person who has justice (*'adala*) necessarily has all other virtues as well. Tusi, who devotes a separate chapter to justice, squarely grounds it in his metaphysical doctrine (*Aklaq,* pp. 114ff.). Unity is the absolute good and is, in fact, God himself; those things that are nearer to God have the greatest share of unity. Unity and justice are twins, as it were, since, in the same way that lack of unity is diversity, lack of justice is the antagonistic plurality of extremes; hence, unity is the same as 'balance', a positive unity synthesizing extremes."

is also rhapsodised by Plato in his ecstatic account of the soul's ascent to the summit of contemplation:

> It is there that true being dwells, without color or shape, that cannot be touched; reason alone, the soul's pilot, can behold it, and all true knowledge is knowledge thereof. Now even as the mind of a god is nourished by reason and knowledge, so also is it with every soul that has a care to receive her proper food; wherefore when at last she has beheld being she is well content, and contemplating truth she is nourished and prospers, until the heaven's revolution brings her back full circle. And while she is borne round, she discerns justice, its very self, and likewise temperance, and knowledge, not the knowledge that is neighbour to becoming and varies with the various objects to which we commonly ascribe being, but the veritable knowledge of being that veritably is.[91]

III. 'Ali, Champion of the Art of Spiritual Combat

When it comes to discussions centred around the practice of *jihad* in Islam, 'Ali's name is always mentioned as one of the foremost champions of the campaigns of early Islam. It is well known that along with Hamza and Zubayr, 'Ali was renowned for his single-handed charges against the enemy; at Badr he was said to have killed more than a third of the enemy single-handedly, for instance.[92] However, among the Sufis, 'Ali's moral might rather than physical prowess is more often celebrated. Just as 'Ali always appears as a champion of conflict resolution and forgiveness in the above stories narrated by Suhrawardi, it is his knightly character on the battlefield rather than his skill as a fighter which Sufis praised. This character is reflected in Junayd's mystical view of 'Ali as a 'holy warrior' narrated by 'Attar:

> A sayyid [descendant of the Prophet] named Nasiri was preparing to set out on the Pilgrimage journey. When he reached Baghdad, he went to visit Junayd. They exchanged greetings, and the master asked where he was coming from. When the visitor said that he was from Gilan (Gilan) [Iran's northwestern Caspian Sea province], the

---

[91] Phaedrus, 247d. trans. R. Hackforth, in *Plato: The Collected Dialogues,* ed. Edith Hamilton and Huntington Cairns, Bollingen Series 71 (Princeton: Princeton University Press 1999, 17th printing), p. 494.

[92] I.K. Poonawala, "'Ali b. Abi Talib. 1. Life," in *Encyclopedia Iranica,* I, p. 839.

[93] 'Attar, *Tadhkirat al-awliya'*, p. 436.

[94] Rumi's source for this tale is apparently Ghazali's *Ihya' 'ulum al-din;* see Badi' al-

master asked about his genealogy. The visitor claimed descent from the Prophet's cousin and son-in-law, 'Ali. The master said:

"Your forefather 'Ali wielded his sword against two foes: the unbelievers and his passionate soul (nafs). You say you are his descendant," continued the master, "but against which of these two foes do you wield your sword?"

At these words the sayyid burst into tears, Throwing himself down before the master, he cried, "O master! My Pilgrimage is here! Show me the way to God!"

"This breast of yours," said the master, "is the elect sanctuary of God. Try your best not to let anything profane enter these sacred precincts."

"So be it," affirmed the visitor.[93]

'Ali's balancing of spiritual struggle with military warfare expressed by Junayd's Sufi view in the above anecdote is best understood by studying the tale in the first book of Rumi's Mathnawi (I: 3721ff.) concerning Ali's encounter with a man who spat in his face during mortal combat on the field of battle.[94] Instead of slaying his foe in 'retaliation' for this gesture of abuse, 'Ali stepped back and left off the fight. Stunned by this change of tactics, he asked 'Ali why he did not kill him when he spat in his face. "I am fighting to quell anger, not because I am stirred by anger," came the reply. In choosing to refrain from battle until vanquishing his own anger, 'Ali thus appears in Rumi's account as the supreme model of the Sufi ethics of forgiveness. He distinguishes himself by conquering psychological foes and interior enemies: anger and lust, thus exemplifying the virtue of forbearance (hilm),[95] proving also by his selfless and altruistic conduct[96] that an ethics of mercy and forgiveness animates his conduct. "Anyone not adept in prayer is swept away by the wind of anger, the wind of lust, the wind of greed,"[97] Rumi moralizes.

In brief, 'Ali incarnates the Sufi ethic of forgiveness. The "sword of merciful self-restraint" (tigh-i hilm), as Rumi calls it,[98] that he wields is sharper than any sabre of steel. His martial prowess on the battlefield

Zaman Furuzanfar, Makhadh-i qisas u tamthilat-i Mathnawi (Tehran: Amir Kabir 1362 A.Hsh./ 1983; 3rd ed.), p. 37, no. 33.

[95] Mathnawi, I: 3746, 3763

[96] Ibid., I: 3787-91

[97] Ibid., I: 3796

[98] Ibid., I: 3746.

[99] Mathnawi, I: 3988-89

[100] See D. T. Suzuki's Zen and Japanese Culture (New York: Bolligen Series LXIV,

is subordinate to his subjugation of passion. His real courage lies in the application of the difficult morality of Sufi contemplative disciplines on the battlefield of daily life.[99] In this respect, he resembles the Japanese Zen Buddhist swordsman, whose aim is to wield the ego-less 'Sword of Mystery'.[100] Transitory and temporal as his forbearance was—occasioned by a chance incident on a battlefield in ancient Arabia—the moral admonition derived from his conduct is as universal as these verses of Shakespeare:

> He who the sword of heaven will bear
> Should be as holy as severe:
> Pattern in himself to know,
> Grace to stand, and virtue, go:
> More nor less to others paying
> Than by self-offences weighing.
> Shame to him whose cruel striking
> Kills for faults of his own liking.[101]

Just as in Suhrawardi's tales of 'Ali's deliberate camouflaging of extramarital relations, 'Ali's clemency on the battlefield proves a stronger and more effective instrument of religious conversion than his physical, martial prowess. His magnanimity and self-restraint caused his enemy to see the light of Islam. By virtue of his high-minded chivalry, 'Ali converted not only his opponent but fifty others of his clan who were impressed enough by his altruistic conduct to profess the Muslim faith. Rumi's moral, which seems to outwardly celebrate 'Ali as a champion of Islamic *jihad,* conveys in fact the subtler truth that the lesser holy war without the greater holy war is of little value, since the spirit of forgiveness and the exercise of self-restraint are in the end stronger weapons against one's enemies than the sword wielded in passion. What 'Ali in self-restraint applied, William Blake in rhyme versified:

> But vain the Sword & vain the Bow,
> They never can work War's overthrow.

Pantheon Books 1959), esp. his two chapters on "Zen and the Swordsmanship," in which cf. his discussion of Yaqyu's "Sword of Mystery" and "Sword of No-abiding Mind," pp. 162ff. and Tesshu's "Sword of No-Sword," pp. 193ff.
[101] *Measure for Measure,* III, ii: 254-61; Vincentio (the Duke) to Escalus, concerning Angelo.
[102] This is particularly the case amongst the Kubrawi Sufis, such as Shaykh 'Ala' al-Dawla Simnani (659/1261–736/1326), who cites with approval 'Ali's dictum in the

The Hermit's Prayer & the Widow's tear
Alone can free the world from fear.

For a Tear is an Intellectual Thing,
And a sigh is the Sword of an Angel King,
And the bitter groan of the Martyr's woe
Is an Arrow from the Almightie's Bow.

IV. 'Ali as Sufi Gnostic and Sage

With the rise of institutional Sufism in the fourth/tenth and fifth/
eleventh centuries, one finds many references in classical manuals to
'Ali's sapiential insight and possession of gnosis ('ilm-i laduni). His
possession of esoteric knowledge is often emphasized by the Persian
Sufis[102] as well as Shi'ite authorities. Abu Nasr Sarraj of Tus (d.
378/988), in his Kitab al-luma' notes that when Junayd was asked
about 'Ali's knowledge of Sufism (tasawwuf), he answered that: "Had
'Ali been less engaged in wars he might have contributed greatly to
our knowledge of esoteric things (ma'ani) for he was one who had
been vouchsafed 'ilm al-laduni."[103] The reference here is to the Sufi
interpretation of Koran XVIII: 65, where the 'esoteric knowledge'
('ilm-i laduni) of Khidr, who was said to possess 'knowledge by divine
inspiration' (wa 'allamnahu min ladunna 'ilm^{an}), is mentioned. In
Persian Sufi accounts of the encounter of Moses with Khidr, Moses
represents exoteric reason, incarnating the literal letter ('ibarat) of the
Shari'a, and he is contrasted to Khidr, portrayed as an exemplar of the
esoteric symbolic lore (isharat) of the higher esoteric truth (Haqiqa)
beyond the Law. Commenting on this verse in his Treatise on Esoteric
Knowledge, the famous Persian Sunni Sufi theologian Abu Hamid al-
Ghazali (d. 505/1111) underlines the importance of 'Ali's possession
of 'ilm-i laduni as follows:

Nahj al-Balagha that "God never leaves the earth vacant of someone who stands up
as demonstrative proof (qa'im bi-hujjat) [of the divine Light and God's Existence],
and who sews the seed of the [esoteric] sciences in worthy hearts [through the light
of divine invocation (dhikr)]." Simnani, Al'Urwat li'l-ahl al-khalwat wa'l-jalwat, ed.
N.M. Harawi (Tehran: Intisharat-i Mulla 1362 A.Hsh./1983), p. 292 [102r]; sections in
brackets are Simnani's Persian interpolated translation of the Arabic.

[103] Kitab al-luma' fi'l-tasawwuf, edited. by R.A. Nicholson (London/Leiden: Luzac &
Co. 1914), p. 129. Cited by Trimingham, The Sufi Orders in Islam, p. 136.

[104] Cited by Wa'iz-i Kashifi Sabziwari, Futuwwat-nama-yi sultani, p. 173. Another
textual variant of this dictum, often quoted by Shi'ite thinkers, goes: "The Prophet

(Referring to this same esoteric knowledge as well), the Commander of the Faithful 'Ali b. Abi Talib – may God's benevolence grace him – confessed, "He (the Prophet) placed his tongue inside my mouth, and a thousand chapters of knowledge (*bab min al-'ilm*) opened in my heart, and another thousand other gates within each of those gates."[104] He also pronounced, "If a cushion were be to set down for me,[105] I would recline on it and administer justice out to the followers of the Torah according to the Torah, pass judgment on the followers of the Gospel according to the rule of the Gospel, and arbitrate amongst the followers of the Qur'an according to the Qur'an's law."[106]

Now, this degree is not attained simply by submission to human instruction (*al-ta'allum al-insani*), but rather, this rank is only realized by a man through the power of esoteric knowledge. 'Ali also said that the exegesis of Moses' scripture would amount to some forty camel-loads [speaking of the day and age of Moses], then adding "Were God to give me permission to compose a commentary on the meanings of the *Fatiha,* I could expand my exegesis to such a sum—that is to say, up to forty camel-loads."[107] Now, this sort of comprehensive amplitude, copious breadth and opening-up of knowledge cannot be achieved by anyone except it come from

taught 'Ali a thousand chapters (or 'a thousand sayings' or 'a thousand words'), each of which gave access to a thousand others." Cited by Amir-Moezzi, *The Divine Guide*, p. 75. "With the growth of Sufi doctrine in the 4th/10th and 5th/11th centuries, increasing emphasis was placed on 'Ali's possession of secret or esoteric knowledge (*'elm al-ladoni*) transmitted to him by the Prophet; many considered it virtually boundless, since he was believed to have even been granted participation in the *ghayb* (e.g. by being granted knowledge of future events...)" noted E. Kohlberg, "'Ali b. Abi Taleb", *EI²*, I, p. 846.

[105] Setting down a "cushion" for someone often designates a special place of honour given to a person in Middle Eastern societies, often constituting the post or position held by a dignitary, similar to the judge's "bench," magistrate's "chair," or minister's "desk" in contemporary Western society.

[106] This is a very popular Hadith of 'Ali and is reported in different versions by various scholars; In *Al-Risalat al-laduniyya* in *Majmu'at Rasa'il al-Imam al-Ghazali* (Beirut: Dar al-Kutub al-Islamiya 1406/1986), III, p. 106. In *Tafsir al-Shahrastani al-musamma Mafatih al-asrar wa masabih abrar,* ed. Muhammad 'Ali Adharshab, (Tehran, Ihya-yi Kitab 1997), vol. 1, p. 200. Ibn Abi'l Hadid, *Sharh Nahj al-Balagha*, ed. M. Abu'l Fa'al Ibrahim, (Cairo, 1961), vol. 12, pp. 196-7. In al-Qazi al-Nu'man, *Sharh al-akbar,* 2nd ed. S. M. Husayni al-Jalali, (Qum, 1414/1993) p.91. Hasan b. Muhammad Al-Mayhadhi relates its longer version in his letter he wrote to the people of Rayy. I am grateful for a number of my colleagues: M.R. Juzi, A. Lalani, and T, Mayer at the Institute of Ismaili Studies in London, for help in locating these and other related references.

[107] Cited as well by , 'Abd al-Razzaq Kashani (d. 736/1335), is his definition of 'esoteric knowledge' (*al-'ilm al-laduni*) in his *Lata'if al-a'lam fi isharat-i ahl al-ilham,* ed. Majid Hadizadih (Tehran: Mirath-i Maktub 2000), p. 422.

a highly esoteric, divine and celestial supernal source (of knowledge).[108]

All understanding and gnosis of God in Sufism thus bears a burden of obligation to the visions and insights of 'Ali, which have served as the basis for so many theological determinations and theosophical propositions, as Junayd stated:

> "If 'Ali Murtada had not in his magnanimity made a certain statement, what would have ever become of the adepts of the Path? And this statement came when some people asked Murtada, 'By what means have you known God Almighty?', and he replied:
> 'By what He has made known of Himself, that He is the Lord for Whom there exists no peer or likeness; that He cannot be apprehended in any respect; that one cannot make any conjecture of Him that can be compared to any creature—for He is near in His distance, distant in His nearness. He is above all things in such a way that one cannot say that there is anything beneath Him. He is from nothing, like unto nothing, and within nothing. Glory be to the God Who is like this, for nothing else beside Him is like this!'"[109]

The most important mediæval Persian Sunni Sufi to expound and dilate upon the subtleties of 'Ali's mystical theology was Ruzbihan Baqli (d. 606/1209), whose writings, in the words of Carl Ernst, "constitute a vast synthesis and rethinking of early Islamic religious thought from the perspective of pre-Mongol Sufism ... a vital resource for understanding the experiential basis, not simply of Persian Sufi literature, but of Sufism and indeed mysticism in general."[110] Ruzbihan's magisterial position in the elaboration of Sufi thought is especially visible in his magnum opus *Sharh-i shathiyyat*, a commentary on the paradoxical sayings of the Sufis. In this text he devotes an entire chapter to explication of 'Ali's paradoxical sayings on gnosis of God.[111] 'Ali is "a lion in the thicket of esoteric knowledge *(dirgham-i bisha-yi 'ilm-i laduni),"*[112] he states when interpreting Ali's saying, ""God appeared to His devotees in the Koran."

[108] Ghazali, *Al-Risalat al-laduniyya,* in his *Majmu'at Rasa'il al-Imam al-Ghazali,* (Beirut: Dar al-Kutub al-Islamiya 1406/ 1986), III, p. 106.

[109] 'Attar, *Tadhkirat al-awliya',* p. 422.

[110] Carl Ernst, *Ruzbihan Baqli: Mysticism and the Rhetoric of Sainthood in Persian Sufism* (London: Curzon Press, 1996), p. x-xi.

[111] Ruzbihan Baqli Shirazi, *Sharh-i shathiyyat,* ed. H. Corbin (Bibliothéque Iranienne 12. Tehran: Departement d'iranologie de l'Institut Franco-iranien, 1966), pp. 71-73.

[112] Ruzbihan, *Sharh-i shathiyyat,* p. 325.

Interpreting 'Ali's saying: "I do not worship a God I cannot see,"[113] Ruzbihan observes that this paradoxical aphorism (*shath*) alludes to the principle that "devotional obedience and divine vision are cheek-by-jowl *('ubudiyyat bi-ru'yat maqrunast).* " In other words, Ruzbihan comments, this saying alludes to the innermost dimension of Islam, which is virtue or *ihsan,* which of course refers to the Prophet's famous definition of *ihsan* is that it involves "serving (or worshipping) God as if you see Him, because if you do not see Him, He nonetheless sees you."[114]

Another saying by 'Ali used by both jurisprudents and Sufis in the context of this same theological debate concerning the vision of God (*ru'yat*) in this world and the hereafter is "If the veil [before the invisible world] were to be raised from before my eyesight, it would in no way increase my certitude."[115] Ruzbihan refers specifically to this statement while interpreting this saying of Hallaj:

> The master [Hallaj] says: "He brings us tidings of contemplation and the locus of divine intimacy by means of apprehension of the Divine Qualities through those very Qualities and the understanding of the Divine Essence through that Essence, eradicating all doubt about beholding Eternity's Existence (*ru'yat-i wujud-i qidam*). Returning (from drunkenness) to sobriety in order to thwart his passions' molestations and the devil of his own sobriety, he behaved as if he were still drunk. In the intoxication of beholding God, he was free of doubt, and in sobriety he was untroubled by the opposition of passion." He said: "I am constantly contemplating the Invisible Realm; through God I see God directly. If the veil beyond these heavens were to be raised before me, that would not increase my certitude since my presence is absence and my absence presence."[116]

[113] The very idea of the vision of God in the heart—a commonplace tenet of all later Sufi thought—which was considered to be one of the key conditions of faith in God in much Islamic theology, seems to have originated partially from an anecdote about 'Ali's interrogation by a sharp-witted man, Dhi'lib, who asked, "Have you seen your Lord?" The Imam replied: "Would I worship that which I see not?" Dhi'lib then asked: "How do you see Him?" The Imam replied: "Eyes see Him not through the perception of outward vision, but hearts see Him through the realities of faith." William Chittick, trans., *A Shi'ite Anthology* (London: Muhammadi Trust, 1980), pp. 38-39; see also M.A. Amir-Moezzi, *The Divine Guide in Early Shi'ism,* p. 47; the Arabic original is cited by Bukhari, *Sharh-i Ta'arruf,* I, p. 199.

[114] Cited by W.C. Chittick, *Faith and Practice of Islam,* p. 5.

[115] Wa'iz-i Kashifi Sabziwari, *Futuwwat-nama-yi sultani,* p. 49

[116] Ruzbihan, *Sharh-i shathiyyat,* pp. 71-72.

'Ali's pivotal place as a Sufi gnostic is to a large degree due to the popularity of his ecstatic sayings on various subjects relating to Islamic theosophy and wisdom. In his chapter on the unity of the divine essence (*tawhid-i dhat*) and the transcendence of the divine attributes (*tanzih-i sifat*) in his *Misbah al-hidaya*, 'Izz al-Din Mahmud Kashani writes that there are three levels of divine unity. First, the divine unity of faith (*tawhid-i imani*);" secondly, consciously comprehended or 'theoretical' divine unity (*tawhid-i 'ilmi*); and finally, the divine unity of spiritually realized altered states of consciousness (*tawhid-i hali*).[117] The source of the final level of *tawhid,* states Kashani, "derives from the light of divine contemplation (*nur-i mushahada*), while the source of consciously comprehended unity comes from the light of meditation (*nur-i muraqaba*).[118]

What is interesting is that in his discussion of the highest reaches of *tawhid* by means of an apophatic approach to the reality of divine Unity through the *via negativa*, Kashani has recourse to the following saying of Shibli (d. 334/945), which as the editor of the text, Jalal al-Din Huma'i asserts, is derived from 'Ali's highly similar words. Shibli's statement:

> Whoever describes God in words is a heretic; whoever makes allusions to God is a dualist; whoever speaks of him is heedless; whoever remains silent is an ignoramus. Whoever imagines that he has reached union (*wasil*) has lost everything (*laysa lahu hasil*). Whoever points to Him as being near is far away. Whoever imagines that he has found Him has lost Him. Whatever your fancy or reason can discern about Him, however comprehensively true in reality it may seem, is but an artificially manufactured product (of the mind) that should be repudiated, being created and timebound like yourself.[119]

—is almost certainly directly modelled on the following saying of 'Ali: "Whoever speaks of Him is ignorant and whoever remains silent is heedless; whoever thinks he has reached Him makes a baseless assumption. Whatever you distinguish in your estimative

---

[117] 'Izz al-Din Mahmud Kashani, *Misbah al-hidaya,* edited by Jalal al-Din Huma'i (Tehran: Chapkhana-yi Majlis 1946), pp. 19-20. See also Javad Nurbakhsh, *Sufism: Meaning, Knowledge and Unity,* tr. W.C. Chittick, and P.L. Wilson (London: KNP 1981), pp. 85-86.

[118] Kashani, *Misbah al-hidaya,* p. 21.

[119] Kashani, *Misbah al-hidaya,* p. 19. For another similar saying of Shibli, see Ruzbihan, *Sharh-i shathiyyat,* p. 280ff.

judgements, no matter how precise, will divert you from Him and reflect back on yourselves and will be an artefact and a created thing like yourselves."[120] Here, it should be underlined that later radical manifestations of apophatic theology found in sayings of Sufis such as Shibli actually have their roots in the statements of such a seminal exponent of Islamic piety as 'Ali.

Examining another paradox of 'Ali, "He is a near distance and a distant nearness," which describes the transcendence of God as an immanence, this is also quite apparent. Ruzbihan reflects:

> He informed us that God is near unto Himself. His distance is not [real] distance. Nearness to Him consists in your own constancy towards Him. His distance arises from your own lack of apprehension of Him. His nearness is His omniscience towering above you. Neither proximity nor distance are in essence warranted; rather, it is on 'theophany' *(tajalli)* that [the experience of] "Then he drew nigh and came down" (Qur'an LIII: 8) depends. There is substance in nearness and farness, yet you don't grasp that. Go beyond space and time and you will know what is meant.
>
> In the Qur'an, He came near to the common folk while summoning the truthful adepts. The qualities of the wine of love appeared in the goblets of words, so that the spirits were delighted and exhilarated. Having become intoxicated, the spirits flew on the pinions of divine revelations *(mukashafat)* and nourished with the food of contemplative vision *(mushahidat)* into the realm of divine ineffability *('alam-i bichun)*. Riding the steeds of the Qur'an, they approached the source of the Qur'an. [Lo! He Who hath given thee the Qur'an for a law] will surely bring thee home again." (Qur'an XXVIII: 85). That is the Qur'an. They tumbled into the source of Eternity, swimming under conditions of annihilation *(fana')* in the oceans of everlasting pre-eternity.[121]

From Ruzbihan's commentary here it is evident that the paradox of 'Ali relating to God's nearness to man has been digested and internalized in exactly the same way that the sayings of Hallaj, Kharaqani, Bayazid and others of the early Sufi ecstatic masters were interpreted by the later Sufis. 'Ali here appears as a Magus, as a worker of mysteries,

---

[120] I am indebted to Dr. Jalal Badakhshani for this reference, which occurs in Nasir al-Din Tusi's *Paradise of Submission: A Medieval Treatise on Ismaili Thought*, A New Persian Edition and English translation of Nasir al-Din Tusi's *Rawda-yi taslim*, ed./trans. S.J. Badakhshani, (London: I.B.Tauris 2005), chap. 3, p. 28 (no. 33) where, however, the saying is ascribed to the Fifth Imam: Muhammad al-Baqir, not to 'Ali.

[121] Ruzbihan, *Sharh-i shathiyyat*, p. 73.

an inspired adept, whose words are to be deciphered in light of the experience of spiritual intoxication.

This hermeneutical use of 'Ali's words to either expound or decipher the mysteries of Sufi teachings is again evident in Ruzbihan's exegesis of a paradoxical statement by Bayazid of Bistam (d. 261/875): "God looked upon the world, and saw that there was no one adept enough to know Him. So he engaged the creatures in acts of devotion to Him."[122] In his lengthy interpretation of this saying, Ruzbihan emphasizes that for those who are intimate with God, "the worship of God ('ibadat) is nothing but gnosis (ma'rifat) of Him,"[123] and from there he launches into a disquisition on the impossibility of knowing God perfectly. He caps off his explanation of Bayazid's saying as follows:

> The king of kings of the holy family of the Prophet (ahl-i bayt), that lion-moon of the bird-garden of gnosis, 'Ali ibn Abi Talib (may God be content with him) said: "Mercy is bestowed on the poor for their poverty, and upon the wealthy for their wealth, and upon all people because of their paucity of knowledge (kami-yi ma'rifat) of God.[124]

Although there is a wide range of Sufis to whom he refers, Hallaj (d. 310/922) is in fact the main author with whom Ruzbihan deals. So it is quite interesting to find that Ruzbihan compares the paradoxical sayings of Hallaj with those of 'Ali, and in order to justify the abstruseness of the former explains that 'Ali and Hallaj shared the same ecstatic love and possessed the same occult lore of God.

> Do not marvel at the discourses of Husayn (Mansur al-Hallaj) on divine Unity with all of those symbolic allusions and verbal expressions—for whatever he said is but one drop of the ocean of divine unity. Whenever the foaming saliva of 'Ali ibn Abi Talib's (may God be content with Him)—he whose purity was most trustworthy, chief of those who had inherited [divine knowledge] (wasiyya-yi ra'is), the victorious lion of God—love in divine Unity overflowed, pearls of wisdom and divine Unity from the oyster-shell of his unique tongue scattered forth. At that moment, 'Ali gave expression to the transcendent grandeur of the irresistible Power of God (bayan-i tanzih-i 'izzat-i qahr-i Haqq kardi), such that the whole

122 Ibid., p. 93
123 Ibid., p. 94
124 Ibid., pp. 95-96

cosmos and creation trembled before the august splendour of his words, mysteries and symbolic expressions.[125]

V. Conclusion

The achievement of 'Ali ibn Abi Talib as a religious thinker, moral philosopher and sage mystic has been contemplated in the mirror of the literature of the Persian Sufi tradition over the foregoing pages. By way of conclusion, the following description of 'Ali's role in the development of Islamic mystical philosophy and Sufism, penned by the late Persian Shi'ite philosopher 'Allamah Tabataba'i, reflecting his brilliance in the mirror of the Persian 'high theosophical' tradition *('irfan)* in Islam, merits citation:

> Despite the cumbersome and strenuous difficulties which absorbed his time, he left behind among the Islamic community a valuable treasury of the truly divine sciences and Islamic intellectual disciplines. Nearly eleven thousand of his proverbs and short sayings on different intellectual, religious and social subjects have been recorded. In his talks and speeches he expounded the most sublime Islamic sciences in a most elegant and flowing manner. He established Arabic grammar and laid the basis for Arabic literature.
>
> He was the first in Islam to delve directly into the questions of metaphysics *(falsafah-i ilahi)* in a manner combining intellectual rigor and logical demonstration. He discussed problems which had never appeared before in the same way among the metaphysicians of the world. Moreover, he was so devoted to metaphysics and gnosis that even in the heat of battle he would carry out intellectual discourse and discuss metaphysical problems.
>
> He trained a large number of religious scholars and Islamic savants, among whom are found a number of ascetics and gnostics who were the forefathers of the Sufis, such men as Uways al-Qarani, Kumayl al-Nakha'i, Maytham al-Tammar and Rashid al-Hajari. These men have been recognized by later Sufis as the founders of gnosis in Islam.[126]

As Tabataba'i's comments make clear, even the most preliminary examination of the contribution of 'Ali to the evolution of esotericism in Islam would demand a lengthy study of his sermons and sayings in the *Nahj al-balagha,* not to mention his letters. These documents would then need to be placed in proper historical and biographical

[125] Ibid., p. 543.
[126] 'Allamah Tabataba'i, *Shi'ite Islam,* trans. S.H. Nasr (Albany: SUNY 1977), p. 54.

perspective, contextualized within the political and literary history of early Arab Islam, recording in detail the influence of Arabic literature and poetry upon his sayings, & etc.

Although none of these steep canyons of historical thought have been scaled in this essay, nor any of these uncharted prairies of socio-political speculation here surveyed, the above evaluation of several key anecdotes from his life and appraisal of his ecstatic sayings has demonstrated that 'Ali ibn Abi Talib is in the fullest sense the supreme master of the esoteric path in Islam, from whom well up the freshets of inspiration to succeeding generations, animating both spiritual perceptions on the individual plane and ethical conduct on the social. It is clear also that 'Ali's possession of esoteric knowledge, his uncompromising ascetic piety, and wisdom in matters of the Spirit have always been universally acclaimed by the Sufis, regardless of their juridical affiliation. His moral theology is central to the development of Sufi ethics, while he holds a pivotal place in the Islamic chivalric tradition. Perhaps even more important than these traits and characteristics is his *religious tolerance* – his incarnation of a unique kind of mystical justice beyond the letter of the law, sustaining the Sufi ethic of forgiveness – which is as generally universal as it is particularly Islamic.

Calligraphy of the name 'Ali in the shape of a lion.

Appendix: Note on 'Alī ibn Abī T'ālib (c.600-661 CE)

'ALI, THE SON OF ABI TALIB, was the cousin of the Prophet Muhammad, and, by his marriage to the Prophet's daughter, Fatima, also his son-in-law. He is revered by both Sunni Muslims, by whom he is regarded as the last of the four Rightly Guided Caliphs, and by Shi'a Muslims, for whom he is the first Imam and the Prophet's spiritual successor. In the Sufi tradition, 'Ali is regarded as the *wali Allah,* 'the friend/saint of God', the possessor of initiatic and esoteric knowledge.

'Ali was born in Mecca (according to some traditions, within the holy sanctuary of the Kaaba itself) in around 600 CE. His father, Abu Talib, a prominent member of the Quraysh tribe, was the guardian and protector of the orphaned Muhammad. By the time of 'Ali's birth, Muhammad was nearly 30 years old and had been married to Khadija for some 5 years. After the prophetic revelation commenced (around 610 CE), 'Ali immediately professed his faith in God and is consequently considered by all Muslims as one of the stalwarts and exemplars of Islam. He remained one of the Prophet's staunchest supporters through the years of his persecution, sharing in the hardships that were suffered by the early Muslim community, and distinuguishing himself in the wars relating to the establishment of the first Islamic polity. An example of his love and support of the Prophet is the famous episode when the Prophet was confronted with a plot to assassinate him, and 'Ali risked his own life by taking the place of the Prophet in his bed, allowing the Prophet to flee from Mecca to Medina (in 622 CE, the start of the Muslim year). As a warrior (he is sometimes called "*haydar al-karrar*" or "The Charging Lion"), 'Ali was scrupulous in his respect for human life and the sacred underpinnings of the rules of engagement, refusing to strike an enemy in anger.

The death of the Prophet (in 632 CE) raised the question of succession for the Muslim community. The Shi'as believe that the Prophet had unequivocally designated 'Ali as his worldly and religious successor from his lineage, the *Ahl al-Bayt*—most prominently at Ghadir-Khumm, where the Prophet is reported to have said "Whosoever regards me as his master, 'Ali is his master"—while the Sunnis believe that the purely political succession of the first Caliph, Abu Bakr, was a matter of community consensus (*shura*) recommended

147

by the Prophet. Despite the controversy, 'Ali did not openly oppose the three Caliphs (Abu Bakr, Umar ibn al-Khattab and Uthman ibn Affan) who preceded him because he wished to preserve the unity of the Muslim community.

After reluctantly ascending to the Caliphate upon the assassination of Caliph Uthman (in 656 CE), 'Ali strove to unify the divided Muslim communities under his leadership. He relocated the capital of the Caliphate from Medina to Kufa (in Iraq) and replaced his predecessor's lieutenants with his own trusted leaders, including Malik al-Ashtar, to whom he wrote his famous Epistle on Governance. His caliphate, however, continued to face opposition from several quarters includingly, prominently, the Prophet's widow, Aisha—whose army was defeated at the Battle of the Camel, in Basra (Iraq), after which Aisha was, with due dignity, resettled by 'Ali, with a pension, in Medina—and Mu'awiyah, the governor of Syria, Palestine and Jordan, and a relative of Uthman. Upon ascending to the caliphate, 'Ali had requested Mu'awiyah to relinquish his governorship, and the latter refused, denying 'Ali his pledge of allegiance and setting up a rival Muslim state in Syria. Eventually, the two sides engaged in battle at Siffin (in 657 CE) and, on the brink of victory, 'Ali ordered his troops to cease fighting when their opponents fixed copies of the Qur'an to their spearheads—a sign that the scripture taught that it was nobler to mediate or arbitrate than to fight. In the negotiations for peace that followed Siffin, Mu'awiyah's negotiator, 'Amr ibn al-'As, outsmarted 'Ali's negotiator, Abu Musa al-Ash'ari, cunningly persuading him to publicly proclaim that neither 'Ali nor Mu'awiyah should succeed, and then himself publicly endorsing Mu'awiyah but not 'Ali. This outcome disheartened 'Ali's followers, who felt cheated of victory. 'Ali's concession to the enemy was seen by some among his followers as a sign of weakness and led to a split within his ranks by a group that came to be known as the Kharijites or "Seceders". Three discontented zealots plotted to assassinate 'Ali, Mu'awiyah and 'Amr, respectively, for the discontent they had sowed among the Muslims, and while the plot against the latter two failed, 'Ali was slain by the dagger of his assassin while at morning prayer at a mosque in Kufa in 661 CE. He died from the poison of the dagger, three days after receiving his head wound. It is recorded that during his final hours he was concerned for the welfare and fate of his assassin, ordering that he not be mistreated and that, if 'Ali should die, his killer be executed mercifully, with a single stroke, in proportion to the single stroke with which he had felled 'Ali.

A collection of 'Ali's approximately 250 sermons and his various speeches, letters, teachings and sayings, were compiled after his death, and in 420 A.H. were published in a collection by Sharif ar-Radi under the title, *Nahj al-Balagha* or "The Path of Eloquence". Through the wisdom of these teachings, their profound metaphysical insights and practical guidance, and the exemplary life that he led, 'Ali ibn Abi Talib is regarded as a paragon of wisdom, piety and virtue, and is not only a great Muslim but a great religious leader whose universal message of truth is relevant for all time.

NOTES ON CONTRIBUTORS

M. ALI LAKHANI was born in England in 1955. He was educated at the King's School, Canterbury, before reading law at Cambridge University, where he received his undergraduate and post-graduate degrees in that subject. Following in the footsteps of his family, who had emigrated from East Africa to Canada in 1972, Ali settled in Vancouver, Canada, and he has practiced law in British Columbia, primarily as a barrister, since 1979.

In 1998, Ali founded the traditionalist journal, *Sacred Web*, with the focus of identifying the 'first principles' of tradition and exploring their relevance to the issues of modernity. *Sacred Web* is now regarded as one of the pre-eminent traditionalist journals in the English language, and has included essays by the foremost contemporary traditionalist writers, as well as by several prominent religious scholars and writers sympathetic to tradition. In 2001, Ali was invited to address the International Congress on Imam 'Ali in Iran, where he presented his essay on the "*Metaphysics of Human Governance*". That essay, which dealt with the teachings of 'Ali ibn Abi Talib on Truth and Justice, garnered the First Prize in English at the conference, and was awarded at a special ceremony held in Tehran in March 2002. The revised essay is included in the anthology, "*The Sacred Foundations of Justice in Islam: An Anthology of Essays based on the Teachings of Ali 'ibn Abi Talib*", co-published by Sacred Web Publishing and World Wisdom, 2006. Ali is a poet and author. An anthology of his own writings, *The Timeless Relevance of Traditional Wisdom*, was published by World Wisdom in 2010.

REZA SHAH-KAZEMI is a Research Associate at the Institute of Ismaili Studies, London. His areas of research are Comparative Religion, Islamic Studies, Shi'i Studies, and Sufism. He has edited, translated, and written numerous books and articles, including *Doctrines of Shi'i Islam* (London, 2001), *Avicenna, Prince of Physicians* (London, 1997), *Algeria: Revolution Revisited* (London, 1997), *Turkey: The Pendulum Swings Back* (London, 1996), *Bosnia: Destruction of a Nation, Inversion of a Principle* (London, 1996), and *Crisis in Chechnia* (London, 1995). Currently in preparation for publication are: *The Other in the Light of the One: Unity, Universality, and Dialogue in the Qur'an* (London, 2006) and *Justice and Remembrance: An Introduction to the Spirituality* *of Imam Ali* (London, 2006). At present he is engaged on a new, annotated English translation of Imam Ali's *Nahj al-balagha.*

LEONARD LEWISOHN is Lecturer in Persian and Iran Heritage Foundation Fellow in Classical Persian and Sufi Literature, Institute of Arab and Islamic Studies, University of Exeter, England.

INDEX OF ARABIC TERMS

'abd or *'abdu'Llah* (Slave or Servant of God), 11n, 34, 88,

abrar (The Righteous), 96

'adalat (Perfect Justice), 133,

'ahd (Universal Covenant between man and God), 88,

'ahdan (Binding covenant), 88

al-'Adil (Just or Equitable), *xi*

al-'Adl (Justice), xi, xiv

akhir (Last), 22

Amanah (Divine Trust), 7, 20, 28, 29, 32, 46,

'aql (Intellect), 7, 63n,

asma wa sifat (Names of Allah), 10n

awwal (First), 22, 43n, 62n,

baqa (Absorption into the Divine Plenitude), 35n, 43,

batin (Hidden), 21,

dafa'in al-'uqul (Buried treasures of the Intellect), 70

dhat (Divine Essence, or Godhead), 10

dhikr (Invocation), 12n, 32, 100, 101, 102, 137n,

din (Spiritual realm, or Religion), 52, 54, 56, 70,

din al-fitr (Religion of the Heart, religio perennis), 53n

din al-islam (Conventional Islam), 53n

din al-qayyim (Right Religion), 70

dunya (Secular realm, or World), 52, 54

fana (Egoic Annihilation), 35n, 43, 142,

fitra (Primordial Nature), 46, 49, 50, 51, 56, 57, 69, 70

fitrat Allah (Nature framed of God), 70

futuwwat (Fraternities of Chivalry), 118, 119

ghafla (Heedlessness), 8, 32

al-Haqq (Truth, Justice), xii, 21, 70n, 73, 102,

hilm (Forbearance), 89, 135,

hujja (Proof), 63, 137

al-hukama' (Sages), 89

'ibadat (Worship of God), 143

'ibarat (Literal letter of the law), 137

'ibra (Exemplary teaching), 91

ihsan (Virtue, Piety), 55, 140

al-ihtimam (Resolute Determination), 89

ijma (Consensus), 55n

ijtihad (Personal striving for Truth), 55

ikhlas (Sincerity), 100

'ilm-i laduni (Esoteric Knowledge, Gnosis), 137, 139

iman (Faith), 20, 29, 30n, 37, 129n

insaf (Equity), 56, 65n

irfan (Gnosis), 11, 14, 43n, 55, 144

al-isti'ana (Seeking divine assistance), 89

istidraj (Drawing out of punishment by degrees), 78

i'tidal (Sound Equilibrium), 133,

jihad (Striving) xiv, 80n, 134, 136,

jism (Corporeal Existence, Body), 42

kafir (Cover Over or Conceal Truth), 78

kashf (Unveiling), 11, 30n,

khalifah (Vicegerant) and *khalifatu'Llah* (Representative of God), 11n, 34, 88

INDEX OF QUR'ANIC REFERENCES

INDEX OF PROPER NAMES

GENERAL INDEX

Way-mark, 41, 49-51, 56
Worship (see also Prayer), 30,
   31 (fn. 88), 41 (fn. 124), 46
   (fn. 136), 53 (fn. 154), 67,
   75, 95, 98-102, 105-106, 140
   (fn.133), 143

For a glossary of all key foreign words used in books published by World Wisdom,
including metaphysical terms in English, consult:
www.DictionaryofSpiritualTerms.org.
This on-line Dictionary of Spiritual Terms provides extensive definitions, examples
and related terms in other languages.

SOURCES REFERRED TO IN THE TEXT

Anthologies on Imam 'Ali

Nahj al-balagha, Arabic text with Persian translation by Ja'far Shahidi, (Tehran: Intisharat-i 'ilmi u farhangi 1368 A.Hsh./ 1999)

Nahjul-Balagha, Sermons, Letters and Sayings of Imam Ali, translated by Syed Mohammed Askari Jafery, (New York, Tahrike Tarsile Qur'an, Second American Edition, 1981)

Nahj al-Balagha, Tehran: Nahj al-Balagha Foundation, (edited by Shaykh 'Azizullah al-'Utardi), 1413 AH/1372 SH (1993)

Peak of Eloquence, Sayed Ali Reza, (New York, Tahrike Tarsile Qur'an, 1996)

The Sayings and Wisdom of Imam Ali, (The Muhammadi Trust, Zahra Publications, ISBN 0946079919, n.d.)

Living and Dying with Grace: Counsels of Hadrat Ali, translated by Thomas Cleary, (Shambhala, 1995)

Masadir Nahj al-balagha ('Sources of the *Nahj al-balagha*'), 'Abd Allah Ni'mah (Beirut: Dar al-Huda, 1972)

Ghurar al-hikam ('The Finest of Aphorisms') (under the Persian title, *Guftar-i Amir al-mu'minin*), compiled by 'Abd al-Wahid Amidi (d. 1116/510), Persian edition and translation by Sayyid Husayn Shaykhul-Islami (Qom: Ansariyan Publications, 2000)

'Ali-Akbar Rashad (ed.), *Danish nama Imam 'Ali,* a 12-volume compendium of articles on 'Ali's life and thought, (Tehran: Institute of Culture and Islamic Thought, 1380 Sh./2001)

Qada' Amir al-mu'minin 'Ali ibn Abi Talib ('The Legal Judgements of the Commander of the Faithful, 'Ali ibn Abi Talib'), compiled by 'Allama Shoushtari (Tehran: Institute for Humanities and Cultural Studies, 2001)

Supplications—Amir al-Mu'minin, trans. W.C. Chittick (London: Muhammadi Trust, 1995)

Farhang—Quarterly Journal of Humanities and Cultural Studies, vol.13, nos.33-36, (Winter, 2001)

Other References

Mohammad Ali Amir-Moezzi, *The Divine Guide in Early Shi'ism: the Sources of Esotericism in Islam,* tr. D. Streight, (Albany: SUNY 1994)

Sayyid Haydar Amuli, *Al-Muhit al-a'zam wa'l-bahr al-khidamm fi ta'wil kitab Allah al-'aziz al-muhkam* (Qom: Mu'assassa Farhangi wa Nashr Nur 'Ala Nur, 2001)

Tor Andrae, *In the Garden of Myrtles: Studies in Early Islamic Mysticism,* tr. B. Sharpe (Albany: State University of New York 1987)

Muhammad Asad, *Principles of State and Government in Islam* (Berkeley: University of California Press, 1966)

Farid al-Din 'Attar, *Tadhkirat al-awliya',* ed. Muhammad Isti'lami. (3rd ed., Tehran: Zawwar: 1365/1986)

Farid al-Din 'Attar, *Musibat-nama,* ed. Nurani Visal (Tehran: Intisharat-i Zuwwar 1976)

Farid al-Din 'Attar, *Tadhkirat al-awliya',* ed. M. Isti'lami. (3rd ed.), (Tehran: Zawwar: 1365/1986)

William Blake. *Blake: Complete Writings,* ed. G. Keynes (London: OUP 1972)

Abu Ibrahim Isma'il ibn Muhammad Mustamli Bukhari, *Sharh-i Ta'arruf li-Madhhab al-tasawwuf,* ed. M. Rawshan, (Tehran: Intisharat-i Asatir 1363 A.Hsh./1984). 5 vols.

Titus Burckhardt, *Fez: City of Islam,* trans. by William Stoddart, (Cambridge, Islamic Texts Society, 1992)

Claude Cahen, *"Futuwwa,"* *Encyclopecædia of Islam*, 2nd Ed., II: 961-69

William C. Chittick, *Faith and Practice of Islam: three Thirteenth Century Sufi Texts* (Albany: SUNY 1992)

William C. Chittick, *A Shi'ite Anthology* (London, 1980)

William C. Chittick, *Sufism: A Short Introduction*, (Oxford, Oneworld, 2000)

William C. Chittick, *The Sufi Path of Knowledge*, (New York, State University of New York Press, 1989)

Michael Cook, *Commanding Right and Forbidding Wrong in Islamic Thought* (Cambridge: CUP 2000)

Ananda K. Coomaraswamy, *Spiritual Authority and Temporal Power in the Indian Theory of Government*, American Oriental Series, Volume 22, (New Haven, Connecticut, American Oriental Society, 1942)

Ananda K. Coomaraswamy, *Time and Eternity*, (Ascona, Switzerland, Artibus Asiae, 1947)

Ananda K. Coomaraswamy, 'Recollection, Indian and Platonic', Supplement to the *Journal of American Oriental Society*, No. 3, April-June, 1944

Henry Corbin, *En Islam iranien: Aspects spirituals et philosophiques* (Paris: Éditions Gallimard 1971), 4 vols.

Paul Davies, *The Mind of God*, (NY, Touchstone, 1993)

Jalal al-Din Dawwani, *Akhlaq-i Jalali* (Lucknow: lithograph edition, n.d.)

Charles Le Gai Eaton, *Remembering God: Reflections on Islam*, (Chicago, ABC International Group Inc., 2000)

Khaled Abou El Fadl *et al.*, *The Place of Tolerance in Islam* (Boston: Beacon Press 2002)

Carl Ernst, *Ruzbihan Baqli: Mysticism and the Rhetoric of Sainthood in Persian Sufism* (London: Curzon Press, 1996)

Majid Fakhry, *Ethical Theories of Islam* (Leiden: E.J. Brill, 1994)

Claude Field (ed.), *A Dictionary of Oriental Quotations*, (London, Swan Sonnenschien & Co., 1911)

Badiʻ al-Zaman Furuzanfar, *Makhadh-i qisas u tamthilat-i Mathnawi* (Tehran: Amir Kabir 1362 A.Hsh./ 1983; 3rd ed.)

George L. Geckle (ed.), *Measure for Measure: 1783-1920*, (London: Athlone Press 2001)

Abu Hamid al-Ghazali, *Ihya' 'ulum al-din,* (Damascus: n.d.). 10 vols.

Abu Hamid al-Ghazali, *Kitab Adab al-suhbah wa'l-mu'asharah ma'ah asnaf al-khalq,* ed. M.S. al-Muʻini (Baghdad: Matbaʻat al-ʻani 1984)

Abu Hamid al-Ghazali, *Al-Risalat al-laduniyya,* in his *Majmu'at Rasa'il al-Imam al-Ghazali,* (Beirut: Dar al-Kutub al-Islamiya 1406/ 1986).

H.A.R. Gibb, "'Ali b. Abi Talib," *Encyclopedia Iranica*, I, pp. 381-86

Mehdi Golshani (ed.), *Proceedings of the Congress on Imam 'Ali* (Persian articles), (Tehran: Institute for Humanities and Cultural Studies, 2001)

René Guénon, *Le Métaphysique Orientale*, published in English as *Oriental Metaphysics*, (Hanuman Books, 1989, ISBN 09378152410937815241)

René Guénon, *The Multiple States of Being*, translation by Joscelyn Godwin, (New York, Larson Publications Inc., 1984)

Shahla Haeri, *Law of Desire: Temporary Marriage in Islam* (Syracuse: Syracuse University Press 1989)

'Ali b. Abi Bakr al-Harawi, *Kitab al-isharat ila ma'rifat al-ziyarat* (Damascus, 1953), (translation by Josef Meri, *A Lonely Wayfarer's Guide to Pilgrimage*)

Hasan b. Yusuf al-Hilli, *Kashf al-yaqin fi fada'il Amir al-Mu'minin,* Persian translation by Hamid Rida Azhir (Tehran 1329 A.Hsh./1950)

M.G.S. Hodgson, *The Venture of Islam*, vol. 1: *The Classical Age of Islam* (University of Chicago Press 1977 rpt.)

'Ali Hujwiri, *Kashf al-mahjub,* ed. V.A. Zhukovskii, (St. Petersburg 1899. Reprinted Leningrad 1926)

'Ali Hujwiri, *Kashf al-Mahjub*, translated from the Persian by Reynold A. Nicholson, (London, Luzac, 1911, 1936, 1959)

Ibn 'Ata'illah, *Sufi Aphorisms* (*Kitab al-Hikam*), translated and with an introduction and notes by Victor Danner, and Foreward by Martin Lings, (Leiden, E.J. Brill, Netherlands, 1984)

Toshihiko Izutsu, *Sufism and Taoism*, (Berkeley, University of California Press, 1984)

Syed Husain Mohammad Jafri, *Political and Moral Vision of Islam* (Lahore: Institute of Islamic Culture, 2000)

Syed Husain Mohammad Jafri, *The Origins and Development of Shi'a Islam* (Oxford: OUP 2000)

George Jordac, *The Voice of Human Justice*, translated by M. Fazal Haqq, (Qom: Ansariyan Publications, 1990)

Muhammad Kalabadhi, *Kitab al-ta'arruf li-madhhab ahl al-tasawwuf,* tr. A.J. Arberry, *The Doctrine of the Sufis* (Cambridge: CUP 1989 rprt.)

Kamal al-Din Husayn b. 'Ali Wa'iz-i Kashifi, *Futuwwat-nama-yi Sultani,* ed. Ja'far Mahjub (Tehran: Bunyad-i farhang-i Iran 1350 A.Hsh./1971)

Mohammad Hashim Kamali, *Freedom of Expression in Islam* (Cambridge: Islamic Texts Society 1997)

Ahmet Karamustafa, *God's Unruly Friends: Dervish Groups in the Islamic Later Middle Period, 1200-1550* (Salt Lake City: University of Utah Press 1994)

'Izz al-Din Mahmud Kashani, *Misbah al-hidaya,* ed. Jalal al-Din Huma'i (Tehran: Kitabkhana Sana'i, n.d., 2nd ed. 1946)

'Abd al-Razzaq Kashani, *Tuhfat al-ikhwan fi khasa'is al-fityan,* ed. Sayyid Muhammad Damadi (Tehran: Intisharat-i 'ilmi u farhangi 1369 A.Hsh./1990)

'Abd al-Razzaq Kashani, *Lata'if al-a'lam fi isharat-i ahl al-ilham,* ed. Majid Hadizadih (Tehran: Mirath-i Maktub 2000)

Peter Kingsley, *Ancient Philosophy, Mystery and Magic: Empedocles and Pythagorean Tradition,* (Oxford: Clarendon Press, 1995)

M. Kiyani, *Tarikh-i khanaqah dar Iran* (Tehran: Kitabkhana Tahuri, 1369 A.H.sh./1990)

E. Kohlberg, "'Ali b. Abi Taleb." ii. 'Ali as Seen by the Community: Among Sufis" in *Encyclopedia Iranica,* I, pp. 843-48

Muhammad Lahiji, *Mafatih al-i'jaz fi sharh-i Gulshan-i raz,* ed. Muhammad Rida Barzgar Khaliqi and 'Iffat Karbasi, (Tehran: Zawwar 1371 A.Hsh./1992)

M. Ali Lakhani, "'Fundamentalism': A Metaphysical Perspective", *Sacred Web 7* (2001, Sacred Web Publishing, Vancouver, Canada), reprinted in *The Betrayal of Tradition: Essays on the Spiritual Crisis of Modernity,* Harry Oldmeadow (ed.), (2005, Bloomington, Indiana, World Wisdom Books)

M. Ali Lakhani, "Pluralism and the Metaphysics of Morality", *Sacred Web 3* (1999, Sacred Web Publishing, Vancouver, Canada)

M. Ali Lakhani, "The Principle of Verticality", *Sacred Web 14* (2004, Vancouver, Canada, Sacred Web Publishing)

Ira Lapidus, *A History of Islamic Societies* (Cambridge: CUP 1988)
L. Lewisohn (with David Morgan), ed., *The Heritage of Sufism:* III, *Late Classical Persianate Sufism: the Safavid and Mughal Period,* (Oxford: Oneworld, 1999)

L. Lewisohn, "The Sacred Music of Islam: *Sama'* in the Persian Sufi Tradition" in *the British Journal of Ethnomusicology,* VI, 1997: 1-33

L. Lewisohn, "The Esoteric Christianity of Islam: Interiorisation of Christian Imagery in Medieval Persian Sufi Poetry," in Lloyd Ridgeon, ed. *Muslim Interpretations of Christianity* (London: Curzon Press 2000): 127-56

Tage Lindbom, *The Tares and the Good Grain,* translated by Alvin Moore, Jr., (Mercer University Press, 1983)

Martin Lings, *Ancient Beliefs and Modern Superstitions,* (Quinta Essentia, 1991)

Martin Lings, *Muhammad, his life based on the earliest sources* (London: Unwin Hyman 1988)

(Martin Lings) Abu Bakr Siraj Ed-Din, *The Book of Certainty,* (New York, Samuel Weiser, 1974)

Wilferd Madelung, *The Succession to Muhammad—A Study of the Early Caliphate* (Cambridge, 1997)
Muhammad Ja'far Mahjub, *A'in-i javamardi ya futuwwat* (New York: Bibliotheca Persica Press, 2000)

Hafeez Malik (ed.), *Iqbal: Poet-Philosopher of Pakistan,* (New York and London, Columbia University Press, 1971)

Rashid al-Din Maybudi, *Kashf al-asrar wa 'uddat al-abrar,* ed. 'Ali Asghar Hikmat (Tehran: Intisharat-i Danishgahi, 1952-60) 10 vols.

Abu Talib Mir-'abidini & Mihran Afshari, eds., *Ayin-i Qalandari, mush-tamal bar Chahar risala dar bab-i qalandari, khaksari, firqa-yi 'ajam u sukhanvari* (Tehran: Intisharat-i Fararavan 1374 A.Hsh/1995)

Henry More, "On Liberty of Conscience," in David George Mullan (ed.), *Religious Pluralism in the West* (Oxford: Blackwell, 1998): 159-65

'Allama Mutahhari, *'Adl-i ilahi* ('Divine Justice') (Tehran: Sadra Publications, 2001)

Diya al-Din Nakhshabi, *Silk al-suluk*, ed. Ghulam 'Ali Arya (Tehran: Zawwar 1369 A.Hsh./1990)

Seyyed Hossein Nasr, Hamid Dabashi, and Seyyed Vali Reza Nasr (eds.), *Shi'ism: Doctrines, Thought and Spirituality*, (New York, SUNY Press, 1988)

Seyyed Hossein Nasr (ed.), *Islamic Spirituality*, vol.1, *Foundations*. (London: Routledge and Kegan Paul, 1987)

Seyyed Hossein Nasr (ed.), *Islamic Spirituality*, vol.2, *Manifestations*. (New York: Crossroad, 1991)

Seyyed Hossein Nasr, *Ideals and Realities of Islam*, (Boston, Beacon Press, 1972)

Seyyed Hossein Nasr, *Knowledge and the Sacred*, (Albany, SUNY, 1989)

Seyyed Hossein Nasr, *Sufi Essays*, London: George Allen & Unwin, 1972, 2nd ed., (Albany: SUNY, 1991)

Jacob Needleman (ed.), *The Sword of Gnosis*, Penguin Metaphysical Library, (Baltimore, Penguin Books, 1974)

Javad Nurbakhsh, *Spiritual Poverty in Sufism*, trans. Leonard Lewisohn (London, Khaniqahi Nimatullahi Publications 1984)

Javad Nurbakhsh, *Sufism: Meaning, Knowledge and Unity*, tr. W.C. Chittick, and P.L. Wilson (London: KNP 1981)

Javad Nurbakhsh, *Hasan Basri: pir-i payravan-i tariqat u rahnama-yi javanmardan* (London: Khanaqah-i Ni'matu'llahi 1375/ 1996)

Shahram Pazuki, "Tasawwuf-i 'Alawi: Guftari dar bab-i intisab-i silasil-i Sufiyya bih Hadrat-i 'Ali (unpublished lecture text, delivered at the conference on Imam 'Ali in Shiraz, Iran, 1379 A.Hsh./ 2000)

Whitall N. Perry (ed.), *A Treasury of Traditional Wisdom*, Second Edition (Middlesex, Perennial Books, 1981)

Plato, *Phaedrus and Letters VII and VIII*, Translation by W. Hamilton (London: Penguin, 1978

Plato, *Protagoras and Meno*, Translation by W.K.C. Guthrie, (London: Penguin, 1979)

Plato, *The Republic of Plato*, Translation by F.M. Cornford (Oxford: The Clarendon Press, 1951)

Plato, *Plato: The Collected Dialogues,* ed. Edith Hamilton and Huntington Cairns, Bollingen Series 71, 17th printing (Princeton: Princeton University Press 1999)

I.K. Poonawala, "'Ali b. Abi Talib. 1. Life," in *Encyclopedia Iranica,* I, pp. 839-43

Nasrollah Pourjavady, "Opposition to Sufism in Twelver Shiism," in Frederick de Jong, Bernd Radtke (eds.), *Islamic Mysticism Contested: Thirteen Centuries of Controversies and Polemics* (Leiden: Brill 1999): 614-23

Daud Rahbar, *God of Justice: A Study in the Ethical Doctrine of the Qur'an* (Leiden: E.J. Brill 1960)

Fazlur Rahman "Aklaq," *Encyclopedia Iranica,* I, pp. 719-23

Sara Rappe, *Reading Neoplatonism: Non-discursive Thinking in the Texts of Plotinus, Proclus, and Damascius* (Cambridge: Cambridge University Press, 2000)

Lloyd Ridgeon, *'Aziz Nasafi* (London: Curzon Press 1998)

Jalal al-Din Rumi, *Mathnawi-yi ma'nawi,* ed. R.A. Nicholson (Rprt.: Tehran: Amir Kabir 1984, bi-sa'-yi Nasru'llah Purjavadi)

Jalal al-Din Rumi's *Kulliyat-i Shams ya Divan-i Kabir,* ed. B. Furu-zanfar (Tehran: Amir Kabir 1976). 9 vols.

Ruzbihan Baqli Shirazi, *Sharh-i shathiyyat,* ed. H. Corbin (Bibli-othéque Iranienne 12. Tehran: Departement d'iranologie de l'Institut Franco-iranien, 1966)

Husayn Wa'iz-i Kashifi Sabziwari, *Futuwwat-nama-yi sultani,* ed. Ja'far Mahjub (Tehran: Bunyad-i farhang-i Iran 1350 A.Hsh./1971)

Abdulaziz Sachedina, *The Islamic Roots of Democratic Pluralism* (Oxford: OUP 2001)

M. Sarraf (ed.) *Rasa'il-i javamardan,* French introduction and synopsis by H. Corbin (Tehran: French-Iran Institute, 1973)

R. Savory, "Some Reflections on Totalitarian Tendencies in the Safavid State," *Der Islam,* 52 (1976): 226-41.

Frithjof Schuon, *Echoes of Perennial Wisdom,* (Bloomington, Indiana, World Wisdom Books, 1992)

Frithjof Schuon, *From the Divine to the Human,* translated by Gustavo Polit and Deborah Lambert, (Bloomington, Indiana, World Wisdom Books, 1982)

Frithjof Schuon, *In the Tracks of Buddhism,* translation from the French by Marco Pallis (George, Allen & Unwin Ltd., 1968)

Frithjof Schuon, *Logic and Transcendence,* translated by Peter N. Townsend, (London, Perennial Books, 1984)

Frithjof Schuon, *Spiritual Perspectives and Human Facts,* translated by P. N. Townsend, (Pates Manor, Bedfont, Middlesex, Perennial Books, 1987)

Frithjof Schuon, *Stations of Wisdom,* (Bloomington, Indiana, World Wisdom Books, 1995)

Frithjof Schuon, *To Have a Center,* (Bloomington, Indiana, World Wisdom Books, 1990)

Frithjof Schuon, *Understanding Islam*, (London, Unwin, 1976)

Mahmud Shabistari, *Gulshan-i raz* in Samad Muwahhid (ed.), *Majmu'a-i athar-i Shaykh Mahmud Shabistari,* (Tehran: Kitbkhana-i Tahuri 1365 A.Hsh./1986)

Shirazi, Ma'sum 'Ali Shah. *Tara'iq al-haqa'iq,* ed. M.J Mahjub, (Tehran: Kitabkhana-yi Barani 1345 A.Hsh. /1966). 3 vols.

Reza Shah-Kazemi, "Recollecting the Spirit of Jihad", in *Sacred Web 8,* (Vancouver, Sacred Web Publishing, 2001)

Kamil Mustafa al-Shaibi, *Sufism and Shi'ism* (Surrey: LAAM Publications 1991)

Amir Sijzi, *Fawa'id al-fu'ad,* trans. B.B. Lawrence, *Nizam ad-Din Awliya: Morals for the Heart,* (New York: Paulist Press 1992)

'Ala' al-Dawla Simnani, *Al'Urwat li'l-ahl al-khalwat wa'l-jalwat,* ed. N.M. Harawi (Tehran: Intisharat-i Mulla 1362 A.Hsh./1983)

Ayatollah Ja'far Sobhani, *Doctrines of Shi'i Islam*, translated and edited by Reza Shah-Kazemi, (London, I. B. Tauris & Co. Ltd., 2001)

Abu Najib al-Suhrawardi, *Adab al-muridin,* Arabic text with Persian translation by 'Umar ibn Muhammad ibn Ahmad Shirakan, ed. N. Mayil Haravi (Tehran: Intisharat-i Mulla 1984)

D. T. Suzuki, *Zen and Japanese Culture* (New York: Bolligen Series LXIV, Pantheon Books 1959)

'Allamah Tabataba'i. *A Shi'ite Anthology,* William Chittick, trans. (London: Muhammadi Trust, 1980)

'Allamah Tabataba'i, *Shi'ite Islam,* trans. S.H. Nasr (Albany: SUNY 1977)

Ahmad b. Muhammad al-Tusi, *Bawariq al-ilma',* Arabic text with English trans. in James Robson, *Tracts on Listening to Music* (London: RAS, Oriental Translation Fund, vol. 34 NS, 1938)

Khwaja Nasir al-Din Tusi, *Akhlaq-i Nasiri* (Tehran: Intisharat-I Khwarazmi 1360 A.Hsh./ 1981)

Khwaja Nasir al-Din Tusi, *The Paradise of Submission: A Medieval Treatise on Ismaili Thought, A New Persian Edition and Translation of Nasir al-Din Tusi's Rawda-yi taslim,* ed. Jalal Badakhshani (London: I.B.Tauris and the Institute of Ismaili Studies 2005)

Abu Nasr Sarraj al-Tusi, *Kitab al-luma' fi'l-tasawwuf,* edited. by R.A. Nicholson (London/Leiden: Luzac & Co. 1914)

J.S. Trimingham, *The Sufi Orders in Islam* (Oxford: OUP 1998 rprt.)

Wensinck et al, *Concordance et indices de la tradition musulmane,* (Leiden: E.J. Brill 1936-1969)

Jafar b. Mansur al-Yaman, *Kitab al-'Alim wa'l-ghulam* (*The Book of the Master and the Disciple,* translated by James W. Morri s, (London, I.B. Tauris, 2001)

Mehdi Ha'iri Yazdi, *The Principles of Epistemology in Islamic Philosophy* (Albany: State University of New York, 1992)

Mizan al-hikma ('The Scale of Wisdom'—a 10-volume compendium of Shi' *hadith,* thematically arranged) (Qom & Tehran: Maktab al-'Ilam al-Islami, 1983)

"Gabriel shows 'Ali's valor to the Prophet." From the Persian manuscript *Khavaran Nameh*, miniature painting by Farhad Naghash, 15th century. Tehran, Golestan Palace Museum.

SACRED WEB: A JOURNAL OF TRADITION AND MODERNITY

Sacred Web (ISSN 1480-6584) was founded by M. Ali Lakhani in 1998 as a bi-annual traditionalist journal, with the aims of articulating the primordial and universal "first principles" of Tradition (in the sense of *religio perennis* or perennial philosophy), as expounded by the major religious traditions of the world, and exploring their application to the contingent circumstances of modernity.

The journal's distinguished contributors have included HRH The Prince of Wales and His Holiness The Dalai Lama, as well as prominent traditionalists and scholars. *Sacred Web* is now widely regarded as one of the best periodicals in the English language in the field of traditional studies. In the words of an authority on tradition, Seyyed Hossein Nasr: "Along with *Sophia, Sacred Web* is the most important journal in the English language devoted to the study of tradition. Furthermore, it is unique in its interest in the consequences of confrontation between tradition and modernity, an issue which lies at the heart of so many aspects of the life of humanity today."

Another of the contributors to *Sacred Web* is the internationally-renowned writer on religion, Karen Armstrong, who has commented as follows about the journal:

"*Sacred Web* provides scholarly and inspiring access to a form of spiritual understanding that is very little understood in our modern society but which is of the greatest importance for our time. Its varied and excellent articles give the reader an insight into the deeper dimensions of our contemporary problems, bringing to life and giving contemporary relevance to the issues of our day."

Further details about the journal are available at www.sacredweb. com.